THE BI-SEXUALITY OF DANIEL DEFOE

THE BI-SEXUALITY OF DANIEL DEFOE

A Psychoanalytic Survey of the Man and His Works

Leo Abse

KARNAC

First published in 2006 by
Karnac Books
118 Finchley Road. London NW3 5HT

Copyright © 2006 by Leo Abse

British Library Cataloguing in Publication Data

A C.I.P. for this book is available from the British Library
ISBN10: 1-85575-456-8
ISBN13: 978-1-85575-456-0

Edited, designed, and typeset by RefineCatch Ltd, Bungay, Suffolk
Printed in the United Kingdom

www.karnacbooks.com

Dedication

To Ania Czepulkowska
In Love

CONTENTS

ACKNOWLEDGEMENTS

This work could not have been completed without the unsparing aid and advice given me by my amanuensis Frances Hawkins. By sharing with me her considerable knowledge of religious controversies prevailing in Defoe's lifetime, by her preliminary editing and by her infinite patience in dealing with an irascible stroke-ridden deaf old man, she ensured this book reached publication. I am profoundly grateful to her.

A near-nonagenarian needs incitement and encouragement to continue writing. This has been boundlessly given to me by my friends. I am therefore much indebted to: Gillon Aitken, literary agent; Reva Berstock, psychoanalyst; Michael Bloch, biographer; Rabbi Dr Sidney Brichto; Anne Brown, antiques dealer; Alan Cameron, publisher; Stuart Cameron, administrator; Paul Cavadino, penologist; Laura Coy, travel consultant; Stephen Cretney of All Souls; Michael Foot, Renaissance Man; Geoffrey Goodman, editor and biographer; John Gritten, biographer; Anthony Howard, biographer; David Hughes, political editor; Hardy Jones, educationist; Brett Kahr, psychotherapist and composer; Julia Langdon, biographer; Charles Leeming, solicitor; Harry Lloyd, retired magistrates' clerk; Richard Martin, economist; Colin Merton, Savile Club librarian; Christopher Morgan, religious correspondent; Paul Murphy, parliamentarian; David Parfitt, painter; Christopher Phillips, banker; Elizabeth Phillips, biochemist; Dacre Punt, designer; Jeremy Robson, publisher; Andrew Ross, botanist; Sally Rowe, lawyer; Martin Rowson, cartoonist; Ivan Sadka, solicitor and musician; Peter Soar, solicitor, writer and carpenter; Mike Steele, lobby correspondent; Brian Thompson, headteacher; Richard Tilleard-Coles, psychiatrist; Don Touhig, parliamentarian; George Warburg, banker; Ernest Woolf, psychoanalyst.

Since delivery of this work, to my grievous loss, my elder psycho-analyst brother, Wilfred, has died; his impress is on this book. I wish too to express my gratitude for the help and stimulation given me by my poet younger brother Dannie, my historian son Tobias and my daughter Bathsheba Morabito, who has given me the blessing of my grandchildren.

I am much obligated to Raymond Playford, George Lewith and Vidurath Mayadunne, whose medical skills helped me to overcome some of the disabilities caused by my stroke in 2002. And, not least, I give my thanks to my physician Stephen Hirst, who, ever reliable, fulfilled his daring promise to keep me alive to complete this essay.

I would wish in this work to record, as in my previous books, my indebtedness to the Torfaen Labour Party and the electors of the Eastern Valley of Gwent who, for thirty years, with considerable forbearance, gave me the opportunity to observe, participate in and endure the strange life, sometimes ennobling, sometimes demean-ing, which is the lot of the children of the Mother of Parliaments. Without that experience, I would indeed have been ill-equipped to write of the complex political involvements of Daniel Defoe.

An author, I grant, may be deficient in dress or address, may neglect his person and his fortune . . . he may be full of inconsistencies elsewhere, but he is himself in his books: . . . An author's appearance or his actions may not square with his theories or descriptions, but his mind is seen in his writings, as his face is in the glass. . . . Let me, then, conjure the gentle reader, who has ever felt an attachment to books, not hastily to divorce them from their authors. Whatever love or reverence may be due to the one is equally owing to the other. The volume we prize may be little, old, shabbily bound, an imperfect copy, does not step down from the shelf to give us a graceful welcome, nor can it extend a hand to serve us in extremity, and so far may be like the author; but whatever there is of truth or good, or of proud consolation or of cheering hope, in the one, all this existed in a greater degree in the imagination and the heart and brain of the other. To cherish the work and damn the author is as if the traveller who slakes his thirst at the running stream should revile the spring-head from which it gushes.

William Hazlitt
(From the essay *On the Jealousy and the Spleen of Party*)

CHAPTER ONE

The genius of Daniel Defoe

To explore the psychodynamics and psychopathology of a politician, to determine how far the manifestoes he advertises,
the political stances he adopts, are, within the context of the
prevailing social circumstances, mere epiphenomena reflecting his
private travail is, without necessarily being over-reductive, well
within the capacity of psychoanalysis; this I have sought to illustrate
in my psycho-biographies of Thatcher[1] and Blair.[2]

But the puny politicians are one matter, a literary genius like
Defoe is another; for to hope, using the armoury of psychoanalysis,
to hack down the undergrowth covering creativity so that we may
find its source is a vanity. Freud well knew that; when, in his essay
on Leonardo da Vinci,[3] he set up signposts pointing to the source
from which the artist's creativity sprang, he insisted it was a destination that could not be reached. Even though he traced the course
that Leonardo's creativity had taken, even up to his fantasies as a
babe, still Freud acknowledged the presently unknowable Delphic
nature of creativity.

Freud once wrote that one of the most attractive subjects of
analytical enquiry is the connection between the impressions of an
artist's childhood and his life history on the one hand, and, on the

other hand, his works, as reactions to those impressions. But despite his attraction to such an investigation, even as he spelled out the accident of Leonardo's illegitimate birth, the excessive tenderness of his mother, and the barrenness of his first stepmother, all having such determining influences upon his works and discoveries, Freud deliberately subverts any claim to having explained Leonardo's wondrous creativity.

Maybe when we have read him, the Gioconda smile is a little less enigmatic. But Freud stresses that the same external circumstances impinging upon Leonardo's childhood could, in someone else, have resulted in a permanent injury to intellectual activity or to the acquisition of an insurmountable disposition to obsessional neurosis; the especial tendency towards instinctual repressions and Leonardo's extraordinary capacity for sublimating primitive instincts remain mysteries, leaving his creativity inexplicable.

Fretting at Freud's self-imposed constraints, there are some psychoanalysts influenced by the redoubtable Melanie Klein[4] who seem to suggest that her concepts could provide an answer to the question which Freud said was unanswerable; they would have us believe that creative activity is either what they describe as "depressive" or "schizoid"; over-emphasising the role of destructiveness in creativity, they would seek to persuade us that creative activity either represents an attempt to make reparation for early infantile destructive fantasies or is in some way analogous to the delusional system-making of schizophrenia. But this is surely a dusty answer; it does not tell us why some rare people have the capacity to find creative solutions for their depressive or schizoid problems, while most do not. It is difficult not to believe that some of the evident dilemmas of those psychoanalysts, seeking in Kleinian mode to unravel the tangled skein, come from their habit of working and thinking within a causal-determinant framework; they are thus entrapped, for the results of creative activity are, by definition, novel, unexpected and therefore unpredictable, and cannot easily be contained within such a framework. Freud used more guile than these followers. He often realised that he was concerned with meanings, not causes. He entitled his famous work *The Interpretation of Dreams*[5]—not *The Cause of Dreams*.

When, therefore, we engage in a scrutiny of the man who is the first and perhaps the greatest novelist in English, the man who was

"one of the most influential architects of the British national consciousness",[6] who was a fraudster, a compulsive risk-taker, a con
man and most dubious businessman, a hired pen, an astonishing
early feminist, a sophisticated marriage counsellor, the first management consultant, a memorable travel-writer, a spy and double
agent, a superb pamphleteer, a major influence in shaping the office
of Prime Minister, one of the greatest of our journalists and an
inveterate fantasist, we would be wise perhaps to forgo a fruitless
probe into his genius; rather, noting that his life and writings have
lent themselves to what seem limitless interpretations, we should
be content modestly to join this queue of interpreters who, in
Defoe's lifetime as now, so contradictorily present this turbulent
man who lived so dangerously, ever provoking responses that, as
his son-in-law ruefully commented: "ruin and wild destruction
sport around him".

One biographer has him being a martyr to his Whiggish political
and religious principles; another concluded that he was "the greatest liar that ever lived"; some have put him down as an amusing
scoundrel, others as a crusading spokesman for the free press and
the emerging power of the writer. His writings were published by
American revolutionaries as republican declarations—yet they were
printed as Jacobite tracts. Charles Dickens denied him the virtue of
self-control and stigmatised him as passionless; yet others have
raged against his intemperance. In more recent times he has been
both listed in the dictionary of radical writers and abused as
one resembling the worst of the propagandists working for Nazi
Germany.

Yet all these contradictory readings of the man and his works are
not about a man possessed of multiple personalities; he was one,
and whole; and if the protean disguises he loved to assume, as
author or spy, deceive some to judge him as saint and others as
sinner, the man behind the masks was no fragmented being; he was
marvellously intact, able to withstand the disasters that fell upon
him and which he so often occasioned; his extraordinary self-
confidence and lability enabled him to survive bankruptcy, exile,
four prison sentences and the stocks and so many other vicissitudes;
nor did he allow the ever-present apocalyptic anxieties which
enveloped him and his works to crush it.

This was no wraith of a man; he was a conquistador, solid, and, being no cardboard creature, he cast shadows, long shadows. Those who would believe him a chameleon, ever ready to adapt to political circumstances, are mistaken; this great Dissenter was, rather, a most principled man, one who so often pursued his principles in the most unprincipled manner. And those, like Hazlitt, who would have us believe there was a disjunction in Defoe's life, and that as he approached his sixtieth year he abandoned all his lifelong interest in religion and political subjects to write his first novel, *Robinson Crusoe*, and thereafter confined himself to "unsophisticated views of nature and the human heart", are in error. We should not let this artful actor, this master of fictions, confuse us as he hides himself behind the many parts he played, for if we are so entranced, we shall never discover the man.

Like Hazlitt, Karl Marx fell into one of his traps, all designed to ensure that the hunter, not Defoe, should be ensnared. Marx, fascinated by the details provided of Crusoe's work on the island, in his *Capital* gave a critique of Crusoe's life as an exposition of a labour theory of value; Defoe the economist so engaged Marx that he insouciantly dismissed all the spirituality of Crusoe as an irrelevance, mere persiflage, as "recreation".[7] Inevitably such a misjudgement means that the real Defoe has eluded him; once again, Defoe's legerdemain triumphs.

But we must persist and not permit Defoe's impersonations, however exotic, to distract us from peering at the runes embossed on all his published essays, political poetry, pamphlets and late novels, for they are decipherable and do most surely tell us of the concatenation linking all his works. Like the man himself, Defoe's work is of one piece. The aetiology of his literary genius, as of all genius, is undiscoverable but the manifestations of that genius which, misled by his simulations, have so bewildered and confused his interpreters, leading them to such contrary conclusions, are certainly capable of being made more coherent and more intelligible.

That is possible only if we determinedly keep him in our sights, never allowing him to trick us into believing that the disguises he dons are not the man himself. Concealment is his game; this is the marvellous professional spy, the anonymous writer of the most devastating political pamphlets. The defences he cunningly erects are certainly not to be easily penetrated. The recent huge tome by the American professor Maximillian Novak,[8] an intimidating trawl through all the known facts of Defoe and his works all scrupulously posited within the social, religious and political context of his time, ends on a note of frustration, with Defoe, not the author, a victor. Recalling the two weighty nineteenth-century biographies of Defoe, the one wholly adulatory and giving a picture of Defoe as a Whiggish saint, the other judging him as trickster, master prevaricator and schemer, Novak implicitly leaves us, as readers, to choose our Defoe. This is a cop-out; it leaves Defoe swinging in the wind.

It may be forgiven that nineteenth-century biographers took Defoe à la carte, but in the post-Freudian twenty-first century that is not an option available to us. We have the right to look for the answer to the question why Defoe, in all his works, seeks, sometimes so insistently, to dupe us by assuming a disguise. What is he seeking to hide? What is the terrible sin he wishes to conceal? What crime has he committed that leaves all his works so penitential?

We shall not find the answers to these questions, as has sometimes been implied, in the turbulent political and religious environment in which Defoe lived out his life. Certainly they were dangerous times, and the need for the feint and the disguise to protect the determined Dissenter from hated Roman Catholic opponents was sometimes real. Protestantism in Britain was not secured and safe against popery when Charles I had his head chopped off. The Counter-Reformation that was later to follow was a real and continuing threat; in 1708, 1715 and 1745 Jacobites attempted to overthrow the government. And the losers in the prolonged struggle were risking their lives, as Defoe well knew from his experience as a young man in the failed Monmouth rebellion against the Catholic James II, which had led to the execution of some of his closest Dissenting friends. Taking care to cover his tracks was not, therefore, necessarily a paranoiac response; with the continuing violence in today's Northern Ireland, with Ulster Unionists still waving their banners celebrating the victory of William of Orange—the man so admired by Defoe and to whom he was a speechwriter—we are unlikely to underestimate the hazards facing the Protestant protagonists involved in the religious conflict of Britain 300 years ago. Yet it is difficult not to conclude that although the times gave great scope, and some justification, for Defoe to indulge his dissembling, nevertheless the extravagant passion for disguise, rarely absent from all his works, so compulsive and obsessional, lacks rationality. We shall never encompass the man or find answers to our questions if we attribute his strange penchant to an outside source. His dissembling was determined by internal not external necessity; and only if we can find the causation of that necessity are we likely to find the explanations we are seeking.

The zest with which, under assumed identities, he engages in the period's shadowy world of political journalism and pamphlet wars shows him enjoying the fancy-dress genre afforded him; more squeamish Augustine pamphleteers, like Swift, may have chosen, out of intellectual snobbery, to hide their names when descending to gutter pamphleteering but Defoe revelled in the game; he has an evident pleasure in the tease which gave him the opportunity to attack unnamed but well known opponents, and simultaneously to affect concealment of his own identity. In this he was not merely following an external period fashion, he was satisfying an inner need.

Nor should we be satisfied that some single external event precipitated the doom-loaded moods pervading his writings. The view has been canvassed that Defoe, witnessing the awesome ravages of the terrifying Great Plague of 1665, and taught by his father that it was the vengefulness of God upon the wicked, was traumatised; and that it is the reverberations of that trauma we are hearing when we pity the anxiety-loaded protagonists of his fiction.

When, up to his usual tricks, Defoe presents *A Journal of the Plague Year* as if it were a genuine book of memoirs, as if it were a detailed eye-witness account, we should remind ourselves that Defoe in fact was only five years of age at the time of the Great Plague. If we yield to the frequent speculation that Defoe was a child so permanently affected by the sight of the disaster that its consequences were to be an ever-present fraught apprehensiveness lacing his works, again, we are allowing him to give us the slip, colluding with him to find a rational extrinsic cause for the constant and pervading tremulousness; but if indeed the child Defoe was so extraordinarily moved by the sights of plague-ridden London, it was surely because a previous massive apprehension of death and punishment had been re-ignited.

We need to ask, what was the earlier precipitate that caused Defoe to be ever possessed with the threat of a terminator? What was the undisclosed event, or psychical events, that left him throughout his life so enveloped in dread? If we are to discover the real Defoe, it is those concealments that must be divined. But we are engaged with a master-spy who will not give up his secrets easily; to unmask him, counter-espionage of a kind that has perhaps only become available with the advent of the insights of psychoanalysis must be deployed.

★ ★ ★ ★ ★ ★ ★ ★ ★ ★

To succeed in penetrating Defoe's defences, we need to draw up a battle-plan; no direct assault will be of avail, for against such an attack he is too well entrenched. We must approach elisively following the strategy of the few who have had a measure of success in their endeavours to reach the source of creative genius. I know of no one who advanced further towards that impossible goal than the much undervalued art critic, lawyer and psychoanalyst Anton Ehrenzweig. Ehrenzweig eschewed the reductive methodology of those who, using psychoanalytical concepts as their tools, would, in biography, attempt a demolition job upon the artist and then, naively and in vain, search for his creativity amidst the fragmentary ruins.[9]

Ehrenzweig's approach was otherwise; it was essentially holistic. Following the emphases of the nineteenth-century American philosopher William James, he drew attention to the articulatory tendency within our surface perceptions; how we tend, for the most part, when viewing a painting or listening to a composition, to notice simple, compact and precise forms, and at the same time eliminate as "dross" vague, seemingly incoherent inarticulate forms from our visual or auditory perceptions. It is a tendency that can bestow advantages when we seek to present, in a biography, a clear outline of the subject and so depict him free from the clutter which in real life encumbered him; but it can also be profoundly misleading, as Ehrenzweig demonstrated in his critique of contemporary gestalt psychologists who have lauded the value of this tendency.

There is no exact English equivalent of the German word *Gestalt*; configuration, pattern, or a meaningful organised whole most closely convey its meaning; the gestalt psychology is one predicated upon the belief that the whole determines the parts, not that the whole is merely the total sum of its parts; the persuasive exponents of the gestalt theory insist that the phenomena which appear as unitary wholes must have their wholeness respected and can analytically be broken into bits only at the price of annihilating what one intended to study.[10]

At first sight, this thesis seems consonant with our insistence that unless we accept that all the parts of Defoe hang together, we cannot usefully go in search of his genius. There is, however, a fallacy here which, unless remarked, would bar us from scrutinising the elements which are excluded by the gestalt—the incoherent, the bizarre, the inarticulate. Gestalt psychology is a surface not a depth psychology; it studies a selected gestalt in detail but pays little attention to the fate of those seemingly chaotic elements which it has rejected. What Ehrenzweig explicated was that those seemingly irrelevant elements can be revelatory; that a true depth psychology of perception is required to make good the neglect of these significant, too easily dismissed elements. Thus, a depth psychoanalysis of art forms must be a determined effort to reverse the usual articulatory tendency and look out for the seemingly accidental detail in which the unconscious creative process of art can unfold itself, safe from conscious observation. Such an analysis will turn away from the consciously "composed" structure of a painting and will watch for the apparently accidental scribbles hidden in the articulated forms of artistic "handwriting"; and similarly, it will pay less attention to the articulate tone steps of a melody moving as they are recorded by musical notation and, rather, will focus on the apparently accidental *glissando* and *vibrato* inflections or on the slight distortions of rhythm and intensity which defy musical notation and are left to the performer's seemingly arbitrary execution.

If we are to advance further than Defoe's limen, then we indeed need to adopt a similar investigative technique; our task is made easier by his prodigious output, for even as acute a dissembler as Defoe could not in all the 5047 publications attributed to him always so compel us, by artful narrative or fierce polemic, to focus on the gestalt impressed on his publications that we overlook a hinterland upon which at times has lain scattered curiosities, quirks, strange irrelevant anecdotes, bizarre asides and odd musings. These are not debris; oft-times they can yield up valuable clues which help us in our quest to de-code the manifestations of his genius as we wander through the bewildering territory; Defoe's obfuscatory directions often ensure we shall be led astray; but sometimes he is careless and we find the clues strewn across our path. Perhaps nowhere in his works are they more visible than in the strange gift that, as a suitor, he sent to his future wife.[11] Never can a woman have been wooed with a more equivocal and bizarre love letter, and, pruriently, if we are to discover our man, it requires a re-reading.

Notes

1. Abse, L., *Margaret, Daughter of Beatrice: a Psychobiography of Margaret Thatcher*, Cape, 1989.
2. Abse, L., *The Man behind the Smile: Tony Blair and the Politics of Perversion*, Robson Books, 1996.
3. Freud, S., *Leonardo da Vinci*, Standard Edition of the Works of Sigmund Freud (hereafter SE), Volume 11.
4. Klein, M., Infantile anxiety-situations deflected in a work of art and in the creative impulse, *International Journal of Psychoanalysis*, 10 (1931).
5. Freud, S., *The Interpretation of Dreams*, SE, Volume 15.
6. Paulin, T., Fugitive Crusoe, *London Review of Books*, 19 July 2001.
7. Marx, K., *Capital, Volume 1*, J. M. Dent, 1934, p. 50.
8. Novak, M. E., *Daniel Defoe: Master of Fictions*, Oxford University Press, 2001.
9. Ehrenzweig, A., *The Psychoanalysis of Artistic Vision and Hearing*, Routledge & Kegan Paul, 1953; Ehrenzweig, A., *The Hidden Order of Art*, Weidenfeld & Nicolson, 1968.
10. Perls, F. S., Hefferline, R. F. and Goodman, P., *Gestalt Therapy*, Souvenir Press, 1972.
11. Defoe, D., *Historical Collections, or Memoires of Passages and Stories Collected from Severall Authors*, 1683.

CHAPTER TWO

The *Historical Collections*

L ike a peacock spreading his tail and bowing to the peahen when courting, so, it seems, it was customary in Defoe's day for a City gentleman when courting his intended to present her with an anthology of improving texts and stories; his selection was intended to boast elliptically of the wooer's virtues, of the principles he held in regard to marriage, of his moral and religious stances. The aim was both to entertain and flatter his adored and to demonstrate how keen he was on gaining the lady and, of course, her dowry.

When, therefore, the twenty-two-year-old Defoe, as an adorer, sent to Mary Tuffley, still in her teens, his gift of *Historical Collections*, he was following an established convention; and the flowery dedication, the self-abasement before the "Divine Lady" and the declarations of his "own Ignorance and Insufficiency" were all part of a fashion where the would-be lover lay prostrate, an "unworthy Servant" supplicating his "Incomparable" lady. But if the outward form of Defoe's address was extravagantly modish, the content of his submission was most certainly of another order, one that would be thought likely to strike fear and apprehension in a teenager, the protected only daughter of a wealthy merchant.

The stories that Defoe selected for her reading are replete with violence; forty of them involve death and execution with the moral instruction usually accompanying the original texts expurgated; most of the tales are of ruthless heroes—of Alexander and the Great Scanderbergh, the Albanian hero who fought the Turks—men triumphing over their enemies by their wit and remarkable displays of strength; and even the religious tales which he submits to his Mary are no pious homilies but are, rather, interlaced with the recounting of appalling cruelty and violence. Some of the stories are frightening, evoking nightmarish responses; typically, one is of a drunken renegade Englishman who decided to go out, armed with a long knife, and kill a lion; the lion which he discovered was, however, too quick for him; it threw him down, almost suffocating him under its weight, and decided to sit upon the Englishman until it should feel hungry enough to eat him; the Englishman took advantage of the lion's decision to delay by eventually freeing his hand, finding his knife and thrusting it into the lion and killing him.

Another tale was one even more likely to disturb a young girl rather than to arouse tender feelings towards a solicitous wooer. Defoe tells how Mohamet the Great, infatuated with Irene, a beautiful Greek captive, spent most of his time with her. His troops, resenting his prolonged dalliance, and believing him to be satiated by sexual luxuriances, reached the conclusion that he was no longer capable of governing. To disprove the allegation, Mohamet ordered his troops to a temple and brought out his beloved Irene dressed in her most glorious and seductive clothes. Then all present submitted to her charms and agreed that she was a woman indeed worthy of an emperor. That accomplished, Mohamet forthwith pronounced her doom: "But my affections must be Bridled by you my Slaves, and drawing out his scimitar at one Blow he cut off her head. Before them all; saying, 'Now know that your Emperor is able to conquer his Affections as well as his Enemies.' "

Presenting this extraordinary triumphant murderous story of a beloved to Mary as a love token has unsurprisingly bewildered not a few critics; some have, unconvincingly, sought to explain it away as Defoe's way of showing Mary how, heroically, he was ready to place duty before passion, but it is more than unlikely that such austerity would commend itself to a young woman who, like all young women, would look to find ardour in a suitor. The painstaking

Maximillian Novak, keenly aware of the inadequacy of such an explanation and aware that there is a mystery behind Defoe presenting such a turnoff to his "Adored", canvasses an even more convoluted explanation.[1] He suggests that Defoe was conveying to Mary that were she to marry him, birth control by Defoe's heroic self-discipline would govern the bedroom, "that she would not have to have sexual intercourse with him every time he felt a twinge of desire", that with women in Defoe's day dying tragically in childbirth after never-ending pregnancies he was anxious to reassure Mary that that was not to be her fate. If there were any credibility in Novak's claim, it would certainly require explanation as to why Defoe should choose such a bizarre mode of conveying such long-term musings—thoughts hardly likely to occur in the minds of two youngsters engaged in a romantic exchange of letters. And certainly the credibility of the hypothesis is not strengthened by the knowledge that, apart from miscarriages, Mary was to give birth to eight children.

It may perhaps be more persuasively urged that Defoe was displaying the same syndrome that reaches its climax in today's stag nights of young men embarking on matrimony: displaying a scorn and hostility to women and a last defiant macho stand before enduring the perceived entrapment and loss of freedom that marriage entails. Certainly the ambivalence of so many men who both want and resent the status of husband could have played a considerable part in Defoe's protest, one expressed in the slaying of Irene even as he was coveting Mary. But once the tale of Mohamet is put into the context of all the other violent and heroic stories Defoe was recounting to Mary, it can be seen that this story is not fully plumbed if we treat it merely as the age-appropriate, ambivalent response of a young man to an approaching marriage.

What needs to be acknowledged, however, although it may not be immediately obvious, is that this story, like the tale of the lion suffocating the hero and like almost all the stories within the *Historical Collections*, is one of a hero violently triumphing over tyrannical enemies, and this, exotically and sometimes with ornate elaborations, points to the unresolved Oedipal problems of Defoe. Albeit half-heartedly, and often superficially, literary critics acknowledge as much even as they hesitate to explore the full implications. Novak, commenting on the fearsome lion story and aware how frequently in Defoe's novels the protagonists are in terror of being devoured by wild animals, a little grudgingly feels compelled to draw our attention to the fact that "psychoanalytical critics have always read such fears as evidence of the fear of castration".[2] Hesitatingly he points out the likelihood that "the strong patriarchal household of the Defoes must have produced the usual dread of the father and the desire to replace him that we now call the Oedipus complex". Novak could hardly have commented otherwise. When presenting his stories to his future wife, young Defoe has still to attain the cunning in concealment of his older years, and because his selection of tales has rare candour they are more revelatory; above all else, they are a caveat warning us, in our evaluation of the man and his works, not to underestimate the significance of the Oedipal struggles which engaged him to the end of his days.

Notes

1. Novak, M. E., *Daniel Defoe: Master of Fictions*, Oxford University Press, 2001.
2. Ibid.

CHAPTER THREE

The negative Oedipus complex

T he Oedipus complex is often said to be a group of largely unconscious ideas centring on the wish to possess the parent of the opposite sex and to eliminate that of the same sex; it is claimed to be a phase we all pass through between the ages of three and five.[1] The complex, of course, is named after the mythical Oedipus who killed his father and married his mother without knowing that they were his parents.

Presenting it thus, almost as a fairy-tale, Anglo-American psychoanalysts, with but a few dissenters, have allowed our culture to accommodate comfortably to what can be interpreted as a reassuringly normative story; we begin by desiring, and wanting to murder, our parents; registering the horror, not to mention the impossibility, of this project we more or less relinquish it. We renounce our first infantile desires and wait; then, in a diaphasic interlude, we, as adolescents, recapitulate, in disguised form, our early rebellions and eventually, if all goes well, we work through the consequent turbulence, and as adults, find people who are sufficiently reminiscent of our parents to be exciting, but sufficiently different that we can consummate our desires. We want something; but, repentant, we realise the errors of our ways and we find the substitutes that can satisfy us.

The story thus portrayed is one of human development, one that is both possible and potentially satisfying. And, doubtless, in this anodyne developmental version of the Oedipus complex that is pedalled by so many of these psychoanalysts, we end the story by saying that as adults we can live happily ever after.

Indeed, within such a paradigm, the continued preoccupation by Defoe in his early twenties with derring-do fantasies of overcoming tyrants—obvious father surrogates—could be dismissed as merely illustrative of a delayed adolescence; and, within such a benign interpretation of the Oedipus story, it is possible too, as literary critics have sometimes done, to treat the flouting by Defoe, in his extraordinarily reckless business dealings, of his father's deeply conservative attitudes to commercial affairs, and his turning away from his father's wish that he pursue a clerical career rather than be a political activist, as little more than whimpers of disobedience echoing from far-off trauma occasioned by childish tantrums.

Distancing the original Oedipus drama, minimising its awesome and continuing effect in adult life, treating it as a transitory phenomenon, a mere staging post in human development, is, however, surely an avoidance stratagem designed to keep at bay the terror and mystery within the life of another Oedipal text that runs parallel to that spelled out so sweetly by too many British and American psychoanalysts. In their reading we shall certainly find no answer to, for example, the question of why Defoe in his last years so metamorphised himself and became, in effect, a woman and as such, as a female raconteur, give us the novels *Moll Flanders* and *Roxana* that still grip and entrance us; nor will such readings help us to understand why Defoe can not only lay claim to be the first English novelist and the first English journalist but could be acknowledged by Virginia Woolf as perhaps Britain's first feminist.

It is in a darker parallel text of the Oedipus story that we are more likely to find the answers we seek. The psychoanalyst Adam Phillips has elegantly written of the life of this text:

> In this life our desire is ineluctably undistractedly transgressive and therefore unknown to us; in this life we are driven always to approach and avoid the objects of desire, and what makes us feel most alive makes us feel we are risking our lives. . . . In this life uncanniness is weighed in excess of our canniness. . . . Where once

there was security operating, now there is risk; where once safety was virtually the be-all and end-all, now fear is preferred. A sense of aliveness displaces a sense of certainty as a paramount consideration. Surprise and dread are the order of the day. In our transgressive life it is as though there is something—or someone—we seem to value more than our lives, more than life itself.[2]

Within such a text we can be encouraged to seek out our ever risk-taking adventurer, so bold that in some of his works, using the first person technique, without any distance between himself and the narrator, he can renounce his maleness, become a female and permit her to play out, only a little subdued, all her lesbian tendencies. We certainly will not find the source of such breath-taking courage in the sanitised versions of the Oedipus complex that today pass as dynamic depth psychology among too many British psychoanalysts, and which deservedly attract the scorn of the French psychoanalysts who relentlessly mock their Anglo-Saxon squeamishness and pusillanimity.[3]

★   ★   ★   ★   ★   ★   ★   ★   ★   ★

If we are to monitor as complex a genius as Defoe, we require equipment capable of a nice calibration; we will never be able to measure the man with inadequate tools. To understand why today's British psychoanalysis is likely to fail us in our endeavour to encompass our man, and why, contrariwise, many of the French practitioners can help us to capture our quarry, requires a little excursus into the sorry politics of psychoanalysis and into the meta-psychologies of the rival schools of psychoanalysis now prevailing in Britain.

The intelligent layman today, unfamiliar with the bitter quarrels that raged within the psychoanalytical movement in Britain in the past century, accepts as definitive the prevailing tepid version of psychoanalysis that has emerged triumphant out of those disputes; but it is so unthreatening a version, so gentle, so lacking in capacity to administer the analytical shock that alone can break up the stale cultural configurations which now desperately need to be re-shaped, that, unsurprisingly, psychoanalysis beyond the couch is uninfluential and of marginal significance in Britain.

And that has been occasioned, above all else, by its retreat from the sexual, from its abandonment of Freud's insistence that sexuality is a concept relating to the very foundations of the psyche, not one that can be merely limited, as appears so often now, to its immediate manifestations, as a local topic, to be reviewed perhaps only when considering such matters as impotence or frigidity.

In this retreat, Freud's Oedipal complex, the most awesome explosive within the psychoanalytical armoury, has been jettisoned, too charged with sexuality and, in particular, with bi-sexuality, to be handled by many of our prissy psychoanalysts. That this should have occurred in Britain may be attributed to, above everyone else, the brilliant, wilful and, as I found, incredibly vain woman Melanie Klein, whose disciples have succeeded in dominating British psychoanalysis; and who have singed even those sections within the psychoanalytical institutions which eschew formal allegiance to Klein's meta-psychology. One of the spin-offs of the Kleinian coup is that we are bereft of the insights that, otherwise, more by osmosis than from formal instruction, could have seeped, to our considerable benefit, into our general culture; and it is symptomatic of the resultant deprivation that applied psychoanalysis of the Kleinian kind can give us so little elucidation of the wonders and perplexities of Defoe's life and works.

The key issue, but not the only one, in the vehement debate between Klein and the Freudians bears on the primitive mechanisms which govern infantile sexuality. Klein taught her followers that all aspects of sexual behaviour in adult life must be related back to their initial prototypes; that is, in her view, to the relationships between mother and suckling child that come into existence at the breast in the early months of life. This supposition amounted to a profound alteration of Freud's theory of infantile sexuality, for once our libidinal development is linked so conclusively and irreversibly to orality, it has in fact only one developmental phase: the first.[4]

All other phases are no more, it is claimed in the Kleinian view, than superficial derivatives of that phase, and that they make every opportunity to return to their origin. The Freudian view of our libidinal development postulates an initial oral phase too, but insists that it gives way to two successive phases attached to erogenous zones other than that of the breast—to the anal and then to the phallic phases which herald the arrival, redolent with sexuality, of the fullblown Oedipus complex. There is not said to be a specific oral libido, anal libido and general libido; there is but one libido which may be displaced from one erogenous zone to another, but forces may sometimes be at work that resist such a displacement, remain fixed, and such fixations can be seen embossed upon an adult's character structure. At its extreme, Kleinian doctrine is essentially dyadic, mother and child; with Freud, the triad is relentlessly emphasised, the father is never absent from our lives, in infancy, in adulthood, right up to our deathbed. The Kleinians accuse the Freudians of patriarchy, the Freudians mock Klein's matriarchy. With every informed commentator on Defoe emphasising the influence of the values and lifestyle of his father upon him, the expectation that we shall glean, in our quest, more from a Freudian than a Kleinian is likely to be met.

The layman may be inclined to dismiss these disputations among the psychoanalysts as tiresome, as storms in a teacup; and indeed, not a few younger psychoanalysts today, far removed as they are from the 1940s and the Hampstead battlefields of yesterday's warring psychoanalysts, and following the hermeneutical trends of contemporary psychoanalysis, also look askance at the fierceness of the old debates between Kleinians and Freudians. Nowadays it is claimed by some that their competing theories of a linear orderly sequential development should all be doubted. Not only in psychoanalysis but in other disciplines, from history to brain studies, fashionable "chaos" perspectives abound; so-called "catastrophe theories" enthusiastically proliferate, endorsing the notion that our world, and our personal development, includes discontinuity, manifest disorder and jaggedness.[5] The caveats of these proponents of non-linear dynamical systems theory, although often dangerous and excessively admonitory, can alert us to the dangers of any crude simplistic reductive assessments, attributing specific psychological behaviour in an adult to one specific developmental derailment at a particular moment in childhood; growing up is far too complex to be so encompassed. But in the 1930s and 1940s there was in place no examination of other overviews of childhood development that could perhaps have tempered the angry exchanges between the Kleinians and Freudians. The protagonists, so many of them exiles from their own countries, believed, rightly, that there was a great divide between them. The full storm that had been brewing for almost twenty years broke out in the British Psycho-Analytical Society in 1943, and tore it asunder.

Melanie Klein had long been based in London when Freud and

his daughter Anna, escaping from the Nazis in Vienna in 1939, arrived; the comparative ease with which Klein had seduced a substantial portion of the British Psycho-Analytical Society with her ideas now ceased. The Freuds, together with the doughty Scottish analyst Edward Glover, and Melitta Schmideberg—Klein's daughter who had become disaffected with Klein's theories—became the focus of a Viennese group of analysts who opposed Klein. There is an irony that soon, at the very time the civilised world was engaged in a life and death struggle with the Nazis, and when the bombs were raining down upon London itself, disdainfully, seemingly almost insulated from the outside world, the continental titans of psychoanalysis in their self-created Hampstead ghetto almost bled themselves to death.

Some fifteen years later, in the early summer of 1958, I met Melanie Klein. Those were days when I was too immersed in my law-books and tending to my legal practice in Cardiff to have concerned myself with what I would have then regarded as the minutiae of psychoanalytical politics and, although I had read a little of Klein and much more of Edward Glover, I was certainly unaware of the full significance of the gulf between the rival psychoanalytical groupings. A local doctor whom I knew well had recently married an American analyst who had been a fervent supporter of Klein in the United States and I accepted an invitation from him for my wife and myself to join him for the weekend in his comfortable country cottage in the Vale of Glamorgan; the only other guest was Melanie Klein.

It proved to be a turbulent encounter. At seventy-six years of age, Klein was to my eyes one of the most beautiful and commanding of old ladies I had met; but as a political missionary myself, I could not fail to become immediately aware that her good looks and accompanying vanity were matched by a missionary zeal; she was ever seeking converts. Only such evangelism could explain the persistence with which she sought to persuade me to become a believer. As a provincial lawyer, a layman with no pretensions to profound psychoanalytical learning, and no claims to recognition beyond being a prominent burgher, I was but a minnow; but still she was determined to catch me in her net. Only her evangelism could explain her persistence. When midnight came and I was concerned that my resistances were tiring her, still she would not desist; she withdrew for an interlude then, refreshed and newly powdered and painted, returned to the fray until the early hours.

Although all this occurred forty-five years ago and since then for thirty years in the Commons I duelled verbally with so many skilled debaters, Klein, who succeeded in turning the whole British psycho-analytical movement upside down, still remains with me as one, at least in private, of the most formidable of polemicists. And thus perhaps, given the impact that the dynamism of the woman made upon me, it is not surprising that I have a recall of far more than an outline of the disputation in which I had been involved that weekend.

The trouble began when a comment by my wife about some novel she had recently read led to a discussion about style; I remarked on Freud's wondrous clarity and the irony that although he never was awarded the Nobel Prize for his clinical discoveries, he had, deservedly, received the Goethe Prize for Literature. Klein picked up the vibes and perhaps she was right in thinking that, albeit unconsciously, I was criticising her writing for, although she has been well served by some of her interpreters,[6] no one could suggest she was a great stylist. Kleinian apologists, defending her, claim that much of the obscurity and inaccessibility of Kleinian thought comes about not only because it is framed in a patient's own experiences but because those experiences are so very remote from conscious and verbal thought and too difficult to communicate in a manner that is very far outside the particular analyst–patient partnership.[7] Klein herself, telling of the baby's primitive fantasies upon which she placed so much emphasis, once wrote: "The descriptions of such primitive processes suffer from a great handicap for these fantasies arise at a time when the infant has not yet begun to think in words."[8] However, in my encounter with her, she was certainly not lacking in articulateness when explicating her viewpoint.

And when, over dinner that evening, my host, prompted by a report in the local press of a terrifyingly violent wretch whom I was then defending, turned the subject to crime, I again became entangled with Klein. Blissfully unaware at that time that Edward Glover was her *bête noire*, that she had fought him tooth and nail as he unremittingly resisted her dilution and emendation to classic orthodox psychoanalytical theory, I praised the man; and told of my indebtedness to him for illuminating in his works on crime the bewildering behaviour of so many of the lost brutes I was then daily defending in the courts.

The exact details of the dialogue during that bumpy dinner are now inevitably, after forty-nine years, beyond my recall; but it was certainly then that I became aware of a chasm between Glover and Klein, and understood the lamentable consequence of her insistence that genitality is always subordinate to orality, that the babe's precocious genital activity can only be an attempt to escape orality; within such a meta-psychology, unlike the Freudian phallocentric approach, the penis is depreciated. As one of the leading French psychoanalysts, André Green, recently arrestingly emphasised, Klein never wished to reflect on the symbolic signification of the Phallus, with all its references to power, to sovereignty and, above all, to pleasure directly related to adult sexuality, not babyish suckling.[9]

Klein was set upon re-casting psychoanalytical theory in accordance with a gynocentric perspective; the mother and daughter were to take the floor in contrast with the phallocentric vision of Freud; and the father could thus be airbrushed out of the equation. At the time of my encounter with her, I was not equipped to identify fully my unease, as perhaps I now am, with the paradigm within which she operated, but already my criminal clients had taught me that I would have no understanding of them if I did not determinedly focus on their relationship with the father.

When, years later, as a member of the Home Office Advisory Committee on Penal Affairs, I failed to follow what I had learned, I seriously misled myself. Together with my fellow-member and friend Robert Mortimer, then Bishop of Exeter, I insisted, when considering the prison regime which long-term prisoners should endure, that the issue of conjugal visits should be considered; this caused predictable consternation at the Home Office but, more strangely, it caused, as we were to discover, equal consternation among the possible beneficiaries. The men we interviewed were, for the most part, professional criminals, thoroughly committed to a life of crime, who had mixed freely among the criminal underworld, physically tough and vigorous and under thirty-five years of age; many had committed homicide or near-homicide in pursuance of robberies and were violent and ruthless. Most of their crimes were ambitious and daring: jewel thefts and massive wage snatches were all part of their way of life. Yet these desperadoes, including some of the train robbers whom I met, were, beneath their bravado, quivering like jellies when one discussed with them the possibility of conjugal visits.

It is not easy to discuss sex, within a prison environment, with an inmate. Apart from the obvious difficulties that the prisoner discerns speedily the sexual viewpoint of the enquirer and so gives a reply deemed to be acceptable even if distorted, there is also the danger that genuine confidences in this domain can become a sort of sexual complicity between the subject and the investigator. The complicity can be experienced as embarrassment or bluster and, in either event, the confidences may bear little relation to reality. The investigation, insensitively conducted, can indeed falsify its objectives and I fear that, initially, unaware of the dangerous ground upon which I trod, I proceeded most clumsily.

I was, therefore, taken aback to find that most of these men proffered to me all the arguments against conjugal visits that I had heard less skilfully assembled by their gaolers. All the practical difficulties of arranging conjugal visits in conditions that combined security with decency were elaborated upon to me by these prim thugs; and they were certainly not slow to damp down my liberal reforming zeal by pointing out the consequences of the many fatherless children likely to be born. But the tension I sensed when the matter was broached, and their eagerness to shift the conversation to other minor grievances, when seen as a recurring pattern, put me on guard and eventually gave me more insight into their problems.

I was, in fact, cheating, and they did not like it. The rules of the game were well understood by them and the prison authorities, and I was not observing well established regulations. A conspiracy existed between gaoler and gaoled; the prisoner was reduced to the desired level of a pre-pubertal child and, in return, he received tranquillity. The pretence that it was his confinement, not his fear, that prevented an adult sexual attitude was, under no circumstances, to be commented upon. While in the maximum security blocks, with their walls covered with pin-ups, these gangsters swaggered and boasted of their past criminality; they had the excuse that only the prison walls prevented them from being great lovers also. The truth was otherwise; the overwhelming majority of them had no regular sexual relationship with a woman at the time of their arrest.

In the prison they were back in childhood; even as, when infants, father—often their stepfather and so frequently a brutal father—was the law imposing his will upon them, so now, as an adult, on the occasion of his transgression, he was subject to an all-powerful authority and they were accepting their quiescent sexuality with relief, for these were flawed men.

All of us must, after puberty, break through parental authority in order to become sexually mature; but to achieve such adulthood means a revolt against the father; we rebel successfully only if we can do this without excessive fear; such men yearn to shelter behind an authority, behind the prison walls, renouncing their maleness in return for protection even as they had, out of terror, subjected themselves to paternal authority. For all the killers and brutes came from rejecting, disordered and deprived homes; and these miserable men had received no love from either father or mother to temper the fear all must overcome to replace our own fathers. It was not surprising that the talk of conjugal relations disturbed them; they knew it was not of sex that we spoke, but of the constrained freedom of adulthood limited by obligations of family, friends, work and society; and this was a type of freedom which frightened them out of their wits. They wanted to be left to their childish sexual activities, and so, indeed, I thought it prudent and kind to leave them in peace to their onanism.

I would not, in the first place, have inter-meddled with them so clumsily if I had followed more closely the guidance in Edward Glover's works,[10] for no one elucidated more, when tracing the behavioural problems of the male criminal, the links between his anti-social conduct and his unconscious conflicts over infantile incestuous impulses directed towards the father. Glover was unsparing in emphasising, not retreating from, the all-pervading sexuality enveloping us as we participate as infants in our Oedipal struggles.

Some years after my meeting with Klein, when I was in Parliament, Glover evidently having noted my intervention in Commons debates on crime, invited me to join him on the Council of the Institute of Scientific Treatment of Delinquency,[11] over which he presided. The picture of Glover presented by the "victorious" Kleinians, as a rigid authoritarian ideologue whose intemperate vehemence fatally damaged his criticism of Klein and caused his resignation from the British Psycho-Analytical Society—a portrayal of the man still substantially accepted by present-day historians of the psychoanalytical move-ment[12]—does not accord with the sage, gentle, receptive committee man with whom I happily worked until his death in 1972. Others may have found him disconcerting but certainly I enjoyed and approved of his peremptory dictatorial closure of our meetings, which he never allowed to be prolonged beyond their usefulness; and the accusations by his detractors of abrasiveness certainly find no validity in the warm relationship he had with the polymath and child psychiatrist Emmanuel Miller and the criminologist Hermann Mannheim, who acted as his co-editors of the *British Journal of Delinquency*, which was so successfully published under the aegis of our Institute for the Study and Treatment of Delinquency. But Glover was contemptuous of pusillanimity and was fiercely unaccommodating to those who would de-sexualise the practice of psychoanalysis; he regarded them as cowards, running away from terrifying forces which their clinical work had uncovered.

Nowhere is that cowardice more apparent than among those content, in and out of the world of psychoanalysis, to accept what Freud described as the "simple Oedipus complex"—the one that is now so glibly bandied around in our culture—but who draw back in horror from what Freud insisted was "the complete Oedipus complex". He wrote:

> the simple Oedipus complex is by no means its commonest form, but rather represents the simplification or schematisation which . . . is often justified for practical purposes. Closer study usually discloses the more complete Oedipus complex, which is two-fold, positive and negative, and is due to the bi-sexuality originally present in children; that is to say, a boy has not merely an ambivalent attitude towards his father and an affectionate object-choice towards his mother, but at the same time he also behaves like a girl and displays an affectionate feminine attitude to his father and a corresponding jealousy and hostility towards his mother . . . it may even be that the ambivalence displayed in the relations to the parents should be attributed entirely to bi-sexuality and that it is not . . . developed out of identification in consequence of rivalry.[13]

Freud's belief in the importance of bi-sexuality went back a very long way. In 1899, replying to his friend Wilhelm Fliess who had written to him emphasising the significance of bi-sexuality, Freud, noting how powerfully all of us carry within us maleness and femininity, replied: "Bi-sexuality! I am sure you are right about it. And I am accustoming myself to regarding every sexual act as an event between four individuals." Already in 1905 he had written: "Without taking bi-sexuality into account I think it would scarcely be possible to arrive at an understanding of the sexual manifestations that are actually to be observed in men and women."[14]

When, therefore, following Freud, we do not tiptoe around the homosexual aspect of the Oedipus complex, we can, when scrutinising Defoe, be emboldened to advance an hypothesis that can claim to be validated by any serious reading of his works. With Defoe there is abundant evidence that, whatever may have been the constitutional factors or particular shaping experiences that brought it about, he never completed the rite of passage which in more usual development leads to at least a partial renunciation of that early Oedipal desire to be possessed by the father.

The psychoanalyst Otto Fenichel,[15] in his classic textbook, emphasising that love and competition are not mutually exclusive, describes how: "The normal identification of a boy with his father, characterised by the formula 'I should like to be like father', 'I should like to have a penis like father's', 'I should like to participate in father's penis', may, in certain cases, grow into a kind of love which may best be described as an apprentice complex, a feminine submission to the father in order to prepare oneself for a later masculine competition with him."

Defoe never graduated from that apprenticeship. The novels he wrote are weighed down with repentance; we remain puzzled that what appear to us to be little more than peccadilloes by a novel's penitential protagonist are depicted as deadly sins; Robinson Crusoe is condemned to twenty-eight years' isolation on an uninhabited island merely because, like so many youngsters, he disobeyed his father by running away to sea. The disproportionate punishment alerts us; it is occasioned not by adolescent defiance, which Defoe, wearing one of his masks, proffers as the reason; uncovered, it reveals the Great Sin which Defoe never ceases to tell us has been committed; and that, in reality, but impossible to be acknowledged by Defoe, is the breaking of the ultimate taboo, that of incest, and, even worse, homosexual incest.

Always under threat that the tug of his early Oedipal years would destroy him, ever striving to ward off the punishment that the acting out of his forbidden feminine submissiveness would precipitate, to our great benefit as readers, he marvellously displaces and enjoys his womanhood in his creations, in *Moll Flanders* and in *Roxana*. There, safely distanced, he could romp as Moll and, as Roxana, could revel in cross-dressing: "dressed in the Habit of a Turkish Princess, in a Robe of fine Persian damask, with the Ground white and the Flowers blue and gold, and the Train held five yards and with a Vest embroidered in gold . . ." Whether in real life Defoe was a secret cross-dresser can only be a speculation, but none can gainsay that the fantasy of cross-dressing was his favourite sport.

In the characters who people his novels, vicariously, he was seeking to indulge his fantasies without assuming personal responsibility for their deviance; but his efforts to gain enjoyment free of guilt failed. Without adequate justifying explanation in the texts, the confessional ever took over. The ventriloquist could not silence his puppets, a Crusoe-Defoe would weep:

> Now I looked back upon my past life with such horrour, and my sins appeared so dreadful, that my soul sought nothing of God but deliverance from the load of guilt that bore down all my comfort. . . . And I add this part here to hint to whoever shall read it, that whenever they come to a true sense of things, they will find deliverance from sin a much greater blessing than deliverance from affliction.

The bewildered reader may find little in the Crusoe novel to justify the flagellation Defoe imposed upon his creation, little to expect that Crusoe-Defoe had led the "wicked, curs't, abominable life" which he claimed was the past of his days. But although no evidence is provided to prove his "abominable" life—an adjective so often in biblical and ecclesiastical law associated with sodomy—Defoe was aware that forces were operating upon him which he could not control or even dare to name beyond calling them "ill fate":

> But my ill fate pushed me now on with an obstinacy that nothing could resist . . . I had no power to do it. I know not what to call this, nor will I urge that it is a secret over-ruling the creed that hurries us on to be instruments of our own destruction, even tho' it be before us, and that we rush upon it with our eyes open. Certainly nothing but some such decree'd unavoidable misery attending, and which it was

impossible for me to escape, could have pushed me forward against
the calm reasonings and perswasions of my most retired thoughts.

Among his "most retired thoughts", out of reach of insight, the
unconscious guilt of his fantasised primal incestuous crime remained
firmly in place. The depiction by Freud of *Homo sapiens* as Guilty
Man was never more apposite than in the case of Daniel Defoe.

A diagnosis of Defoe's extravagances, crushing guilt and extraordinary feminine identification as symptoms of his unassuaged
childish yearnings to be possessed by the father is, of course, discomfiting; it involves an acknowledgement of our bi-sexual natures
and for many that will prove frightening. The temptation is to take
each of Defoe's bizarre manifestations separately and to attribute its
causation to different external circumstance. His life as the perpetual penitent can be persuasively presented as a consequence of
his strict guilt-ridden upbringing, since as a child he was soaked in
the Old Testament; as a boy he had been required to copy out in
shorthand the whole of the Pentateuch;[16] he certainly learned much
of God's anger with humans who disdained His warnings and the
terrible retribution that fell upon sinners. And again his ever pertin-
ent penitential stance can be attributed to his "survivor guilt", a
view most persuasively presented by Tom Paulin,[17] who has drawn
attention to the continuing remorse afflicting Defoe, the escapee
from the Duke of Monmouth's failed 1685 Protestant Rebellion,
which resulted in the hanging of his less fortunate comrades.
Similarly, doubtless, it would be possible for one to be content to
deduce that his lingering erotic handling of the dresses and finery,
with which he adorned the women he created, springs from his
place in the family constellation; as the only boy, with two sisters a
little older, nostalgic for a childish paradise lost, he could again in
his novels ape his siblings as perchance he once had while dressing
up in their clothing.

Giving such varying explanations for each of Defoe's quirks may
often bring to us intimations of the environmental influences that
teased out, reinforced or corroborated his initial disposition; but
while we acknowledge their considerable significance, they must
not lead us away from an insistence that this very significance arises
because of the resonance they struck; external events detonated
an explosion, releasing the galaxy of Defoe's works, only because

they touched off highly charged, underground, imperfectly buried, negative Oedipal impulses of the man.

And it is those negative impulses which so frequently guide the selection in the *Historical Collection* of the violent stories with which Defoe, in his strange wooing, regaled his future wife. The tale of the wrestling between the lion and the renegade Englishman is, as Novak points out, "like a nightmare". The man is depicted as being almost suffocated by the oppressive weight of the beast which has decided to sit upon his victim and postpone devouring him until meal-time arrives; only the flashing, phallic knife thrust into the beast at the last moment saved the Englishman from that fate. It is a story which anticipates another nightmare: "the terrible dream" which Crusoe endured. In that terrifying dream the attacker is not disguised as the King of Animals; in the context, he is almost named as the father, the man with the "long spear":

> In this sleep I had this terrible dream. I thought that I was sitting on the ground on the outside of my wall . . . and that I saw a man descend from a great black cloud, in a bright flame of fire, and light upon the ground. He was all over as bright as a flame, so that I could just bear to look towards him; his countenance was most inexpressibly dreadful, impossible for words to describe; when he stepped upon the ground with his feet, I thought the earth trembled . . . and all the air looked, to my apprehension, as if it had been filled with flashings of fire.

> He was no sooner landed upon the earth, but he moved forward towards me with a long spear or weapon in his hand to kill me; and when he came to a rising ground, at some distance, spoke to me, or I heard a voice so terrible, that it is impossible to express the terror of it; all that I can say I understood, was this: "Seeing all these things have not brought thee to repentance, now thou shalt die"; at which words, I thought he lifted up the spear that was within his hand to kill me.

> No one that shall ever read this account will expect that I shall be able to describe the horrors of this terrible vision; I mean, that even while it was a dream, I even dreamed of those horrors; nor was it any more to describe the impression that remained upon my mind when I awaked and found it was but a dream.

The continuing presence of the nightmare in waking life, as experienced by Defoe-Crusoe, has oftimes been remarked. Early in the nineteenth century, in 1836, the physician Robert Macnish was writing:

> The illusions which occur are perhaps the most extraordinary phenomena of nightmare; and so strongly are they often impressed upon the mind, that, even on awaking, we find it impossible not to believe them real. . . . In many cases, no arguments, no efforts of the understanding will convince us that these are merely the chimeras of sleep.[18]

Victorian and Edwardian medical authorities ascribed such fearsome anxiety attacks to digestive or circulatory disturbances and, by so doing, illustrated once again how the advance of medicine in the material field can lead to the "forgetting" of much discomfiting knowledge, for healers of earlier centuries were well informed about the sexual origins of the condition. It was left to Freud's colleague and biographer, Ernest Jones, one of the most distinguished Welsh thinkers of the past century, to re-discover anew the pathogenesis of the phenomenon in his monumental work *On the Nightmare*.[19] There he elucidated the nightmare by telling us it is:

> a form of anxiety attack, that is essentially due to intense mental conflict centring around some repressed component of the psychosexual instinct, characteristically reactivation of the incest wishes of infancy, . . . repression of the feminine, masochistic component of the sexual instinct rather than that of the more masculine is apt to engender the typical nightmare. . . . The latent content of a nightmare consists of . . . a normal act of sexual intercourse. . . . Special emphasis should be laid on the circumstances that wishes fulfilled in this way always belong to the most powerfully repressed ones . . . with a nightmare the object is always a person whom the inhibiting forces of morality exclude from the erotic sphere. It is therefore comprehensible if the psychoanalysis of such dreams regularly showed them to be linked to a near relative, most usually a parent. . . . The latent content represents fulfilment of a repressed sexual wish, usually an incestuous one.

When writing the above in 1910, Jones emphatically predicated the bi-sexual nature of incestuous nightmare experiences, and in his introduction to the work forty years later he makes clear that he would, upon further reflection, lay even greater stress on the nightmare's bi-sexual characteristics. Thus encouraged by the great clinician, the evidential value of Defoe's nightmares becomes weighty; still enslaved to his infantile negative Oedipus complex, Defoe conjured up and doubtless endured nightmares that are exotic presentations of his dilemmas; to put it bluntly, and in a manner likely to be regarded by some as outrageous and to induce the maximum resistance to the hypothesis, Defoe was in his unconscious lusting to be fucked by his father and throughout his adult life carried all the guilt attached to that incestuous desire.

If this appears unnecessarily provocative, it is because I am weary of the circumlocutions that in my public life I was often forced to use in order to achieve desperately needed law reforms. During the 1960s, when I was repeatedly endeavouring to end the criminality of adult homosexual conduct, I was constantly lying in Parliament, affecting that the homosexual belonged to a totally different group, quite unlike the absolutely normal male members of the Commons; only thus could I allay the anxiety and resistance that would otherwise have been provoked. Homosexuals had to be placed at a distance, suffering a distinctive and terrible fate so different from that enjoyed by Honourable Members blessed with normalcy, children and the joys of a secure family life. Because of that wealthy endowment, they could surely afford charity. To have pleaded Freud would have alarmed too many in the House, insufficiently secure in their own heterosexuality to acknowledge their homosexual disposition. My discomfort with my own mendacity was considerable for I was, of course, well aware from Freud that:

> by studying sexual excitations other than those that are manifestly displayed, it is found that all human beings are capable of making a homosexual object choice and have in fact made one in their unconscious. Psychoanalytical research is most decidedly opposed to any attempt to separate off homosexuals from the rest of mankind as a group of a special character.

But, to achieve my end, I had no alternative but to plead compassion towards a separate disabled group. Even to hint that the homosexual component in a man's nature plays a large part in helping him to understand and so form a profound relationship with a woman would have been too disturbing; and to point out that the conduct of some of the philanderers in the House, compulsively chasing women, was determined by a ceaseless flight from their feelings for men, would, of course, have been disastrous. Even my intellectual dishonesty did not succeed in containing the fear of many of my colleagues; it was with only one vote in hand in the Report stage of the Bill that I did finally succeed in putting on to the Statute Book in 1967 my Act which ended the criminality of private homosexual conduct between consenting adults.

By the 1970s I was, albeit very tentatively, to be a little less guarded. During a debate on a Nullity Bill I was able to introduce successfully, and in bolder terms, arguments which led to more financial protection being given to transsexuals who, after undergoing a physical operation giving them an artificial vagina, had married. I said:

> Not all the human race can be neatly divided into two—and only two—separate compartments. Nature does not obey man-made laws and although this may be inconvenient to lawyers and legislators, we would be unjust and unfair if we persisted in continuing to believe that nature is not often shamelessly untidy.

Today, fortunately, the bi-sexuality of all of us can be acknowledged in less constrained terms, and it is to be hoped that laying stress upon its implications need no longer be an act of daring but can be merely a mature acknowledgement of its universality. Nevertheless, the continued diffidence shown by literary critics towards introducing the consequences of the condition when considering the curious collection of tales Defoe presented to his adored, which inevitably has led to the most strained explanations for the inclusion of some of them, shows how resistible even today is the injection of the subject of bi-sexuality into discourse. Yet only when one focuses upon the nature of the intense relationship between father, or father-surrogate, and son which governs the Oedipus complex is it possible to effectively explore the unconscious motivations determining Defoe's choice of texts for his *Historical Collection*; and that exploration reveals far more than the illumination of the choice of horrific stories of Mahomet the Great and his decapitation of his loved Irene; although, inevitably, the accusation will be made that we are engaged in a Procrustean exercise, that the selfsame unconscious motivations, if our hypothesis is well founded, should remain in place and be found when scrutinising the remorse which is so singularly attached to Defoe's guilt, or the punishments he courted through his fraudulent and risk-taking commercial enterprises, or, indeed, in his relationship with William of Orange.

But our exploration will be a foolhardy expedition if it depends for support on the aetiolated version which, with a few notable dissenters,[20] is too often accepted as valid within the Anglo-American psychoanalytic culture; these wan versions are the consequences not only of the influence of the Kleinians with their depreciation of the role of the father and their emphasis upon the mother's breast as the determinant in character formation, but also of other groupings in psychoanalytical circles that emerged in the second half of the twentieth century.

The "object-relations" school has as its central position an emphasis upon our need to relate to others, in contrast to the weight the Freudians place upon our need to reduce instinctual tension; and in the United States of America the "Self" school of analysts, following the brilliant and innovative probings of our narcissism by their master Heinz Kohut, while making their genuflections to the classic versions of the Oedipus phase, claim to be "enriching" it even as they put in the doubtful claim that the experience of the Oedipus complex does not fall to all, and that it is wholly dependent upon the particular developmental case history of an infant in his pre-Oedipal stage.[21]

And in Britain the benign influence of Donald Winnicott, the paediatrician-psychoanalyst, whose teachings have happily so penetrated the work of all working in the field of childcare, has also played a major part in deflecting attention away from the intense relationship which flares up in the Oedipal phase between father and son, and turned the searchlight on the first year of life of the human infant. There, Winnicott finds, the emotional development of the babe starts with the birth experience; and in his studies of the evolution of personality and character he warns that we must not even ignore events of the first days and hours.[22] Such an approach inevitably leads to rapt attention being given to the nature of the care bestowed upon, or withdrawn from, the baby by the mother; the nature and responses to the maternal feelings become all-important, and so single-mindedly have some of Winnicott's followers acted upon his guidelines that their extravagances have led to the accusation that Winnicott in his work ignores sexuality and passes over the role of the father in total silence. Winnicott evidently found it necessary to ward off the charge, for he once wrote:

> Freud did the unpleasant things for us, pointing out the reality and force of the unconscious, getting to the pain, anguish, conflict which invariably lie at the root of symptom formations, also putting forward, arrogantly if necessary, the importance of instinct and the significance of childhood sexuality. Any theory that denies or bypasses these matters is unhelpful.[23]

But his caveat appears to have gone unheeded; and that may well be because of the prevailing Zeitgeist. The excesses of the gender-feminists who, in the 1970s, expressed themselves in a depreciation of the penis, in a celebration of the clitoris orgasm, in soaring purchases of dildoes, and in declarations that a preference for mount-and-thrust sex was a confession of enjoyment in oppression, have faded, and affirmation of the joys of mutual masturbation between the sisters, making the male superfluous, now lacks stridency; but, with the coming of *in vitro* fertilisation, and the visibility of children born without copulation, and with the collapse of man's role as the sole family breadwinner, the notion that the father, during an infantile Oedipal phase, plays an all-important part that determines the destiny of the adult woman as well as of the man is unwelcome; the gender tricoteuses with their hostility to any hint of male power have certainly contributed to the creation in Britain and the United States of a climate of opinion which avoids acknowledging the full consequences of our sojourn within an Oedipal phase.[24]

But, distanced from the Anglo-American hegemony, in Israel, as in France, the student and the lay public are often encouraged to face unblinkingly Freud's exposition of the Oedipal complex and to gaze upon its terrors and pervading sexuality. In the United States and Britain, usually in the context of courses of general psychology and personality theory, Freudian thought reaches the undergraduate in most universities only through courses offered by professors coming from outside psychoanalysis and critical of it; the textbooks used only provide thematic and partial views of Freud, and the complexity of his exposition of the Oedipus complex is put aside in favour of very formal and inadequate presentations; the student rarely reads Freud direct. In Jerusalem, however, at the Hebrew University, in-depth studies of Freud are available; indeed, graduating students in clinical psychology are required to take a specific course on the Oedipus complex;[25] and that means that they are directed to the source which causes Freud boldly to insist that long before the babe has even differentiated the mother as a distinct object, the infant carries an identification with the father.

Freud, who never minimised our constitutional and philo-genetic inheritances, posits: "the child's first and most important identification is . . . his identification with the father in his own personal pre-history".[26] The close tie to the father is posited as innate; the conflicts and ambivalences which arise after the baby is born, during the Oedipal phase, have been historically anticipated. In his *Totem and Taboo*, Freud claims that in pre-history the sons

> hated their father, who presented such a formidable obstacle to their craving for power and their sexual desires; but they loved and admired him too. After they got rid of him, had satisfied their hatred and put into effect their wish to identify themselves with him, the affection which had all this time been pushed under was bound to make itself felt. It did so in the form of remorse.[27]

In this presentation, the murder of the father assuaged the son's hatred and, although severely tempered by remorse, his now-liberated affection for his father becomes boundless. Determined by this pre-history in the present, an infant, according to Freud, plays out the selfsame drama. The beloved father will again be the recipient of the same passive adoration when the little boy enters the Oedipal phase; but if the infant fails to negotiate successfully the pitfalls within that phase he will, as an adult, be ever wrestling with his passive femininity; and his desire to be the seducer and the sole love of his father will, in his unconscious, remain in place.

From this perspective the odd selection by Defoe, as a suitor, of the story of Mahomet and his murder of his loved one becomes less bewildering. More than one reading of the gruesome tale is no doubt possible but the dominant leitmotif is the renunciation by Mahomet, the great idealised father figure, of Irene in favour of a total untrammelled bonding with his soldiers; his slave troops would "bridle his affections" and no woman, however alluring, would distract this father from his submitting sons. However inept the recounting of such a tale by a suitor may be, Defoe nevertheless found its telling irresistible; this was a story of an exclusive love between father and son, and subliminally it echoed all Defoe's yearning. Within the negative, inverted Oedipus complex, the little boy's mother may be loved but she is seen as a rival coming between him and the father; she is the depository of his most ambivalent wishes; she is loved but he wishes her elimination even as was the case for Irene. The congruencies between Defoe's predicaments and the narrative of the Mahomet tale resound.

There is another significant concordance between Defoe and the content of the Mahomet tale. The Oedipus complex is enveloped in fantasies of castration; in its negative phase, in the surrender to the father, maleness has to be denied; castration is the physical pre-condition if consummation is to be achieved; and in its positive phase, it is the matching prohibitory threat that the father will cut off the boy's penis if he does not desist from his desire for the mother that plays a major part in the creation of castration anxieties. Normally, some traces of the Oedipus complex continue into the positive phase;[28] but where what Freud has called the "complete" Oedipus complex is only very hesitantly reached, it follows that the infant carries into adulthood an especially heavy load of castration anxieties since the anxieties stemming from the never-relinquished desire to be his father's lover are added to those arising from his incestuous desire for his mother.

Castration anxieties of this nature hover over the Mahomet tale, and it is not a strained reading—although one of a number—to suggest that the story recounts an attempt to be freed from their oppressiveness. The public decapitation by Mahomet of Irene is a symbolic castration. In Freud's works the castration fantasy is iden-tified behind a variety of symbols: the blinding of Oedipus in the seminal Oedipal legend is but one of many displacements that mask an assault on the penis: "the act may be distorted or replaced by other attacks upon the wholeness of the body",[29] and chopping off Irene's head with a scimitar is a thin disguise of a castration ceremony.

Nor should we be deceived or confused by the assault being made upon a woman, not a man; for the attack is essentially a retaliatory one, the riposte of a Samson against the castrating hair-cutting Delilah who would deprive him of his strength and mightiness. For most men the Delilah or Medusa lurks; those with an especial castration anxiety are particularly fearful of their powers; "the mythological creation of Medusa's head", Freud has written, "can be traced back to . . . fright at castration".[30] The early psychoanalyst Ferenczi cited this mythological horror—Medusa's head—as the source of the fears experienced by the boy in his sightings of the female genitalia void of a penis;[31] unworthy boys with incestuous wishes could suffer the same fate. When Mahomet cut off the head of Irene, the woman seen by his men as emasculating him, he committed an act of defiance against the Medusa castrating woman; the castrating woman was herself castrated. No one would be more likely to respond to such bravura than Defoe; a tale that told how in one blow a provocateur of lowly castration anxieties could be eliminated and that, untroubled any further, a father and son could live locked in an exclusive embrace, was indeed a happy ever after fairytale which Defoe could relish. Seemingly indifferent to the effect it might have upon his bride-to-be, Defoe, for his own sake, to gain a temporary catharsis, a transitory relief from his castration anxieties, placed it in his *Historical Collection*; but one cannot too forbear to muse that unconsciously the gift contained an encoded threat to his adored; men fear the Medusa in the woman they desire—Defoe much more than most—and in the death of Irene, over-determinedly, he was warning of the consequences were Medusa-powers ever to be dared to be directed against him.

He was to continue fighting against such castrating Medusa powers even in his sixties when, with guile, he wrote, as a woman, *Moll Flanders* and *Roxana*. For, in such works, he used the transvestite's trick of being a woman and yet keeping a penis. One fact always becomes obvious to little boys: the clearest sign that they are males is their penis. It is therefore what stands between them and a dreadful sense of inferiority and damage; and its penile sensations make it a most highly valued organ for pleasure. For Defoe, afflicted with a double dose of castration anxiety, the threat that, because of his passive feminine yearnings, he could lose it, would have been terrifying. He dealt with it in the fashion described by the American psychoanalyst Stoller:

it is just the future transvestite who feels so threatened with this loss because of his feminine wishes. He handles this danger by the thought that if males are evidence of a state of penislessness, the cause is not hopeless if there are women with penises. What better proof can there be of this than if one is such a creature oneself? Thus, in fantasy, does the transvestite make himself into a "woman".[32]

Defoe's "fantasy" was creatively displaced as he rustled his hidden penis underneath the folds of the skirts of Moll and Roxana.

Defoe's choice for Mary of the Mahomet story should be seen as an early tactic within his anti-castration strategy that was to culminate in the late novels in his last decade. How Mary received his gift we, of course, do not know. She would have been a very serious teenager indeed to have pondered on all its didactic moralising and all its bizarre tales. More probably, as so often in gifts given by lovers with serious intentions, the recipient would have been more intrigued by the significance of the token rather than its content. But for posterity the curious selection of pieces proves a boon, a rare occasion when Defoe, in his effusions, lowered his guard and so gave us more than a glimpse of the hinterland from which his genius emerged.

Notes

1. Ryecroft, C., A Critical Dictionary of Psychoanalysis, Nelson, 1968.
2. Phillips, A., The soul of man under psychoanalysis, The London Review of Books, 29 November 2001.
3. Green, A., Play and Reflection in Donald Winnicott's Writings, Karnac Books, 2005.
4. Green, A., Chains of Eros: The Sexual in Psychoanalysis, Erebus Press, 2000.
5. Thom, R., Structural Stability and Mortho-Genesis: An Outline of a General Theory of Muddle, Benjamin, 1975. Galatzer-Levy, R., in International Journal of Psychoanalysis (April 2004).
6. Segal, H., Introduction to the Work of Melanie Klein, Hogarth Press, 1973.
7. Hinshelwood, R. D., A Dictionary of Kleinian Thought, Free Association Books, 1989.
8. Klein, M., Notes on some schizoid mechanisms, International Journal of Psychoanalysis, 27 (1946), 99–110.

9. Green, *Chains of Eros*.
10. Glover, E., *The Roots of Crime*, Imago Publishing Co., 1960.
11. Abse, L., Introduction to E. Saville, *A History of the ISTD*, Institute for the Study and Treatment of Delinquency, 1992.
12. Kuhn, P., in *Psychoanalysis and History*, 3 (Summer 2000).
13. Freud, S., *The Ego and the Id*, SE, Volume 9.
14. Freud, S., *Ego and the Super-ego*, SE, Volume 19.
15. Fenichel, O., *The Psychoanalytic Theory of Neurosis*, Routledge & Kegan Paul, 1946.
16. Defoe, D., *Review*, 2, 408, quoted in Sutherland, J., *Defoe*, Methuen, 1950.
17. Paulin, T., in *London Review of Books*, 19 July 2001, and *Crusoe's Secret*, Faber & Faber, 2005.
18. Macnish, R., *The Philosophy of Sleep*, 1830.
19. Jones, E., *On the Nightmare*, Liveright, 1971.
20. Stoller, R. J., *Sex and Gender*, Hogarth Press, 1968; Blos, P., *The Gender Conundrum*, Brunner-Routledge, 2002.
21. Kohut, H., *The Restoration of the Self*, International University Press, 1977.
22. Winnicott, D., *The Family and Individual Development*, Tavistock Publications, 1965.
23. Winnicott, D., *Human Nature*, Free Association Books, 1988.
24. Abse, L., *Fellatio, Masochism, Politics and Love*, Robson Books, 2000.
25. Blass, R. E., The teaching of the Oedipus complex, *International Journal of Psychoanalysis*, 82 (2001), 82–105.
26. Freud, *The Ego and the Id*.
27. Freud, S., *Totem and Taboo*, SE, Volume 13.
28. Fenichel, *The Psychoanalytic Theory of Neurosis*.
29. Laplanche, J. and Fontalis J. B., *The Language of Psychoanalysis*, Hogarth Press, 1973.
30. Freud, S., *Revision of Dream Theories, New Introductory Lectures*, SE, Volume 22.
31. Ferenczi, S., On the symbolism of the head of Medusa, *International Zeitschrift fü Psychanalyse*, 9, 69 (1923).
32. Stoller, *Sex and Gender*.

CHAPTER FOUR

The thrills of risk-taking

In 1684, after a hesitancy of twelve months, Mary Tuffley yielded to Defoe's importunings and married him. She brought with her the not-inconsiderable dowry of £3700. By 1692, Defoe, the young trader, had lost it all, was a bankrupt and, not for the last time, was imprisoned for debt.

His wild schemes had undone him; nothing was too extravagant a venture to engage him. Not content with trading in clothes and wine, he became involved in the most bizarre enterprises. His immediate ruin was occasioned by two madcap promotions; one was the setting-up of a civet cat-farm with the intention of using the glands of the cats, which exude a strong and lasting scent, to enable him to become a manufacturer of perfumes; the other was an involvement with a patent-monger in a company that was to manufacture a diving engine capable of finding buried treasure in the ocean. Unsurprisingly these ventures proved disastrous, but not before Defoe's friends and his mother-in-law, duped by Defoe, had lost money by trusting in his misadventures.

These escapades were not simply the flightiness of a fey young man, nor do they demonstrate an incompatibility between a young day-dreaming future novelist and the man of business, for right into his sixties Defoe was to be forever involved in dicey trading; at various times in his life he is to be found dealing in horses, oysters, cheese, fishing, brick manufacture, tobacco importing, hose as well as clothing; and almost always he would leave behind, as he moved from one speculation to another, a trail of litigation arising from his failure to meet the debts his adventures had incurred.

Risk-taking for Defoe was irresistible; always he would choose to operate off-piste. "As a businessman", his latest biographer concedes, "he was essentially a gambler, excited by new deals, new prospects. What we see in many of the speculations is an almost compulsive interest in taking risks."

But what is especially intriguing about Defoe's risk-taking is not his compulsive commercial gambling—there are many literary figures who have been compulsive gamblers—but that, by beguiling paradox, this most reckless of men, one who has often attracted the soubriquet of "Britain's first novelist and first journalist", can, improbably, also claim to be our first management consultant; that is an assessment indeed which, in effect, was made of him in the nineteenth century where the instruction and advice which he gave in his *Compleat English Tradesman* to the nascent entrepreneur was treated with boundless deference, as perhaps it would be today in the Massachusetts or Manchester Business Schools. Such respect, however, was certainly not accorded to him in his day. Then a contemporary, telling of Defoe's reputation, wrote: "Daniel Defoe, the author of *The Review* is no Frenchman, but born here in England, bred an Hozier, and followed that trade 'til he broke for a considerable Sum. His Creditors run him into an Execution of Bankruptcy but to no purpose, he having fraudulently, as they seem assured, Concealed his Effects so that His Reputation amongst ye Fair Dealers of the City is very Foule. He is a profest Dissenter, though reckoned of no morals."

This was not the man presented in nineteenth-century biographies;[1] there his work was commended to be read as prophetic texts heralding the rise of Britain's economic power; with the approbation of this seer, the trading bourgeoisie of the century could bask in their own complacency and discover morality and religion in their sales. All their faults and obsessions, their regulation of time, their tunnel-visioned dedication to the mastering of the language of their trade undistracted by the schemes of projectors or the lure of politics and society, became highly commendable visions and would be rewarded, work being no burden but an untold delight "raising the trader above the world".

Such is Defoe's art—one that, as Anthony Burgess reminded us, is too much concealed to seem like art, and hence is frequently discounted—that even readers with no vested interest in believing in his heaven in the counting-house could nevertheless be persuaded of its reality; and in the nineteenth century, in the burgeoning capitalism of the time, there were indeed many believers happy to respond to his call to achieve liberation and joy through work.

Defoe wrote:

> Now in order to have a man happily heartily, and pursue earnestly the business he is engag'd in, there is yet another thing necessary, namely that he should delight in it to follow a trade, and not to love and delight in it, is a slavery, a bondage, not a business; the shop is a Bridewell, and the warehouse a house of Correction to the Tradesman, if he does not delight in his trade; while he is bound, as we say, to keep his shop, he is like the galley-slave chained down to the oar; he tuggs and labours indeed, and exerts the utmost of his strength for fear of the strapado, and because he is obliged to do it; but when he is on shore, and is out from the bank, he abhors the labour and hates to come to it again.
>
> To delight in business is making business pleasant and agreeable; and such a Tradesman cannot but be diligent in it; this according to Solomon makes him certainly rich, makes him in time, raises him above the world, and able to instruct and encourage those who come after him.

The sentiments chimed with the times of the nineteenth century. The biographers of that age enthused about *The Compleat English Tradesman*.[2] William Chadwick thought the work was not only Defoe's best book but "the best book that ever was written in the English language".

Such enthusiasm, telling of the book's influence, engenders further bewilderment. Almost all the precepts which Defoe laid down as the route to a commercial nirvana were those he persistently and flamboyantly transgressed; one important exception, to our great advantage, was his insistence that all communication by a trader must never be in a "rumbling bombast style" for "the easy free concise way of writing is the best style not only for the tradesman but for everyone". He continued:

> If any man was to ask me what I supposed to be a perfect stile, or language, I would answer, that in which a man speaking to five hundred people, all of common and various capacities, Ideots and lunaticks excepted, should be understood by they all, in the same manner with one another, and in the same sense in which the speaker intended to be understood, this would certainly be a most perfect stile.[3]

With such a style Defoe, preaching what he never practised, eloquently laid down the cautions and the rules which the novice trader must follow if he is to be a happy and successful businessman.

Was Defoe, then, an appalling humbug? All of us at some time fail to live up to our own ideals; but Defoe's duplicitous business dealings are too many to be forgiven as simply a one-off fall from grace. Yet his wild schemes are far too imaginative for us to believe that he was a confidence trickster who deceived others but never really believed in his own commercial fantasies; and, again, given his calamitous commercial CV, what causes him, late in life, after the success of his *Crusoe* and *Moll Flanders* and seemingly under no pressure, to write *The Compleat English Tradesman*, a work so totally at odds with his own lifestyle, one which praises the sedate and diligent and is free from the risks, thrills and misadventures which Defoe had endured all his days? To deal with this disconcertion the book precipitates, we shall have to do more than dismiss it as massive hypocrisy. It calls for more sensitive and persuasive enquiry.

* * * * * * * * * *

When Defoe's father died, in 1706, his will showed his scrupulous regard for paying all his debts; he died as he had lived, an upright merchant, a most respected member of a City livery company, the Butchers Company, and had been honoured by being made First Assistant Warden; his selection as a trustee in many wills bears further witness to his reputation as an honest and dependable businessman. He was, it is generally accepted, the model Defoe used to depict the ideal tradesman whom he canonised in his *Compleat English Tradesman*. And there are too many congruencies between the father Defoe gave to Crusoe and that of his own father to hesitate in identifying them with each other.

The admonition given by Crusoe's father to his son tells us much of the values that James Defoe had sought to inculcate in his son Daniel, and the agonising within Robinson Crusoe's defiance of his father corroborates the tortuous subversion which moved Defoe in his life to transgress so persistently against the advice which his father had proffered:

> You told me it was for men of desperate fortunes on one hand, or of aspiring, superior fortune on the other, who went abroad upon adventures, to rise by enterprize, and make themselves famous in undertakings of a nature out of the common road; that these things were either all too far above me, or too far below me; that mine was the middle state, or what might be called the upper station of low life, which he had found by long experience was the best state in the world, the most suited to human happiness, not exposed to the miseries and hardships, the labour and sufferings of the mechanic part of mankind, and not embarrassed with the pride, luxury, ambition, and envy of the upper part of mankind. He told me I might judge of the happiness of this state by this one thing, viz., that this was the state of life which all other people envied, that kings have frequently lamented the miserable consequences of being born to great things, and wished they had been placed in the middle of the two extremes, between the mean and the great; that the wise man gave his testimony to this as the just standard of true felicity when he prayed neither to have poverty or riches.

> . . . The middle station had the fewest disasters, and was not exposed to so many vicissitudes as the higher or lower parts of mankind; nay they were not subjected to so many distempers and uneasiness, either of body or mind, as those were who by vicious living, luxury and extravagances on one hand, or by hard labour, want of necessities, and mean or insufficient diet on the other hand, bring distempers upon themselves by the natural consequences of their way of living; that the middle station of life was calculated for all kinds of vertues and all kinds of enjoyment; that peace and plenty were the handmaids of a middle fortune; that temperance, moderation, quietness, health, society all agreeable diversions, and all desirable pleasures, were the blessings attending the middle station of life.[4]

When, in Defoe's script, through the voice of Crusoe's father, we hear James Defoe speaking so passionately and with such conviction, we know that it belittles the struggle being enacted in the interior life of Defoe to treat his commercial escapades as simple but masked rebellious responses to his father's conservatism; that view, one sometimes hinted at, is only a half-truth, one that is disrespectful to the algedonic combinations of desire and horror to be found embossed upon Defoe's relationship with his father. Those more sensitive to the agonising that lies beneath his continuous flow of pamphlets on finance will divine the causation of this compulsive gambler's fears and never-ending denunciation of all gamblers engaged in the professional market of his day. In 1719, in his *Anatomy of Exchange Alley*, he lashed the stock-jobbers in words that might indeed be appropriately applied to many of today's investment bank analysts: "If you talk to them of their Occupation there is not a Man but will own, 'tis a Compleat System of Knavery . . ." And this man, whose reckless taking of credit would lead him at least twice into the debtors' gaol, could, with a sophistication that amazes contemporary financial editors, spell out the effects of money and credit upon prices;[5] yet Defoe's perspective and interest in the nature of credit could not save him from his folly. It was of no avail that he had an acute sense of the difference between intrinsic value and market price: "The setting of a Price upon the Stock is the work of Artifice, and perhaps of Knavery, and is too often in the power of the most scandalous Sharpers of the Alley." Still he would, rejecting his own counsel, continue on his disastrous commercial misadventures.

When, in editing his newsletter *The Director*, Defoe mocked the panic-stricken investors caught by the collapse of the South Sea Bubble, he ably pinpointed their irrationality, but not his own: "If we saw a whole street of inhabitants in an uproar, crying fire, calling for water, some running for engines, others breaking up the pipes, others hurrying away their wives and children for fear of their being burned in their beds, others throwing their goods out of windows and doors for anybody to run away with them, and all this while no fire was discovered, no smoke seen or smelled, should we not all say, 'The people are mad?' "[6] Not all are free who mock their chains, the German poet Schiller once reminded us; the "madness" Defoe saw in others was his own compulsive addiction to gambling. Not all his tremendous inveighing against its evil could protect him from its lure. Predictably, in accordance with his secret wish, this extraordinary financial expert would die in poverty.

$$\star \quad \star \quad \star \quad \star \quad \star \quad \star \quad \star \quad \star \quad \star \quad \star \quad \star$$

Vain though it proved to be, Defoe's attempt to use weighty and cautionary financial pamphlets as material for the construction of a defence, keeping at bay his yearning for wild commercial spec-ulation, was creative and extraordinary; but the syndrome that prompted this heroic effort was ordinary and commonplace. He was playing the game that, as legal adviser to one of the largest book-makers in Britain, I often saw being dis-enjoyed by chronic gambling punters. I learned the reason for the equanimity of the bookmaker as he suffered huge losses when chronic gamblers had a winning streak: he knew these punters would soon return to squander the winnings on losing bets, never satisfied until all was lost, for the compulsive gambler, unconsciously, plays to lose, not to win.

Risk-taking aimed at loss, gambling to lose, is a phenomenon explored in some revealing and startling asides within Freud's essay *Dostoevsky and Parricide*.[7] Freud found the causality of the com-pulsive gambler's habit in a particular variation of the Oedipus complex, one in which the negative and inverted elements play a malign role; it was one which in Defoe, as in Dostoevsky, had a shattering impact on adult life. Freud, in his essay, once again emphasised how when the child is in his Oedipal phase—in intense rivalry with his father and resenting the father's possession of the mother—he not only has parricidal wishes against his "rival" but simultaneously has the desire to be the father's love-object. This bi-sexuality, prompting the boy's wish both to become his mother's lover and to be taken by his father to displace the wife can, in adverse external circumstances, bring about intolerable dilemmas which often reach into adulthood.

The boy fears that his wish to slay the father may bring him the retaliation of castration; at the same time he fears submission as a feminine love-object will bring about the same result. The ideal reso-lution of these dilemmas may never be possible, but most of us, from fear of castration, in the interests of preserving our masculinity, give up the wish to possess our mother and to slay the father, and confine both impulses—hatred of the father and being in love with the father—to the unconscious. There, albeit imperfectly, they remain repressed but still prompting in all of us a feeling of guilt and a need for expiation. Freud finds, however, that in those whose bi-sexual disposition has caused them especially to fear the consequences of their feminine attitudes, a pathogenic intensification of their feelings of guilt arises. In adulthood such boys are prone to attempt to relieve their guilt by placing themselves at the mercy of Fate and demanding that *it* provides a means of resolving their impossible dilemmas.

For, in the Freudian view, gambling is in essence provocation of fate, forcing it to take decisions for or against the individual. With every throw of the dice, with every turn of the card, with every spin of the wheel, the questions being asked over and over again reflect the earlier Oedipal dilemmas: am I omnipotent, able by my secret wishes to kill my father, and have I, if he is in fact dead, killed him? And simultaneously—since formal logic is not part of the unconscious—am I the belovèd of my father? He loves me, he loves me not. If the gambler wins, he receives affirmative answers to all his questions. He is the killer and the belovèd. But in either case he must pay the price of emasculation, a totally unacceptable and terrifying conclusion. So, to remain intact, the compulsive gambler never desists; he is determined to continue until he loses in order to survive. Only by losing does he gain relief from his guilt as killer and lover, for then he obtains the punishment he deserves for his parricidal and incestuous wishes.

During the years that I observed my bookmaker-client supplying these masochistic needs to thousands of customers, it was clear that although the punters, to maintain their psychic equilibrium, were determined to lose their money, the thrills that they had en route were sustaining them. Those joyless thrills were paralleled by Freud to masturbation. Indeed, Dostoyevsky himself described the tremulous excitement which losing afforded him and pointed out that the punishment of total loss at the end of a losing run led to orgasm. Thus the psychic masochist pursues his lonely path, producing pleasure out of displeasure.

From dangers we gain our thrills; always we must fear some risk, but from the ultimate risk, that of emasculation which was the threat menacing Defoe, as all compulsive gamblers, we seek to distance ourselves; our thrills are less intensive, the dangers we court less threatening. We ski on these steep slopes and sometimes dare to risk going off-piste, we skate and toboggan, we rock-climb, sail, speed in cars, dive from heights, we whirl around on breathtaking contraptions at funfairs and some are driven, in their search for thrills, to heighten their anxieties and so increase their pleasures by greater, more terrifying dangers, by sailing alone in small boats around the world braving tempestuous storms. So often the thrills, when described, intimate that sexual undercurrents are operating, as when we tell of those taking a virginal route to a mountain peak or exploring virginal lands.[8]

The thrills we enjoy in our games, in our sports and in our exploratory adventures into strange lands or with strange women are compensations for our renunciation of the thrills of our early infantile incestuous desires; but that renunciation, in the case of a chronic gambler like Defoe, was far from complete. If we trace Defoe's morbidity to his father fixation, we must too ask about the mother whose presence in more usual circumstances would surely have ensured that Defoe moved through the Oedipal rite of passage and not remained throughout his adult life so fatefully enamoured in fatal bondage to his father.

And of Defoe's mother we know very little. Suspiciously, only once in his writings did Defoe mention her, and that was in an aside which suggested she would put up with no nonsense from young Daniel. When, to vex her, he wilfully refused his dinner, she ensured he was left hungry. His biographer, James Sutherland, concluded she was "a severe mother"[9] and certainly, if we can equate her with the mother of Crusoe as depicted by Defoe, the son found her extra-ordinarily difficult and unapproachable, never ready to intercede on his behalf to mitigate her husband's rulings. In this strict Puritan Defoe household we find that such rulings required Daniel, as a boy, to copy in his own hand the whole of the Pentateuch.[10] He would have found that Moses and other commanding father figures abound, but no succouring Mary. On the basis of the few facts at our disposal, it seems improbable that a mother's warm responses were available to Daniel; if they had been in place, perhaps young Daniel, with such encouragement, would have dared to desist from his masochist obeisances to his father.

When he was to pursue Mary Tuffley, it may well be that it was not only her dowry that attracted him but the qualities she pos-sessed that were reminiscent of his mother, for evidently Mary was a "tough cookie", described as a shrew by Anthony Burgess[11] and certainly notorious for her verbal aggressiveness. And the oyster-wench mistress that Antony Burgess tells us Defoe possessed could hardly have been a gentle flower; a fish-market woman has other qualities. Pope, writing of Defoe's son Norton, in *The Dunciad* remarked on his mother's lashing tongue:

> Norton, from Daniel and Ostroea sprung,
> Blessed with his father's front, and mother's tongue,
> Hung silent down his never-blushing head;
> And all was hushed, as folly's self lay dead.

The masochistic lover seeks out the dominatrix. Such adult diversions all suggest a desire for the chastisement he originally received from his mother.

For punishment was ever his secret goal; only thus could he expiate his Great Sin, his intemperate passion for the father. To possess the father for himself alone, he sought to erase the mother from his biography; she was to be expunged from the record but the father, a tallow chandler named Foe, was reborn as an aristocratic Defoe descended from "*Antient Norman* family of the name of De Beau-Foe", and the blood of Sir Walter Raleigh flowed in his veins. Defoe's pretentious elevation of his father's status is a typical over-valuation by a besotted lover of the attributes of a belovèd.

But the love he proffered was tainted; and, acknowledging his guilt, he thus submitted to the suffering he knew his perversion deserved. A lesser man would have been totally destroyed by the flagellation he imposed upon himself, but Defoe would not succumb to his torture. By his marvellous capacity to displace and sometimes contain his masochism within his works he ensured he survived to become so significant a figure in British history. Never was masochism more creatively transmuted.

Notes

1. Chadwick, W., *The Life and Times of Daniel Defoe*, 1859; Wilson, W., *Memoirs of the Life and Times of Daniel De Foe*, First & Chance, 1830.

2. Chadwick, *The Life and Times of Daniel Defoe*; Wilson, *Memoirs of the Life and Times of Daniel De Foe*.
3. Kelly, A., *The Compleat English Tradesman*, 1969.
4. Defoe, D., *The Life and Surprizing Adventures of Robinson Crusoe*.
5. Chancellor, Edward, *Prospect*, 2002.
6. Defoe, D., *Defoe's Financial Pamphlets*, Pickering & Chatto, 2000.
7. Freud, S., *Dostoevsky and Parricide*, SE, Volume 21.
8. Balint, M., *Thrills and Regressions*, Hogarth Press, 1959.
9. Sutherland, J., *Daniel Defoe*, Methuen, 1950.
10. See Chapter 3, p. 33.
11. Burgess, A., Introduction to *A Journal of the Plague Year*, Penguin Classics, 1966.

CHAPTER FIVE

Cannibalism

C annibalism was a strange but continuous preoccupation of Defoe; so often the protagonists in his tales fear they will be devoured. In *Robinson Crusoe* the horrors of cannibalism are often depicted and the spectacle of savages inhumanly feasting upon the bodies of their fellow-creatures is condemned as the "pitch of inhuman hellish brutality and the horror of degeneracy of human nature".

In the sequel to *Robinson Crusoe—The Further Adventures*—an allegorical note is struck: Defoe seeks to teach that people can come together as a nation under the threat of a grave external danger. On Crusoe's island it is the prospect of being devoured by invading cannibals that stills the strife between quarrelling, marooned Spaniards and Englishmen. A fictional Spanish captain is given by Defoe the script reciting the consequences of falling into the hands of the man-eaters:

> The Sight had fill'd them with Horror, and the Consequences appear'd terrible to the last Degree, even to them, if ever they should fall into the Hands of those Creatures who would not only kill them as Enemies, but kill them for Food as we kill our cattle. And they

profess'd to me, that the Thought of being eaten up like Beef or Mutton, tho' it was suppos'd it was not to be until they were dead, had something in it so horrible, that it nauseated their very Stomachs, made them sick when they thought of it, and filled their Minds with such unusual Terror that they were not themselves for some Weeks after.

But long before these stories were written, Defoe would be found extravagantly justifying English colonial expansion, pleading that otherwise, under incompetent Spanish administration, the inhabitants would "Eat up one Another". Such quirky judgements are not irrelevancies. There is a haunting and revelatory quality in Defoe's fantasies of the gastronomy of savages banqueting on human flesh. Such gluttony outrages him; when he rails against the obscenity of cannibalism, it is against his own imagination that his anger is being directed. His was a need to condemn an appetite which he found alluring. He was struggling to distance himself from the oral-cannibalistic phase which, Freud has taught us, as suckling babes, we all must pass through in our advance towards genitality.[1] Each time, as a result, in each oral kiss we bestow upon our loves, nostalgically, we evoke the sweet memory of the nipple, and each time too, subliminally, we recall both the vengeful anger felt at each withdrawal and our thwarted desire to incorporate, devour, the bestowing breast so that irrevocably it would belong to us alone.

The daring early follower of Freud, Sandor Ferenczi, wrote of how the nursling is in the main an ectoparasite on his mother, just as in the foetal period he lives on her endoparasitically.[2] Just as he lorded it in the mother's womb, and finally compelled the mother, his liberal host, to push the presumptuous guest out of doors, so also the babe behaves more and more aggressively towards the nursing mother: "It emerges from the period of harmless oral eroticism, sucking, into a cannibalistic stage; it develops within the mouth instruments for biting with which it would fain eat up, as it were, the beloved mother, compelling her eventually to wean it."[3]

But that weaning, unless handled delicately, can be a severe trauma for the babe; the consequences of his first traumatic experience, the birth trauma, can be mitigated by the solicitous mother providing the illusion of the intra-uterine state, bestowing warmth, the darkness and the quiet which are requisites to that illusion. And similarly, the empathic mother, by soothing reassuring nursing, can reduce the terror of the child as it finds itself bereft of its sustainer: the breast. Comfort and love are needed as never before if the rage of the babe suffering deprivation is not to be all-consuming.

Freud's collaborator Karl Abrahams postulated that each of us pass from a pre-ambivalent oral phase to a second stage, a sadistic one, the oral-cannibalistic phase;[4] if no or insufficient compensation flows from the mother, if the babe is denied the needed reassurances that the mother belongs to him but is made to feel that all his former omnipotent control over the mother is irretrievably lost, then, as Melanie Klein has described the situation, the babe's fantasy of the good breast, which has been confirmed by gratifying experiences of love and feeding by the real mother, is replaced by a fantasy of a persecutory breast.[5] Against that enemy, all the oral-cannibalistic rage is hurled. Only a mother's empathy can temper such vengefulness; a brusque controlling strict mother—such as Defoe appears to have possessed—can be disastrously provocative.

All in adulthood bear the impress of our oral phase; indeed, none display it more explicitly than the garrulous politicians with whom I dwelt for thirty years in the Commons; but for all of us, it is the oral experience of satiation at the breast which furnishes the prototype for our later fixated wishes for a specific person; desire and satisfaction are for ever marked by our first early oral experience,[6] and so is the accompanying sadism and aggressiveness which laces the behaviour of every adult. Defoe's exaggerated apprehensions of cannibalism tell us of the fears of retaliation, of a terror that the breast he wished to devour will devour him.

In an attempt to allay the fears of the retaliatory consequences of his own sadistic yearning, Defoe repudiates his gruesome appetite and projects it upon the savages that he conjures up within his wondrous tales. Yet, ever simmering beneath the surface of the stories, frightful menaces swell; Crusoe's discovery of a man's footprint on the sand immediately arouses fears that he will be eaten; but no cannibals are lurking. What are surfacing are the repressed hideous desires of Defoe; he cannot banish them from his imagination; all the artifices of the elaborations of his story-telling cannot exorcise his fear of yielding to his dangerous primal appetite for human flesh, for the breast that had been denied to him.

Is this the fear that haunts so many of Defoe's works? Always and

about the external dangers that he brings to threaten the security
of protagonists of the stories, beyond the impending or potential
disasters that is their lot, there looms a harbinger of disaster, an
unnamed, unidentified terminator who will ensure that Defoe's her-
oes/heroines, whether Roxana or Moll Flanders, will be unmasked,
their impersonations revealed, their worlds utterly destroyed.

The tension heightens as we see his characters teetering on the
edge; we identify with them, as did Defoe, under a compulsion to
learn whether they are fated or will escape their doom. Yet somehow
we sense that it is not the recorded events of which we have been
informed that are determining the outcome; there are ghosts abroad
and these are not under the novelist's control. They have come from
another world, from Defoe's unconscious. Crusoe's/Defoe's "preoccupation with the fate of being devoured by cannibals seems to
evoke a psychological nightmare rather than reality", comments his
biographer, Maximilian Novak.[7] But although the stalking ghosts
are invisible, they are ever-present and, with care, we can hear their
lamentations as they mourn their loss of the suckling breast; we hear
too their cry for vengeance against the betraying persecutory breast
which has cruelly deserted them.

All the ambivalences within the lament of these invisible pursu-
ing furies are echoed in Defoe's libretto; indeed, those apparitions
provide the frisson and the fascination of Defoe's highly charged
depictions of cannibalistic savages. One marvels again that whereas,
for many, the legacy of an unempathic mother may be found in the
whining or defeatism of the adult son, with Defoe the disadvantage
is so opportunistically and creatively seized. The enraged frustrations of his earliest orality, displaced and finding expression in
adulthood, were to give us England's most savage and effective political pamphleteer; no cannibal dismembered his meat with greater
relish than did our Daniel as he tore to shreds the pretensions of his
opponents. And certainly no primitive man-eater mocked his prey
more mercilessly. His fierce lambastings infuriated those he lashed.
Unsurprisingly, to silence him, he was at various times put in the
stocks and also gaoled. But the cries of the furious rage within the
man were not easily stilled.

His aggression, given its primal source, was limitless but not
undirected. The bitter irony of *The Shortest Way with Dissenters*, an
outrageous parody on the fanaticism within the Anglican Church of

his day, was as intolerant a lampoon of intolerance as has ever been written; and never more than today has his poem *The True-Born Englishman*, the most frequently reprinted poem of the reign of Queen Anne, been more relevant. His onslaught on those stirring up prejudice against foreign immigrants and his raillery against English insularity, xenophobia and absurd pride in purity of descent should be on the curriculum of every school in the land. If there were sad occasions in Defoe's life when expediency caused him to bite his tongue, we should nevertheless applaud the courage he displayed when on so many occasions he released it and, paradoxically, for this we may be indebted to deficient sensibilities of his martinet mother.

For we are indeed formed in our mother's arms as well as within her womb. If the babe has not through tender care felt trust, if a secure relationship with the breast, his first object, has not been established, if, during the regime of the teething stage—when the teeth cause pain from within and when one of the few ways the babe has of obtaining relief is by the biting of nipple and breast—the breast is unsympathetically and brusquely withdrawn from him, then teething becomes of especial proto-typical significance;[8] the same cold mother who impatiently wards off the babe distances the infant when, a little later, he enters the Oedipal phase; to work through the negative beginnings of the phase, to give up his desire to be possessed by his father, and to move forward on his way to genitality, requires the infant to yield to the seductions of his mother; biological maturation in itself in no way guarantees access to genitality. It is the play, teasing and fondling of the mother that ensure the infant will choose her as the desired object and give him the courage to quit his role as a submissive catamite and to become the rival to his father.

But it would appear that no welcoming mother awaited Daniel and no warm encouragement was available; an indifferent mother would not woo him but would leave him in thralldom to his father, never able to achieve the emancipation which would have freed him to experience what Freud has named as the "complete Oedipus complex". Exposed as a baby to similar circumstances and emotional deprivation, another man might perchance have become a snarling loudmouth or a passive homosexual or developed a paranoid personality; Defoe's particular and extraordinary capacity creatively to sublimate and displace the wounds which his early disadvantages had occasioned therefore remains a mystery; but, by identifying the ecology within which his genius flourished, we are left no less enchanted but certainly less bewildered by it. Listening attentively to the fearsome war-cries of his savage cannibals, we hear in the background the whimpering of an angry babe denied the breast; marvellously, out of that cacophony, the genius of Defoe emerges.

★　★　★　★　★　★　★　★　★　★

Are we being misogynistic in attributing to the unempathic mother sole responsibility for so many vicissitudes which, to his disadvantage and our advantage, befall him as he fails to free himself from his initial early bondage to his father? When he displaces on to savage cannibals his own rage, do the attacks he fears and envisages tell us too of frustrations felt even earlier when he experienced his mother's grudging breast? There are hungers, other longings, variously described by some discerning psychoanalysts as "father-hunger"[9] or "father-thirst".[10] The birth of an infant son brings about an ambivalent dyadic relationship; love, pride and devotion may be the father's manifest emotions but darker shadows can be felt by the father seeing his infant son's exuberant lust for life. Negative feelings, unacknowledged, unconscious, can drift into the relationship; hostile emotions of envy, resentment and death wishes can be reduced to insignificance by the joy and elation evoked by paternity but sometimes they are not so benignly neutralised; and then they can affect the early son–father relationship. That relationship, which has the potential to endow the babe with a feeling of being protected and loved, of being saved from helplessness, can be damaged and leave the infant insecure, ever to be hungry in later life for love and security.

Clinicians noting from their findings the ubiquity of this phenomenon often cite as illustrative corroboration aspects of the Greek myth of King Laius,[11] who set out to kill his son Oedipus by abandoning him in the wilderness to certain death: "The inference that the unnatural deed Laius committed was initiated by the voice of the oracle only speaks of the ubiquitous danger of hostile emotions which the birth of an infant son unleashes to the father."[12] For my part, my lawyer's experience as a divorce practitioner sometimes brought to me instances of the destructive consequences that may fall upon a man who, in adult life, can never come to terms with the hostility of a father which he had felt as a babe. I recall the dismay of a young woman married to a very successful professional man who, following upon an unplanned pregnancy, gave birth to a boy; the husband, declaring he could not share his love, immediately walked out of the home; she brought me a sheaf of letters from him begging her to place the child for adoption so that he could return and they could enjoy, as before, their wondrous exclusive love; he refused counselling, and she refused his impossible request; a divorce followed.

Such displays of hostility by a father to a new-born son are fortunately rare but clearly some of the nutrients that the father can provide to ensure the growth of a healthy and expansive enrichment of the babe's incipient personality were denied to Defoe. Behind his tales of devouring cannibals there looms not only a mother begrudging the breast; there is too a father unable or unwilling to give the emotional nourishment for which the boy was clamouring. It was an under-nourished babe that was to give us tales of dismembering cannibals gorging themselves on human flesh; in fantasy, Defoe has the banquets his parsimonious parents had refused him; no wonder, feeling guilty, he was ever in fear that he would suffer retaliatory punishment, that he too, one day, would be gobbled up. Perhaps in the telling of the story, although quickening our own unconscious apprehensions, Defoe was helped a little to still his own nerves.

Notes

1. Freud, S., *Three Essays on the Theory of Sexuality*, SE, Volume 7.
2. Ferenzci, S., *Thalassa*, Karnac Books, 1989.
3. Ferenzci, *Thalassa*.
4. Abrahams, K., *Collected Papers*, Hogarth Press, 1927.
5. Klein, M., *Envy and Gratitude*, Tavistock Publications, 1957.
6. Laplanche, J. and Pontalis, J. B., *The Language of Psycho-analysis*, Hogarth Press, 1973.
7. Novak, M. E., *Daniel Defoe: Master of Fictions*, Oxford University Press, 2001, p. 153.
8. Erikson, E., *Childhood and Society*, Pelican, 1965.
9. Herzog, A. M., Sleep disturbance and father-hunger, *Psychoanalytical Study of the Child*, 35 (1980), 219–33.

10. Avelin, E., The role of the father in the separation individuation process, in *Essays in Honour of Margaret S. Mahler*, Inter-University Press, 1971.
11. Ross, J. M., Oedipus re-visited: Laius and the Laius complex, *Psychoanalytical Study of the Child*, 37 (1982), 169–200.
12. Blos, P., Son and father, Plenary lecture for meeting of American Psychoanalytical Association, New York, 17 December 1982.

CHAPTER SIX

The plague: defying Thanatos

I n his superb essay on Defoe, Michael Foot, as one great journalist to another, pays tribute to the man he describes as "the father of English journalism" and tells how, at sixty, during the last decade of his life, "the genius of Defoe suddenly sprouted into a winter blossom unexampled in the whole range of literature".[1]

Defoe's miracle year was 1722. *Crusoe*, his first novel, had been published only three years earlier and had been followed by the sequel *The Further Adventures*. Then, out of a frenzy of creative work, there came *Moll Flanders* and *Colonel Jack* and *A Journal of the Plague Year*—and all this while he was carrying in his mind *Roxana*, which was to be published in 1724. All these were novels excepting the *Journal*, which was the account of the pestilence that, when Defoe was a child, had devastated London; that work was *sui generis*.

However the *Journal* may be described, it would be singularly inappropriate to call it a novel; neither is it history, nor is it fiction. Defoe's usual stratagem of gaining verisimilitude by presenting fiction as fact is here much used, but this work nevertheless is no mere "faction"; for the work includes an account of a profound religious experience, an expression of a deep conviction that the life of man is providentially ordered; it is governed by "Providence's

chequer-work"; even so appalling a calamity as the plague was a con-
vulsion in a microcosm[2] and if we were to understand its meaning,
we must look to "the vast open field of infinite power".

This affirmation, made by "HF", the anonymous narrator of the
dreadful visitation, does not, however, go unchallenged: "Is it the
fruit of faithlessness to shun the Plague?" It is the subject of a theological debate which Defoe causes HF to hold with his brother—
whether to remain in London and submit to fate or to flee to the
country and there escape its commands. Does not the deity who
sends pestilence also send life? Should not a man take responsibility
to preserve himself instead of throwing himself on the mercy of
providence? The debate between the brothers reveals all the continuing ambivalences of Defoe to the demand that the paternal edict
of providence must be unquestionably obeyed; it also tells us of
Defoe's hesitancy to escape, to be a rebellious son and, emancipated,
without crushing guilt to make his own choices.

Echoes from the Oedipal clashes of Defoe's earliest years therefore
resound throughout the theological debate; but to treat it seriously,
to regard it merely as a platform on which, in disguised form, Defoe
could attempt to work through his Oedipal struggles, would belittle
the grandeur of the disputation. What we are witnessing is an
endeavour by the profoundly religious Dissenter to come to terms
with the Enlightenment, for an unqualified belief in Providence
leads to an acceptance of plague as punishment, as an instrument of
divine wrath, a notion so utterly contrary to the rationalist spirit of
the Enlightenment.

But even positing this engagement of Defoe as a vital sub-text
of the work, we are still left with the unanswered question as to
why, when he was so fanatically involved in his story-telling, he
should turn aside to write a dense work not only wrestling with
the theological and philosophical dilemmas of his day but doing
so in the context of an exhaustively researched and documented
historical chronicle; such a change from the beguiling romanticism
to the unremitting realism is startling, and although his picaresque
novels oft-times show pity for the individual sinner, nowhere in his
works do we hear such a moving threnody for the general human
condition.

The extraordinary meditation on the human predicament is the
essence of the work; to regard it as a product of the moment and seek

to explain away the occasion of its publication as a response to contemporary events is persuasive but ultimately unconvincing. It is, of course, attractive to regard the *Journal* as the creation of a great journalist and it suggests that although he was writing of the Plague of 1665, plague in 1772 had a topicality which Defoe found irresistible. Plague was in the news. It had broken out in Marseilles two years earlier, and a recall of the manner in which the 1665 outbreak had reached London from the ports of Holland and an address of the question whether the infection would now spread from the port of Marseilles were apposite. Others have advanced the view that the *Journal* is pseudo-history,[3] written by a superb pamphleteer in the service of expert political propaganda, designed to give support to Walpole's unpopular Quarantine Act, a preventative measure which Defoe thought necessary.[4]

But it is an inadequate reading of the *Journal* to consider it solely as a commentary on some contemporary events; it is not an isolated, idiosyncratic work. It is a culmination of a persistent interest in plague expressed in Defoe's writing for at least a decade before he wrote the *Journal*. "The very idea of plague seems to have been an abiding fact in his consciousness", Louis Landa opined.[5]

Landa's speculation that this may have been "implanted in childhood memories" may be less well founded, since Defoe, aged five years and before the Great Plague entirely overwhelmed London, was taken to the country. However, the terror that was beginning to be felt by the citizens of London would, given Daniel's precocity, hardly have been unnoticed by an alert and curious child, but his exposure to the plague would have been slight and therefore to attribute his preoccupation in later life with the plague directly to his awareness of it as a five-year-old would be misleading; such an attribution would be too simplistic, leading us away from a diagnosis of the temperamental condition which precipitated Defoe's constant outpourings against the dangers of plague. He was writing as early as 1709 about the danger to England of an epidemic and continued to sound the tocsin until the autumn of 1720 when his fears were aroused by the Marseilles epidemic.

No homophobe, fiercely blaming the prevalence of AIDS on homosexual activity, could more starkly reveal his fear of his attraction to that which he condemns; Defoe, in his alarums on the dangers of plague, reveals his fear of his morbid attraction to fatality. The homophobe fears his desire for homosexual sex; Defoe fears his attraction to the lures of death; such forbidden lascivious dreams of attaining consummation within death's embrace contributed to the making of Defoe the eternal penitent. This was an element within the Great Sin to which, through his characters, he always hurried to plead guilty. Immersed in religious doctrine, no one knew better that choosing one's death was a privilege reserved for the elect; Christ could choose the Cross, the Saints their martyrdom; for others it was an unforgivable presumption. *The Journal of the Plague Year* is a depiction of one man's epic struggle to quench that blasphemous masochistic presumption.

★ ★ ★ ★ ★ ★ ★ ★ ★ ★

The societal and religious condemnation of the suicide in Defoe's day was continued well into the twentieth century. The proclaimed ukase was unequivocal. Stigmatising masochistic practitioners curbed mimesis, punished the lese-majesty of the impertinent ones denying the glory of life and ensured that identification with the cross should be free of excess; there were no shortcuts to heaven and anyone taking an alternative exit would find it led to hell.

All these warnings still had coercive back-up when, in 1958, I entered Parliament. Successful perpetrators of suicide could not be pursued for their criminal behaviour but those who had failed in their efforts at self-destruction could; attempted suicide was a criminal offence. A lone voice in the Commons, Kenneth Robinson, a back-bencher later to become Minister of Health, had in vain been seeking to alter this barbarous penal law and I soon joined him in efforts to end this scandalous harassment of the defeated, men and women who could neither live nor die. I had learned through my criminal clients how terrible and fascinating death can be to those whose genetic endowment and, by chance, their particular environment could leave them defenceless against their own masochism. Few thus afflicted can unload themselves and escape out of their dilemma as did Defoe, who projected his own self-tortures on his imagined writhings of plague victims.

The worst consequences of an untamed, uncontrolled masochism were illustrated to me by my client murderers; their agony was expressed differently but did not differ fundamentally from those of so many would-be suicides. One murderer whom I was defending, and who for no apparent reason had cut his wife almost to shreds in the bathroom of their suburban home, once courteously and gently explained his conduct to me: "It was absolutely necessary for me to kill her," he said. "If I had not killed her, I would have had no chance but to have killed myself." And, for good measure—with the attendant prison officers fortunately within sight but, in accordance with prison rules, out of hearing—he explained insistently that some years earlier he had killed a young man in the north of England for exactly the same reason. His madness may have been unusual but his motivation for murder was sadly orthodox.

The lure of self-destruction, the attractions of death, are often warded off only by turning outwards the aggression which is threatening to destroy the potential assailant. The terrible injuries wreaked upon his wife by this murderer were a measure of his destructiveness from which, at another's expense, he had just saved himself. Suicide or murder is often the option; and the conscience, temporarily stilled or undeveloped, as events are balanced on a razor's edge, leads by chance to murder, not *felo de se*.

The ultimate intention, however, may only have been temporally shelved; one-third of the murderers in Britain commit suicide before being brought to trial, and many more make determined attempts; sometimes, indeed, with a high sense of occasion, as I once found on arriving at the prison to interview a murderer client who timed the appointment so that he was able to receive me with a freshly cut throat.

The Janus-faced suicide demon is directed not only towards destruction and death but also towards human contact—and often those clients of mine possessed by the demon turned their gaze at the very last moment towards life; then they found themselves in the dock charged with the criminal offence of attempted suicide, leaving me to seek to mitigate their felony, as, listless and depressed, they sat wondering why they should be punished for their yearning to stop living, for wanting to die. They were part of the long procession of 7000 attempted suicides who were, for the ten years from 1946 to 1956, convicted by the courts; more than 300 during that period found themselves thrown into prison without the alternative of a fine. My quota of desperate and melancholy clients inevitably included some doctors; one in every fifty male doctors kills himself, having failed in his attempts to ward off his own death-wishing by keeping his patients alive.

Involvement in such incidents made me uncomfortably aware that the law had categorised as criminals more than 500,000 of my fellow-citizens who had made suicide attempts. The possibility of life imprisonment was the riposte of an enraged society, still governed by a cruel rule—a late, relatively sophisticated invention of Christianity more or less foreign to the Judaeo-Hellenic tradition—which made suicide a grievous felony. Equally jealous of murderers and suicides, divining the same motivation within the murderer and the self-slayer, society declares them both criminals.

To de-criminalise suicide was a tough task, therefore, for those of us wishing to reform the law. Eventually, however, a committee appointed by the Archbishop of Canterbury cautiously recommended that the offence of suicide should be abolished, provided that a second-class burial service could be used in those cases of suicide—quaintly described by the Churchmen as "manifestly selfish". And then, ultimately, after long persuasion, and the inevitable tardy reference for review of the offence to the Criminal Law Review Committee, the judges came back with recommendations sufficiently tough upon the survivors of suicide pacts to enable the proposition, without loss of face, to be put to the House, by way of a Government Bill, that attempted suicide should no longer be a criminal offence. The Government's ambivalence to the Bill was nicely expressed in the affectation that so little time was available that it needed to be rushed through almost unnoticed in the fag-end of a Friday afternoon. By a ruse, much to the vexation of the Government, I succeeded in gaining a full-scale debate to complete the Bill, for I believed that it was not the passing of a civilised Act by an interested cabal in Westminster which would make the nation more humane; it is the public affront to evil history that must, with anguish, be metabolised by the whole community if a nation is truly to move forward.[6] Always I have found in my parliamentary life that those who sought to thwart my legislative ambitions were those most jealous of the perpetrators of the conduct I was seeking to de-criminalise or mitigate; for these envious ones, savage penal laws were necessary to contain their own repressed sado-masochism. They feared that the sight of a successful suicide, an unashamed homosexual or a triumphant murderer would detonate their own self-destruction. Freud has written:

If one person succeeds in gratifying the repressed desire, the same desire is bound to be kindled for all members of the community. In order to keep the temptation down the transgressor must be denied the fruit of his enterprise; and the punishment will not infrequently give those who carry it out an opportunity of permitting the same outrage under cover of an act of expiation.

When it fell to me to carry through the Commons the Bill finally ending capital punishment, nothing vexed my opponents more than my assertion that hanging was an incitement not a deterrent to murder;[7] like many other defence lawyers I had found, when the gallows were still in place, that many murderers deeply resented our efforts to diminish their responsibility, and so save them from state strangulation. They wished to hang from the rope. They killed to die; and we were cheating them of their most profound masochistic desire.

That profound desire, however manifested, is ever feared. Any courtesies extended to the suffering masochist are regarded with suspicion. The advocacy of compassion, not condemnation, arouses acute anxiety among those who need unyielding prohibitions to ward off temptation; they insist, therefore, that those who, out of pity, collude with the afflicted to circumvent those prohibitions must be ruthlessly punished.

It was, therefore, to avoid being overwhelmed by those anxieties that I was once caused, contrary to my usual practice, to introduce a Bill not with challenging fanfare but with stealth. The little Bill was aimed at giving some relief to those who, after years of tending a loved one, were guilty of having yielded to the importuning of a terminally ill sufferer begging aid to accelerate their own death. The rules governing the offence of abetting a suicide were unbending: even if a judge found that punishment was wholly inappropriate, still any material benefit that could flow from the suicide's estate to an offender was forfeited. If the offender, in her sixties, had given her whole adult life to keeping alive and succouring her chronically ailing mother, she was to be turned out of the shared house which, together with its contents, would go to undeserving distant relatives.

My Bill simply gave the judge a discretion, if he thought the special circumstances merited it, to modify the forfeiture rule. It was a Bill that so escaped the attention of an indolent and otherwise distracted House that it reached the Statute Book. When, fortunately too late for amendment, its full implications were grasped, my predictable opponents raged that such a breach should have been made in the penal laws that, by its charity, left them exposed to their own murderous and suicidal impulses.

They feared those impulses. All of us are potential suicide bombers. Into denial, we prefer to distance ourselves from such terrorists, attributing mental illness to them from which we are exempt; or we falsely claim that desperation is wholly due to illiteracy or poverty, that having nothing to lose in this world they act in hope of a paradise in the next. All such diagnoses dodge the reality that neither reward nor poverty is the main determinant of their conduct; indeed, research shows that they are better off and better educated than their peers and that they cannot be categorised as mentally ill.[8] Groups that sponsor suicide bombers do not need to dangle prizes before their volunteers; for the eager masochist, free from the taboos that prohibit his self-indulgent desires, death itself is his delicious reward.

The suicide bomber behaves as so many of my fellow legislators feared that, if granted immunity, they might behave; both the bomber and the timorous parliamentarian are bonded to their masochism in similar modes, for the relationship between masochism and sadism is finely tuned; the bomber kills, the legislator punishes. Pondering on their iconoclasm compels the question of how and why Defoe, the most masochistic of personalities, one weighed down with guilt and a sense of shame, summoned up so different and creative a riposte to the dilemma and so perhaps gave us his most artistic and wondrous work.

★   ★   ★   ★   ★   ★   ★   ★   ★   ★

As age advanced upon Defoe, his warning of the terrors of plague became ever more strident. As his fiftieth birthday approached, in six numbers of his *Review* he warned of the risk of infection if British troops went to assist Sweden in the wars against the Second Coalition. In August 1712, in the same paper, he continued to show how many European countries had suffered from outbreaks of plague over the previous eight years, and before long he gave a thunderous reminder of the disaster that had once befallen London and published a copy of the Mortality Bill for the week beginning 12 September 1665, the worst of the whole epidemic, when over 7000 people are recorded as having died of plague. When the 1720 Marseilles epidemic struck, in the pages of several periodicals—*The Daily Post, Applebee's Journal* and *Mist'l Journal*—he took occasion no fewer than ten times within that year to describe the horrors and ravages of the plague in France, and went on to write a book on the subject in which prophesy, admonition and practical advice were all mingled. This work Defoe entitled *Due Preparations for the Plague, as well for Soul as Body*; the sub-title of the book is revealing: *Being Some Seasonable Thoughts upon the Visible Approach of the Present Dreadful Contagion in France, the Properst Measures to Prevent It, and the Great Work of Submitting to It*. This was a work completed before the *Journal*, which was to be published two years later when Defoe had reached his sixtieth year.

For Defoe, the bell was tolling ominously. Advances in medical knowledge have resulted in the present British population being by far the oldest body of persons which has ever occupied our islands; but Defoe in the eighteenth century could not enjoy our expectations of long life. The most for which a religious man would dare to hope was that he would be granted the Psalmist's span. The plague was, for Defoe, but a metaphor; the fears and apprehensions he was raising in his warnings and descriptions of the horrors of plague tell of his anxiety that his own death was now imminent. We have learned from Freud that the "recoil of horror" is the sign of desire;[9] the more Defoe recites, unsparingly, the horrors of the plague, the more we understand how great was his desire to participate in the agonies the plague proffered. Those terrible ecstasies, so beguiling to an impatient masochist, could be anticipated by yielding to death. We shall never plumb the depths of Defoe's extraordinary work unless we acknowledge the significance of the *Journal of the Plague Year* as a bulwark against that temptation.

Despite all the many scholarly appreciations of the work, the failure of critics to see the overwhelming therapeutic importance of the *Journal* to Defoe often results in myopic readings. The literary appraisers find it discomforting to acknowledge the force of an ebbing tide, ever pulling us towards hopelessness and despondency, away from life. They underestimate the significance and importance of uncontained masochism in determining the nature of our society and its institutions. Yet, if Freud's contention is right and masochism is indeed older than sadism, then man's history of wars and violent struggles is part of man's frantic attempts to ward off his yearnings for the ultimate nirvana; by directing his erotically loaded aggressiveness away from the interior life, for a little while man postpones the joys of his capitulation to death. The challenge which Freud gave the twentieth century, illuminating the potency of sex in our lives, has been only superficially met. Gripped with panic, we dodge the awkward implications of a hypothesis that a biologically determined instinct, bathed in an exciting sensuality, draws us to our nemesis, and that we can only advance a little the date of our masturbatory death by deflecting some of the force of this terrible instinct into sexually inspired cruelty against our fellow-men.

Freud has taught us that the meaning of civilisation's evolution is no longer obscure:

> It presents the struggle between Eros and death, between the instinct of life and the instinct of destruction, as it works itself out in the human species. This struggle is what all life essentially consists of and the evolution of civilisation may therefore be simply described as the struggle for life of the human species.

In the battle of these giants, Eros and Thanatos, it is not difficult to perceive which of the adversaries is today, at least temporarily, gaining the upper hand.

We should, therefore, well understand how intensely Defoe, given his age and temperament, was overwhelmingly afraid of Thanatos; for the great Dissenter, living, as we do now, in an age of transition, had, with deliberation, abandoned and savaged the old Roman Catholic faith which, with considerable artifice, had traditionally acted as the container of man's masochism and saved so many from self-immolation. This resource was not available to Defoe; his vitriolic attacks on the Pope and Roman Catholics and any infiltration of their influence in the Anglican Church were unremitting. For him the ecumenical approach was suspect; he regarded Dissenters as the bulwark against the hegemony of the Roman Catholic Church and was ever alert to any signs of the import of Catholic persecution from the continent. For Defoe the religious wars of the seventeenth century had not ended. He was contemptuous of the Catholic attachment to religious images and he mocked the veneration of relics. The supportive techniques, practised by the Catholic Orders, particularly in times of plague, to the aged and dying which saved them from despair were not available to so severe a Dissenter as Defoe. He was on his own; he was his own man. Ministrations to comfort the dying were not absent from the Dissenters' code, but not for them the sprinkling of holy water and the presence of a priest bestowing absolution. Such dependency was demeaning, indeed, abhorrent.

But the assertion of his individuality by the Dissenter demanded a great renunciation; to scorn the solaces of the Roman Catholic Church, to abandon the props the Orders had so ingeniously crafted to help Tragic Man to endure life's sorrows, left Defoe singularly bereft. Unrestrained identification with the Passion, making a little lighter the load of masochism carried by the penitent by sharing it with the suffering Christ, were settings denied to austere Non-conformists. Indeed, although Defoe himself demurred, many Dissenters insisted that the notion of the Trinity was not grounded on firm historical evidence. The Crucifixion certainly did not have the centrality in the belief of the Dissenter as it had in Catholicism.

We should not minimise the resulting deprivation. In the face of catastrophes like plague, the Catholic Church had developed an extraordinary sophistication; by anchoring masochism to the Passion, it had at its command prophylactic and healing balms unavailable to fastidious Nonconformist Protestantism eschewing the theatre and art of the Catholic ritual.

In the communal hall of the Dissenters where Defoe prayed, the Old Testament ethos prevailed and the Father was God, an obeisance that matched his unconscious desires to submit to his own sire. In the glorious cathedral the altar was a stage reserved for the Son, a usurpation that for Defoe would be a frightening presumption inviting reprimand. The difference between Dissenter and Catholic was profound, not resting upon mere shibboleth; and never is that gulf more apparent than, when facing disease and death, the Protestant stoically accepts affliction as God's punishment for his transgressions, while the Roman Catholic clings to his Saviour for redemption.

When Defoe, the determined Dissenter, scorned Catholic blandishments, he was c urageously forfeiting the very gift that the Catholic Church was, in times of need, always able to offer a plague-ridden flock; it was a bribe, tailor-made to allow the sufferer to enjoy a heavy flirtation with his masochism without totally yielding to its deathly embrace. But Defoe and his incorruptible fellow-Dissenters would never accept or apply the Catholic Church's proffered emollient, however attractively packaged. Their refusal is all the more extraordinary when we witness how lavishly, through art, the Catholic Church advertised its wares; this was a refusal that indeed was a renunciation; it was a refusal to accept the part in a wondrous Passion play.

The most powerful production of that play, the one illustrating the lure of the theatre which the Puritans and their Nonconformist heirs would never attend, is to be found in France in Colmar. There we can find how the masochism endemic to mankind can be marvellously transmuted. There we find one of the most staggering demonstrations by the Roman Catholic Church of the deployment of masochism in the service of mankind. In Colmar there stands Mathis Grünewald's Isenheim altarpiece, one of Europe's greatest religious paintings and one which was deliberately conceived as a therapy for plague victims. It contains the most harrowing image of the Crucifixion in Western art. The altar, a polyptych, was commissioned by patrons of the mendicant order of Antonites, founded in 1080, who had always dedicated themselves to the care of the sufferers of the various sicknesses which successive plagues brought. As a first stage of the healing programme, before the victims were brought into the hospital to be fed, the patients were required to contemplate Grünewald's image and only then were deemed to be sufficiently receptive to receive medical treatment. It was a psychological purging, for it was believed that the patient's spiritual well-being was a prerequisite to the regaining of physical strength. And, above all, the image upon which they gazed, and which is the most haunting part of the altarpiece, is the Crucifixion where there is no circumspection in the painter's portrayal of the agony of Christ.

Grünewald made no attempt to dilute the awfulness of the event. Exhausted by pain and degradation, this haggard figure hangs down with such terminal heaviness that his shoulders are wrenched from their sockets. Hammered nails tear at his palms. A distinguished art correspondent has vividly described the scene:

> Although his fingers stab in protest, he can do nothing to arrest the relentless process of deterioration. With head lolling forward, and

mouth open because he no longer retains the strength to keep it
shut, the defeated Christ is in a death agony almost too gruesome to
scrutinise. Blood oozes from the gangrenous feet, the one skewered
hideously on the other by a gleaming bolt.

His sweaty pallor proves that the end is close, but nothing is going
to hasten the last excruciating moments of his torture. Pitched against
the dark void unalleviated by signs of divine intervention, he is condemned to writhe until his body seems unable to withstand any more
punishment.[10]

The Christ is depicted alone and isolated, the Virgin and the
anguished Mary Magdalene unable to help, yet the sores erupting
all over his body tell the plague-stricken viewers that they are not
alone in their predicament, and, by identifying themselves with
the battered and festering body of Christ, they must have gained
immense reassurance, and an emancipation from the humiliating
stigma attached to their condition.[11] And to comfort them further
Grünewald presents another panel, an astounding one of the resurrection, stressing the miraculous exhilaration of life after death, a
dazzling purified apparition that, although Christ holds up His
hands still bearing the red marks of His wounds, now they cause
Him no pain. It is unsurprising that this great ensemble of panels
has resonated in so many creative works in the twentieth century,
from the novels of Nobel Prize winner Elias Canetti to the sym-
phony and opera of the German composer Hindemith and more
recently the prose poem of W. G. Sebald.[12] It is the most convincing
representation Europe has of the belief that the Passion can turn
around masochism and bring boundless hope.

But for Defoe, as for his austere co-religionists, the Second Com-
mandment was inviolable; no graven image, no replica of the
Godhead, no painting, could bestow Hope; to crave from art a bene-
diction warding off self-destructiveness was a mark of idolatry. The
relief and protection which the beauteous mediating influences of
Catholic art, granting absolution, offered the sinner were, for Defoe,
gifts from Satan. The determined Protestant Dissenter would have
little empathy with the art of Grünewald and none, of course, with
the later Jesuit-inspired counter-Reformation artists. This was occasioned much more by religious prejudice than that of sensibility, for
Defoe can never be accused of lacking visual acuity. Indeed, in his

Tour thro' the Whole Island of Great Britain, he describes himself as having "some Pretensions to Judgement in Pictures" and gives us his assessment of some of the paintings in the great country-houses he visited.

The works he enjoyed were essentially secular, even when they recounted biblical tales; he never really sought spirituality in art. We find him, rather, slyly lingering over paintings that subliminally doubtless afforded him some sado-masochistic pleasures. He was much taken by Luca Giordano's "fine piece of Seneca bleeding to death in the warm bath and dictating his last morals to his scholars, their eager Attention, their generous Regard to their master, their vigilant Catching at his Words and some of them taking Minutes that it is indeed admirable and inexpressible". Then, when viewing Raphael's Cartoon at Hampton Court, he relishes the rendering of the death sentence upon Ananias, of the countenances of the faces witnessing his death as well as the main figure surprised by "Terror and Death". And the painting of Tintoretto which he finds irresistible is a subtle appreciation of abasement, a condition so appealing to Defoe, that of Christ washing the feet of the disciples.

But the innuendoes in these paintings which evidently so delighted Defoe, the supreme voyeur, were mere titillation; they were not, and were not intended to be, as in the work of a Grünewald, an invitation to an awesome contemplation which could assist the viewer to overcome and transmute threatening masochism. Defoe's favourite, Giordano, when working in the Escorial, amazed the Spanish painters by his virtuosity, since they were more accustomed to painting saints, not randy Olympian gods. Speed, shock, surprise, a dash of eroticism, not stillness, were his hallmarks; he was known in Italy and Spain for the record time in which he could cover the vaults of palaces with flying figures, all in different styles; not for nothing was this famous decorator, whose paintings are as noisy as his native city Naples, called "Fa Presto".

Nor was there any quietude in Defoe's other favourite, Tintoretto, whose rendering was vivid, crisp and furiously energetic, and told of tumultuous external events, not of the struggles of the inner life. As the art critic Eric Newton instructed us: "He was essentially an interpreter of happenings, and especially of the larger, dramatic implications of those happenings."[13] The happening which, over all else, obsessed Tintoretto was that of miracle. That was the theme of his Venetian work at the Scuola of the Plague Saint, San Rocco, where he worked for many years depicting the miracles of the Old and New Testaments; but the miracles he shows are the consequences of divine intervention. The world does not shake, reverberating to the movement of the troubled inner spirit of man. It is the journalist Defoe whom we find responding to the action, the event, the concrete imagery, the similitude, the reporting of a happening, the immediacy, which Tintoretto always brings.

Defoe's interest in painting was certainly not perfunctory. His involvement is clear from his earliest writings, in which he expressed a longing to be able to make his prose function as clearly and concretely as a painting or drawing in getting close to a representation of what he called "the Thing itself". His usual term for a false argument was "a *deceptio visus*", or optical illusion, and Novak suggests that his growth as a writer owes much to this impulse. The clarity and explicitness of his prose no doubt gained much from Defoe's appreciation of the realism and directness of the painters he admired; but his rapport with painters of the High Renaissance, who so often used religion merely as a peg on which to hang a secular narrative, could not extend to the genuine servants of Rome; their visions of an inner peace and harmony, of intimations of paradise, were to be shared only by those first prepared to endure the frenzy and mystical ecstasies of the saints they so marvellously depicted. But these were precisely the extravagances the Dissenter found intolerable. He was not beguiled; he was wholly scotomatised to their charms.

The sedations prescribed by Catholic art as a physic for the relief of sinners of their fears and the attractions of death were not for Defoe; the effect on the determined heretic would have been wholly iatrogenic; he scorned the palliatives so persuasively offered. Yet if he was not to die before his death, a victim of his own death-wish, some response was necessary to the importunings of his masochism that, as he grew older, were, as his plague writings reveal, becoming ever more clamorous. He could have chosen another technique, one so frequently and fruitlessly practised by those who refused to acknowledge the inevitability of death, that of denial. Such denial today is perhaps even more widespread than in Defoe's day. As a solicitor I found it widely practised in superstitious Wales where the making of a will was regarded as a death warrant; the resulting intestacies brought confusion and bitter family quarrels to many family homes.

And refusal to face the reality of death can, too, have extraordinary and malignant consequences not only for an individual but a whole nation. Sebald, in a recent disturbing posthumous publication,[14] has told how a collective refusal by the Germans to recall or discuss or write about the gruesome death of 600,000 German civilians, victims of the Allies' carpet-bombing air-raids, continues to damage the German psyche: a massive disavowal of the destruction of 3.5 million homes, leaving 7.5 million homeless, persists. Such unassimilated trauma can induce angst and neurosis in a nation and its political leadership as surely as it causes behavioural problems for a soldier suffering an untreated "Gulf War Syndrome". It is understandably appallingly difficult for Germans to accept that their fathers' provocations brought about in one terrible night in Hamburg the deaths of 50,000 of their fellow-countrymen and caused, in Dresden, the extermination in a few days of nearly as many German civilians as the number of Jewish children the Nazis had thrown into the gas ovens.[15] Thanatos, however, cannot thus be gainsaid. He does not vanish because you turn your gaze away. Out of the rubble of Hamburg and Dresden ghosts emerge and continue to haunt the German imagination.

But Defoe scorned the use of such inadequate defence mechanisms to protect himself from death's encroachment. No man could have been more vulnerable than Defoe to death's seductive handmaid, masochism; but, marvellously, he abjured her beguiling inducements to lead him to her master, and using all his guiles as a supreme confidence trickster, he induced that fickle servant temporarily to desert her master and to enter into his service. Relentlessly he put her to work. The *Journal* was essentially the product of that exploited labour. Once again, Defoe transmutes his masochism into creativity.

In the *Journal*, Defoe unloads his masochism and, thus displaced, the fascinated reader is condemned to suffer shock and horror. In an arresting essay Novak convincingly opines: "Few readers of the *Journal of the Plague Year* would argue with the notion that the most compelling aspect of the book involves the terrible scenes of pain and death, the cries of the victims ..."[16] HF, Defoe's alter ego, is indeed unsparing in detailing the carnage. The plague pits were, he wrote,

full of Terror, the Cart had in it 16 or 17 Bodies, some were wrapt up

> in Linen Sheets, some in Rugs, some little other than naked, also
> loose, that what Covering they had, fell from them in the shooting up
> of the Cart and they fell quite naked among the rest; but the Matter
> was not much to them, or the Indecency much to anyone else, seeing
> they were all dead, and were to be huddled together into the common
> Grave of Mankind, as we may call it, for here was no Difference
> made, but Poor and Rich went together.

Such passages show us Defoe not under the control but in control of
his masochism. With an icy detachment, almost free from affect, he
does not depart from his role as an observer, never permitting himself the indulgence of an excessive identification with the tortured
victims. Thus insulated, the plague cannot claim him; the death-
wish is fulfilled by others. HF brazenly looks death in the face, gives
a nod of recognition, and then insolently passes on.

Indeed, it has well been remarked that those who consort with
death are sometimes treated by HF more as enemies than as victims.[17]
In a startlingly biblical reference, HF says of the survivors of plague
that they were like "the Children of Israel, after being delivered from
the Host of Pharaoh when they passed the Red-Sea, and looked back,
and saw the Egyptians overwhelmed in the Water". Here the plague
sufferers have become conquered enemies, deserving to be punished
for their sin of acting out, not resisting, their death-wishes. Defoe is
determined that his protagonist will survive untainted by such infec-
tious desires. When, almost miraculously, he does emerge, triumphant, in manic mood, he rounds off the *Journal* in a celebration of his
victory in harnessing his masochism in the service of creativity:

> I shall conclude the Account of this Calamitous Year therefore with a
> coarse but sincere Stanza of my own, which I plac'd at the End of my
> ordinary Memorandums, the same Year they were written:—
>
> A dreadful Plague in London was,
> In the Year Sixty-Five,
> Which swept an Hundred Thousand Souls
> Away; yet I alive!

And, alive and continuously writing, Defoe remains for nearly
a decade, his masochism servile and sublimated to his literary

purposes. But, like Defoe himself, who had as a spy been a double agent, so was his servant who ultimately betrayed him. Defoe's power to control the retainer was spent. In his seventieth year he died, with his physician recording the cause of death as the "Lethargy". There has been produced an air of mystery surrounding his death. Where precisely he died is certainly unknown; it appears that he was holed up all alone in some down-at-heel boarding-house in a lugubrious quarter. Perhaps, as ever, he was hiding from his debtors. More likely, as an old lion approaching his end seeks out a secluded spot, so he sought solitude as his final hour approached. But, quite unnecessarily, a mystery has been conjured up about the cause of his death.

The "lethargy" diagnosis has been challenged and sometimes mocked by Defoe's biographers, who seem to regard the doctor's verdict as quaint; they cannot accept that a man with such inexhaustible energy would have departed the world so quietly. Some have preferred to double guess the physician and suggest Defoe died in his sleep of a mild stroke; others canvass the theory that the fatal condition had its origins in his encounters, on the five occasions that he was imprisoned, with the typhus and other diseases which killed off far more prison inmates than did the gallows; again, some would have us accept that his death resulted from the strains and pains imposed on his body by his travels on horseback through the British countryside among storm and cold; and, since he had become bitterly estranged from his children, some portray him as a wandering King Lear, no more able to withstand the obloquies hurled against him by his enemies. There is a marked reluctance to concede that Defoe died of the disease which he well understood, the Lethargy which he had once described as the cause of the death of Moll Flanders's severely depressed bank manager.

But Defoe's doctor was no dunce. His description of the malady was apposite; Defoe's treacherous servant had lured him to Lethe, the river of the underworld whose waters ensured oblivion; from the waters of Lethe, alone, and as isolated as Crusoe, guiltily, shamefully, yielding to the temptation, he drank the fatal potion. But for Thanatos it was a victory too long delayed; the *Journal's* defiant taunts against his omniscience were never to be erased and remain embedded in a classic of plague literature bearing comparison with Thucydides and Boccaccio.

The manner of Defoe's death may have confused his unimaginative biographers but there was at least one man who understood
Defoe's struggle against his forbidden death-wish and who, through
that understanding, gave his wandering and lonely death the mythical quality it merits. The lapsed Catholic James Joyce, brought up
and tutored in a Dublin ever oppressed with the shame of original
sin, ended a Triestian lecture on Defoe by telling of his condition,
and perhaps the condition of all of us:

> And so, sometimes man, born into shame, will also bow before the
> shame of death, not wishing others to be saddened by the sight of
> that obscene phenomenon with which brutal and mocking Nature
> puts an end to the life of a human being.

Notes

1. Foot, M., *Debts of Honour*, Davis-Poynter, 1960.
2. Landa, L., Religion, science and medicine: introduction to *A Journal of the
   Plague Year*, Oxford University Press, 1969.
3. Richetti, J. J., *Defoe's Narratives: Situations and Structures*, Clarendon
   Press, 1975.
4. Henderson, A. J., *London and National Government, 1721–1722*, Duke
   University Press, 1945.
5. Landa, Religion, science and medicine.
6. Abse, L., *Private Member*, Macdonald, 1973.
7. Ibid., Chapter 6.
8. Atran, S., *The Times*, 7 March 2003.
9. Phillips, A., Bored with sex?, *London Review of Books*, 6 March 2003.
10. Cork, R., A miracle of healing, *The Times*, 1998.
11. Abse, L., *Fellatio, Masochism, Politics and Love*, Robson Books, 2000.
12. Sebald, W. G., *After Nature*, Hamish Hamilton, 2002.
13. Newton, E., *Tintoretto*, Longman, 1952.
14. Sebald, W. G., *On the Natural History of Destruction*, Hamish Hamilton,
    2003.
15. Abse, L., *Wotan, My Enemy*, Robson Books, 1994.
16. Novak, M. E., *Defoe and the Disordered City*, Modern Language Associ-
    ation of America, 1977.
17. Roberts, D., Introduction to *Journal of the Plague Year*, Oxford University
    Press, 1998.

CHAPTER SEVEN

The storm

F reud explains the distinction between moral masochism and other intimations of the accursed life-destroyer and has told that it could often be awakened not by another but by "impersonal powers and circumstances"; and it is the moral masochist "who always turns his cheek whenever he has a chance of receiving a blow".[1] When, therefore, disaster, not even of his courting, fell upon Britain in 1703, Defoe thus received a delicious bonus, one in which he was to revel, and which, three hundred years later, has deservedly helped to earn him the title of "Father of Journalism".

The storm of 26 November 1703 remains the worst storm recorded in British history. Not until the German blitz in 1940 did Britain receive such punishment. Between midnight and 6.00 a.m. on 27 November an extra-tropical cyclone of unusual ferocity hammered into Britain from the North Atlantic, cutting a 300-mile wide swathe of destruction across southern and central England and Wales. During those hours it claimed the lives of more than 8000 people on land and the unbelievable seas. The Queen, in a public proclamation, accurately described the event as "a Calamity so Dreadful and Astonishing, that the like has not been Seen in the memory of any Person Living in this Our Kingdom".[2] Defoe enthusiastically rushed out his tract *The Layman's Sermon upon the Late Storm* and therein called upon his fellow-citizens to join him in his self-flagellation and submit to their deserved punishment. God had chosen the storm to be the vehicle of His wrath, the means by which to chastise London, "a Powerful, Populous, Wealthy and most Reprobate City", in an attempt to direct its forgetful inhabitants towards the path of godliness and repentance. It was a moment when Defoe indeed wallowed in his moral masochism.

But it was, if prolonged, a self-indulgence which he knew could be fatal; survival demanded he renounce the temptation to empathise unrestrainedly with the storm's victims, to linger pleasurably on the punishments that their evil doings had brought upon themselves. His addiction had to be tempered; if he yielded to the pleasures of being tortured even unto death by his own conscience, he was undone. At all costs he must distance himself from the exquisite agonies the terrible storm had so seductively proffered; if he did not disengage, then his fate would be as dire as those who suffocated beneath the ruins of London on that awesome night. And it was that act of disengagement that produced his first full-length book, *The Storm*, a book that remains an unsurpassed model of investigative journalism.

In its arresting preface he insisted it was the work of a historian. He claimed that the occasion and consequence of the storm would be spelt out by the recitation of unadorned facts. Nothing would be recorded but authenticated material, only reliable eye-witness accounts of his own and his correspondents would be admitted, and these were to be told without embroidery or extravagance. This was to be a work that determinedly would not founder through want of "Caution", which was "the Foundation of that great Misfortune we have in matters of ancient History; in which the Imprudence, Ribaldry, the empty Flourishes, the little regard to truth, and the Fondness of telling a strange Story, that has dwindled a great many valuable pieces of ancient History into meer Romance." Here was to be presented an austere history, free from the distortions of empathy and imagination; and, thus insulated, our Daniel, deaf to the masochistic ballads of the sirens who would fain lure him into a life-denying nirvana, would coldly and detachedly tell the grim story.

His allegiance to such a fancy-free, truthful rendering was, of course, given his temperament, not to be consistently sustained, but his lapses were few; fact by fact, statistic by statistic, cumulatively he assembled his "Collection" of eye-witness reports of "Casualties and Disasters"; tables showing the barometer's height as a preliminary to the enumeration, district by district, trees felled, roofs torn apart, churches toppled, animals drowned, barns flattened, houses blown down, women and men injured or killed; nothing that could be classified and then quantified was to be omitted. This is essentially an accountant's report, the catastrophic figures left to speak for themselves unaccompanied by any distraught auditor's troubled report; if emotions were allowed to be intrusive, then Defoe feared he would betray himself, revealing his attraction to the carnage he was depicting.

Unlike the *Journal of the Plague Year*, the book to be written by Defoe some twenty years later, this is not a work of creative imagination; the *Plague* is a threnody mourning all mankind's tragic fate with a libretto provided by a composer who personally knew not the events of which he told. Nor is it an allegorical one like Camus's *La Peste*, which presents a modern city stricken by the plague, where the disease is a figure of a tyrannical occupying power; neither is it a story where the plague, as in Thomas Mann's novella *Death in Venice*, is a threatening corroborative symbol, a centrepiece within the *mise-en-scène* which forms the backdrop to an enactment of disintegration, of the decay of a great writer lusting for the return of his youth. Here, in *The Storm*, Defoe was claiming there would be no exploitation of catastrophe to engage the reader's attention, no embellishments, no "rodomontades", none of the "prodigious Looseness of the Pen" that "has confounded History and Fable". The clear intention of Defoe was to write a work which was anti-literary, one where, sheltered behind a bulwark against a dense and imminent sea of his own desires, he could bear to tell the terrible story.

It was his hope to construct, in the impermeable bricks of statistics which he so relentlessly accumulated, that defensive wall. His efforts, however, proved only partially successful; the worst excesses of his masochism were shut out but still the moral masochism crept through his defences and, albeit reluctantly, in an ambivalent admission, he laments that "in this case . . . the strong Evidence God has been pleas'd to give in this terrible manner to His own Being, which mankind began more than ever to affront and despise".

Our Daniel, despite his protestations, cannot forbear to tell his tale without making his obeisances to God the Father who justly punishes His errant children. He submits to God's will and warns the atheist, and indeed himself, that denying God's will and attributing the cyclone to mere natural causes could provoke a terrible retribution: "If the Atheist is mistaken, he has brought all the Powers, whose Being he deny'd, upon his Back, has provok'd the Infinite in the highest manner and must at last sink under the Anger of him whose Nature he has always disown'd." Defoe's declared aspiration was to tell the story of the storm as it was, to give us a comment-free fact-based account of the event; but a fundamental inhibition prevented him from giving us such a detached overview. A wholly rational presentation, an "atheist's" rendering, would bar him from acknowledging the cyclone as a manifestation of direct divine intervention; for Defoe, that would have been a dangerous display of lese majesty; an atheistic stance, lacking the punctuation of moralistic interpolations, was too risky a posture; it might be mistaken, and thus indeed would be an "unhappy Misfortune and Mistake that it can never be discover'd til tis too late to remedy. He that resolves to die an Atheist, shuts the Door against being convinc'd in time." Ignobly, lacking the courage to take a chance, Defoe stained his pure fact-finding essay with the superstitions of the era which had not yet yielded to the Enlightenment, and submitted himself to God the Father.

But this first full-length book of Defoe was marred not only by this humiliating capitulation; there are other blemishes in the work. It is a fraught telling; a neurotic tremulousness pervades the book; it always teeters on the edge of a full-blown obsessional neurosis. There is no economy in the recital; in each and every district surveyed the devastation is presented in excruciating detail and is repetitively tabulated; anxiety envelops the raconteur, fearful lest there should be any omission, any hyperbole, any departure from truth. The resultant product is superb, meticulous reportage; with imagination and empathy vanished, it is a memorable but desiccated essay. As the noted Defoe scholar G. A. Starr has argued, *The Storm* suffers by comparison with works like *A Journal of the Plague Year*: "The litany of losses has limited emotional impact because they are seldom adequately individualized. From the inventories of drowned livestock, toppled steeples, uprooted trees, collapsed buildings, and foundered ships we do get a sense of enormous damage, but not of human pain of grief."[3] Contrariwise, *The Plague* with its tragic depictions is possessed by a rare élan; untrammelled by leaden prosaic verisimilitude, the work soars. Fact is respectfully acknowledged but more often is enhanced, ever subordinate to Defoe's liberated creative imagination.

It is not difficult to divine from whence springs both the freedom of this later work and the constraints of *The Storm*. In *The Storm*, as a defence mechanism, a faulty floodgate is in place; it is there to save Defoe from being drowned in his own masochism. It is, however, a doubtful device; it leaves him stranded on arid land and, lacking sustenance, he does not flourish. But in *The Plague* Defoe does not attempt to hide behind defensive barriers; he goes on to the offensive, confronts his Tormentor and battle is joined. The struggle is fierce but in the end Defoe, surrounded by corpses, stands out against the bleak devastated landscape, upright and triumphant, declaiming:

> A dreadful Plague in London was,
> In the Year Sixty-Five,
> Which swept an Hundred Thousand Souls
> Away; yet I alive!

Twenty years earlier such an uninhibited display had been beyond Defoe's resources. By his compulsive obsessional rendering of detail, by his mountain of statistics and facts, he was exhibiting the selfsame symptoms that clinicians encounter when endeavouring to relieve obsessional neurotics of their burdens. As early as 1904, Ferenczi was drawing attention to the correlation between suppressed homosexuality and the obsessive behaviour he observed among patients fearing their homoerotic yearnings:

> After the very shortest examination those suffering . . . prove to be typical "obsessional" patients. They swarm with obsessions, and with obsessional procedures and ceremonies to guard against them. A more penetrating analysis finds behind the compulsion the torturing doubt, as well as that lack of balance in love and hate which Freud discovered to be the basis of the obsessional mechanism.[4]

It is such an imbalance we find in Defoe; handicapped by never having worked through his negative Oedipus phase, unconsciously he ever feared that the exclusive intemperate love for his father would lead him into the dangers of a masochistic homosexual submission. He attempted, like a typical obsessional neurotic, to conceal his forbidden desires; Defoe's statistics are not facts, they are camouflage.

But this camouflage reveals, not conceals; vainly does Defoe attempt to be wholly objective, a non-judgemental observer. His manoeuvre fails; it advertises and explicates the moral masochism pervading the work; it is a masochism that is a refined, cerebral, affective displacement of his unconscious wish to submit sexually to his father. A former president of the American Psychoanalytical Association, in another context, following Freud, succinctly illuminated the strange evolution of the desire for homosexual incest into a moral imperative:[5]

> In one of his pithy, all-encompassing observations, Freud[6] noted that moral masochism represents regression from true morality to negative Oedipus complex. . . . Briefly put, moral masochism as a rule develops in the following way. At a certain stage in his development, the male child, under special conditions, adopts a loving, feminine, passive, submissive attitude towards the father. Since sexual submission, however, is unacceptable, this trend is opposed and may be replaced by a painful but nevertheless more acceptable compromise formation: instead of wishing to submit sexually in the manner of a woman, the individual substitutes the wish to be beaten physically. At this level one outcome could be the development of a masochistic perversion. However, in a further defensive manoeuvre, the wish to be beaten physically is replaced by a tendency to be oppressed by moral strictures. At first these strictures can be experienced as emanating from the father figure. In turn, however, they may be replaced by the law and commandments imposed by God and experienced as a constant inner moral imperative.

That moral imperative can cripple a creative artist; Defoe, so maimed, could write his down-to-earth books in spare, lucid prose but not in poetry. What circumstances operated twenty years on in Defoe's dazzlingly creative decade were certainly not in place in 1703; at this earlier stage of his life, in *The Storm*, the inhibition, the legacy of his negative Oedipal phase, was decidedly not overcome. Such work-inhibitions have been much investigated in recent years by French and Italian psychoanalysts seeking to aid writers and painters afflicted by intellectual and artistic blockages.[7] Joyce McDougall, the distinguished French psychoanalyst, who has affirmed that the wish to be the other sex while at the same time keeping the one sex is an unconscious and universal longing, has reported:

> As we have seen from a psychological point of view, people are basically and profoundly "bisexual". The double take of identity construction leads to identification with the parent of the same sex while taking the other sex as its object. The genital sexual relationships cannot alone absorb and satisfy this deep bisexual longing in mankind. The question might then be raised as to where bisexual wishes find sublime or substitute satisfaction . . . one is clinically evident in creative acts and processes that permit people to produce things magically, through coalescence and assumptions of what they conceive to be their masculine and feminine wishes, so that they may, alone, engender their "products". Many work inhibitions and intellectual and artistic blocks are rooted in the unconscious resistance to accept bisexual wishes and conflicts.[8]

Defoe's inhibition was indeed rooted in his attempted denial of the feminine within his bi-sexual disposition.

From McDougall's perspective any creative act can be conceptualised as a fusion of masculine and feminine elements in our psychic structure; she alerts us to the possible benign and malignant consequences of such a coupling. A man's creative capacity is dependent upon his readiness to accept the feminine within his psyche; the creative act is essentially mimetic and no man can give birth to a work of art if he has expelled the woman from his interior life; his sterility, if he claims to be an author, will be advertised in his prose; the penetrating comment of George Groddeck, the father of psychosomatic medicine, is apposite: "In the being we call man there lives also a woman, in the woman too, a man. That a man should think of child-bearing is nothing strange but only that this should be so obstinately denied."[9] The expurgation of any traits of a child-bearing fantasy in the imagination of a would-be artist leaves him presenting us with a work which, however skilfully and cerebrally crafted, and although perhaps vivid, is lifeless rather than life-enhancing; such a work is *The Storm*. Even great journalism is not art. Defoe himself was to demonstrate the distinction when, twenty years after *The Storm*, his inhibitions overcome, he courageously dared to metamorphose himself, become a woman and assume the identities of Moll Flanders and Roxana to give us his great novels.

Notes

1. Freud, S., *The Economic Problems of Masochism*, SE, Volume 19.
2. *London Gazette*, 3975 (13–16 December 1703).
3. Starr, G. A., *Dreadful Visitations: Confronting Natural Catastrophe in the Age of the Enlightenment*, 1999, quoted by Rogers, P., *Times Literary Supplement*, 4 July 2003.
4. Ferenczi, F., On the nosology of male homosexuality, in *Selected Writings*, Penguin Books, 1999.
5. Arlow, J., Bisexuality in Jewish mysticism, in M. Ostow (ed.), *Ultimate Intimacy: The Psycho-dynamics of Jewish Mysticism*, Karnac Books, 1995.
6. Freud, *The Economic Problems of Masochism*.
7. Ferraro, F., Psychic bisexuality and creativity, *International Journal of Psychoanalysis*, 84 (December 2003), 6.
8. McDougall, J., *Plea for a Measure of Abnormality*, Free Association Books, 1990.
9. Groddeck, G., *The Meaning of Illness*, Hogarth Press, 1988.

CHAPTER EIGHT

The voyeur

A n appraisal of Defoe's extraordinary talent as a meticulous investigative journalist, as displayed in *The Storm*, requires an acknowledgement of that work's obsessional nature and of its function as a defence mechanism against the threat of self-destructive masochistic morality. But canvassing such a perception is suspiciously depreciatory, and leaves unanswered the question: from whence came the dynamic that drove Defoe, in 1704, the year after the Great Storm, to launch and sustain his *Review*, a journal that he single-handedly edited for a decade? The constraints and inhibitions to be identified in *The Storm* are certainly not to be found here.

In the *Review* Defoe built a platform from which, untrammelled and in the most apocalyptic terms worthy of a committed Dissenter, he could, like one of the ancient Jewish prophets he so often quoted, rage against sin and vice to be found in the prevailing polity. It was a journal which lived up to its initial declaration of intent. It was to be a political paper "Purg'd from the Errors and Partiality of News-Writers and Petty-Statesmen of all sides, a weekly history of Nonsense, Impertinence, Vice and Debauchery". In the second issue Defoe introduced a prototype gossip column headed "Advice from the Scandalous Club". Here he dispensed advice on morals and manners in a style mixing rectitude with debauchery, ranging through the field of human frailty to cover such vices as duelling, swearing and the lustful drunken section of the clergy—particularly High Churchmen.

The mood of the rumbustious *Review* is in striking contrast with that prevailing in Defoe's austere *Storm*; it is a mood change well illustrating the differentiation Freud insistently made between ethical morality, one so often ostentatiously displayed in *The Review*, and masochistic morality, the type from which *The Storm*'s raconteur, fearing its seductiveness, attempted to flee; Defoe was making a bid to hide himself in a passionless account of the disaster. Some measure of ethical and masochistic morality governs all of us but its distribution can vary enormously. As Freud explicated, "An individual may . . . have preserved the whole or some measure of ethical sense alongside of his masochism; but, alternatively, a large part of his conscience may have vanished into his masochism."[1] Certainly in Defoe's case, much of his conscience-bound morality seeped into his masochism; but such was the underpinning of his ethical conscience, it remained firmly, rigidly in place. And it is the moral fervour that stemmed from that conscience which inspired Defoe's journalism. His polemics, his crusading, his pamphleteering, his rages against injustices, his fiercely expressed prejudices, his marvellous chronicle of the stirrings of the cultural revolution in England, the seismic power-shift in which the mainly middle and commercial class was seizing the initiative from the upper class and landed Tories, all are recited in the mode of a charismatic chapel preacher; he sermonised, writing as from a pulpit, not a desk.

But moral indignation, however abundant, however vigorously expressed, would not have in itself established his claim to be the supreme exemplar for journalists; that rests upon him being in the fullest sense a seer; the moral constant illuminates his eye, endowing it with an extraordinary observational capacity; he focuses, with a microscopic vision, on the quirks, humbuggery, evasions, virtues, vices and tragedies abounding in his society—but yet the moralist in him never loses sight of the eternal verities to be found in the macrocosm. His piercing eye can puncture all pretensions; by his gaze he can strip the mighty of their accoutrements and leave them naked; he is a Peeping Tom *par excellence* and we enjoy his sightings because they are essentially transgressions; the guilt of our moral Daniel gives a piquancy that only the forbidden can provide.

Nowhere more than in the second section of *The Review*, in the "Merry" part, do we find Defoe revelling in the condemnation of sin. His sharp eye spotted all that was scandalous; in those columns he inveighed against debauchery, wrote of the consequences of extra-marital sex, of the status of prostitutes, of women abandoned and betrayed. The House of Commons believed itself not to be deceived by the moral strictures which interlaced his tales of concupiscence and protested to the Bishops about *The Review*'s licentiousness; but there was no stopping Defoe, who, like his growing number of readers, enjoyed the detailed descriptive telling of the antics of devi-ants. The ancestral father of our modern witty columnists, of *Private Eye* and, it must be conceded, of our tabloids is Defoe.

But although Jonathan Swift, like many of the literati of the day, stigmatised *The Review* as being "of a level with great numbers among the lowest part of mankind", Defoe as a journalist is to be distinguished from our contemporary tabloid scavengers and the corrosively cynical and prurient columnists. From the gutter they give us a worm's eye view of the world. Almost without exception, they are amoral practitioners of a spurious homeopathy ever pour-ing their poisonous potions into the gaping wounds of our alienated society. Defoe, contrariwise, commanded by his ethical conscience, wished to be a healer not a destroyer. He was a meliorator, a com-mitted man who would have despised the iconoclasm of so many latterday, jeering journalists who wearily accept the shackles of their paymasters even as they flaunt their superiority in a display of non-partisanship. In none of his writings would Defoe expunge the moral assessment, and even in the near-pornography of some of his *Review* columns, there is a moral fervour that can never be regarded as wholly synthetic. And nowhere is that moral fervour more intriguingly and subtly on display than in his marvellous travelogue *A Tour Thro' the Whole Island of Great Britain*.

★ ★ ★ ★ ★ ★ ★ ★ ★ ★

The astigmatic modern columnist, ever self-hating, ever inviting us to mock our society and ourselves, sees only a joyless world; but Defoe, a believer, is too moral a man to hold such a heretical creed. Man was created in God's image, and His lineaments are beauteous; and though man is wicked and was deservedly expelled from the

Garden, still Eden remains within his sights. Because he possesses a moral vision from either facts or his mind's eye, Defoe conjures for us a picture of a pre-industrial Britain where all could dwell in peace and harmony. In his enchanting idyll—for such it is—he gave us the *Tour thro' the Whole Island of Great Britain*. There, in a happy conjunction of moral uplift and his extraordinary visual acuity, he warmly welcomes us to participate in a joyous celebration of "our Blessed Protestant Country".

The *Tour* has a hidden agenda; it is far more than an eye-witness guide book telling us of the sights he discovered when travelling to much of southern Scotland and through "seventeen very large circuits" in England; it is even more than, as Defoe claims, "a description of the most flourishing and opulent country in the world", inhabited by people with "morals above our Continental neighbours"; it is in fact a missionary work, zealously proclaiming the virtues and the accompanying blessings of the Protestant work ethic. He was asserting that the prosperity of the country was occasioned by the readiness of Britain to uphold that ethic.

All his life Defoe fought the Counter-Reformation, always in his advocacy, in his pamphleteering, in the columns of *The Review* and in his urging of foreign policies designed to contain the Catholic ascendancy in continental Europe, the faithful Dissenter fought his anti-Papist battles. The Pope had at his command his artists, painters like Guercino, one of my favourites still at work when Defoe was born, who in their depictions of the apotheosis of saints, as in their glorious altarpieces in resplendent churches, entranced the masses; for Defoe, with his personal history of armed rebellion against a Catholic king, and with Jacobite alarums ever sounding, certainly did not complacently accept that the full force of the Counter-Reformation was in fact spent. In the *Tour*, yet again he made a riposte; he too painted an apotheosis with whom his readers could inspirationally identify; but it was not an apotheosis of any swooning saint; it was an apotheosis of vigorous Protestant Britain.

What Defoe was assaying in the *Tour* was no dispassionate account; rather, as it has sometimes been described by Defoe scholars, "It is a patriotic celebration or panegyric."[2] It is, however, no vulgar display of racial superiority, for Defoe always complimented the English on the advantage of being "the mongrels of Europe". Nor does the *Tour* attribute the prosperity of England to successful wars. In his *Complete English Tradesman* he writes:

> War has not done it; no, nor so much as helped or assisted to it; it is not by any martial exploit; we have made no conquest abroad, added no new kingdoms to the British Empire, reduced no neighbouring nation, or extended the possession of our monarchs into the property of others; we have gained nothing by war and encroachment; . . . instead of being enriched by war and victory, on the contrary, we have been torn in pieces by civil wars and rebellions.

Defoe claimed that peace and, above all, the moral virtue of hard work have brought about a happy land. No severe Puritan could more extol the delights and rewards of work. Work is idealised; it is the producer of the therapy which can cure all a nation's ills. When he has sight of a town, however ugly may be its approaches, if all there are at work, then in Defoe's eyes it becomes beauteous and is described in rhapsodic passages. When coming to the woollen manufacturing centre of Halifax, the good inhabitants whom he recalls in inimitable style as "zealous Protestants" who "sent 12,000 young men to fight the Popist army then in rebellion", he becomes lyrical. Fascinated by the ubiquity outside every house of a tenter, the wooden framework on which cloth, after being milled, is stretched so that it may dry evenly, he rejoices in its presence as a signal that all inside those homes are diligently at work: "always carding, spinning, etc., so that no hand being unemployed, all can gain their bread, even from the youngest to the ancient. . . . Hardly any thing above four years old but his hands are sufficient to itself."[3] The moral imperative of work, with Defoe, brushes aside any qualms over his enthusiasm for child labour. He is carried away, intoxicated by such a ravishing display of dedicated work. The scene was sublime:

> I thought it was the most agreeable sight that I ever saw, for the hills, as I say, rising and falling so thick, and the vallies opening sometimes one way, sometimes another, so that sometimes we could see two or three miles this way, sometimes as far another; . . . We could see through the glades almost every way, yet look which way we would, high to the tops, and low to the bottoms, it is all the same innumerable houses and tenters, and a white beast upon every tenter.[4]

Buoyed up by such sights, safe in the knowledge that his voyeurism, otherwise suspect, has the sanction, by way of approval of the work ethic, of his moral conscience, confident and relaxed, Defoe rides and strides his way through Britain. He is in good humour, pleased with himself and Protestant Britain, always ready to tell us a diverting tale while regaling us with vivid descriptions of the countryside, communication systems, towns and people he is encountering:

> We came to Ross, a good old town, famous for good cider, a great manufacture of ironware, and a good trade on the River Wye; and nothing else as I remember, except it was a monstrous fat woman, who they would have had me gone to see. But I had enough of divination, and so I suppose will the reader, for they told me she was more than three yards about her wast; that when she sat down, she was oblig'd to have a small stool plac'd before her, to rest her belly on, and the like.[5]

The disguises and confabulations behind which Defoe usually conceals his identity are absent in the *Tour*; of course, he could not possibly have made all the journeys he claims but his homework has been impeccable, and what he tells us is as it is, not fantasy. The recounting is told in the first person and the "I" is Defoe, not a ghost writer. We find him in the *Tour* robust, confident, knowing well the route to take to reach his destinations; he is no irresolute wandering wraith afflicted by agonising existentialist problems. Yet such is the fascination of the characters he, in his novels, has so artfully created that still literary appraisers remain duped into the belief that the unresolved problems afflicting his fictional protagonists always belong in their entirety to their creator, that they are never vicarious. And so they misleadingly present Defoe as a hapless, bewildered man ever vainly searching for his own identity.

The most persuasive exponent of such a wholly mistaken existentialist interpretation is the Nobel Prize winner of 2003, J. M. Coetzee. Born of Boer and English parentage, brought up in apartheid South Africa, living his peripatetic academic life first in England, then in New York and Cape Town, and now in Australia, he is perhaps too vulnerable a subject to be resistant to the attractive existential theme of the footloose rootless artist seeking, through his creativity, to find his identity. When he delivered his Nobel Prize acceptance lecture, it proved to be one of the devious little metaphysical schizoid fragments of which his own fiction seems increasingly to consist;[6] he calls it "He and his man" and the "he" and "his man" were each Defoe/Crusoe. In my lifetime I have had two creative friends, one a man and the other an unrelated woman, both, alas, now dead, who belonged to families cursed by a gene which carried madness; some of the members of their families ended their lives in mental hospitals. My creative friends escaped that fate but there was always a schizophrenic impact upon their mode of thinking. Von Domarus, in his classical paper on schizophrenic thinking,[7] suggested that schizophrenic patients differed from normal in that they were "para-logical", that is, they did not require "identity of all predicates" to state that two objects were identical; they might say that an orange and an house were the same simply because both shared one attribute (say, the colour yellow). On occasion the predicate may be some-thing which is not even apparent to the observer (for example, that both were facing north).[8] This confusion of boundaries, its splitting and odd differentiation of objects, often led my friends to have per-plexing but innovative visions that I did not share. I believe that much of Coetzee's work is redolent of such schizophrenic meander-ings. In his Nobel lecture, he dismembers Defoe/Crusoe, creates a duality which I believe does not exist, and then sends each of them on a vain search to find their *Doppelgänger*:

> How are they to be figured, this man and he? As master and slave? As brothers, twin brothers? As comrades in arms? Or as enemies, foes? ... He yearns to meet the fellow in the flesh, shake his hand, take a stroll with him along the quayside and hearken as he tells of his visit to the dark north of the island, or of his adventures in the writing business. But he fears there will be no meeting, not in this life. If he must settle on a likeness for the pair of them, his man and he, he would write that they are like two ships sailing in contrary directions, one west, the other east. Or better, that they are deckhands toiling in the rigging, the one on a ship sailing west, the other on a ship sailing east. Their ships pass close, close enough to hail. But the seas are rough, the weather is stormy: their eyes lashed by the spray, their hands burned by the cordage, they pass each other by, too busy even to wave.[9]

This portrayal of a disorientated Defoe is an engaging conceit, but it tells us far more of the schizoid element woven into the general fabric of Coetzee's thinking than it does of Defoe's. Here, as in his earlier novel *Foe*,[10] Coetzee plays us a pretty fugue, with one Defoe performing an initial theme and another developing an answering one; such literary counterpoints may, as they clearly have, charm Nobel and Booker Prize judges but those not prepared to collude with our Daniel and accept his impersonations as fact and not fiction will regard with suspicion the existentialist interpretations proffered by Coetzee.

The reality of the true Defoe is to be found in the *Tour*, where, with his two feet firmly on the ground and, on this occasion, donning no mask and clothed in no concealing garb, he confidently and didactically presents himself and his Britain to his readers; and those readers were to be many, for the *Tour* had reached its ninth edition by 1779 and remains today the most often quoted source for early eighteenth-century English social and economic history. The *Tour* is indeed no caprice, no raunchy jaunt taken by a novelist as a relief from the labours of the demanding imaginative story-telling. It is a work for which, as perceptive critics have noted, he had "been preparing all through his life whether consciously or unconsciously".[11]

The *Tour* indeed provides us with a rare opportunity to view Defoe undisguised. With such an opportunity available it would be wilful to join Coetzee and his ilk in their fanciful yarns of a multiplicity of Defoes; with a holistic perspective, and a whole, clearly defined man to be seen in the *Tour*, an attempt can be made to understand the psychodynamics at work which allowed an unabashed Defoe, casting off his inhibitions, to indulge, blatantly and promiscuously, without moral qualms, his unashamed voyeurism. Such an attempt may be taxing, perhaps over-ambitious, perhaps over-speculative, since it must involve an exploration of the earliest months of Defoe's life, of his pre-Oedipal experiences;[12] but since we have found that a scrutiny of his negative Oedipus proved rewarding, we may brave the scoffers of such an attempt and hope that it may result in giving us a little more understanding of the enigmatic man whose compulsive voyeurism, dangerously close to a perversion, was, in the *Tour*, so creatively deployed.

⋆   ⋆   ⋆   ⋆   ⋆   ⋆   ⋆   ⋆   ⋆   ⋆

Dominating London's landscape today, to the delight of most of its citizens, is the Eye; it is a viewing platform which is a most appropriate symbol for a capital city of a nation of voyeurs. Technology

has brought us seedy TV channels, websites saturated with pornography and an abundance of hard-core videos;[13] each week millions
are now engaged in watching others copulating; they empathise
with the performers in the same fashion as did the Peeping Toms
whom, as a young man, I defended in the courts. From those perverse
voyeurs of couples I learned that, while watching, they invariably
identified in fantasy with one of the partners and, more usually,
with both. So do most of today's viewers; contemporary capitalism,
abusing and harnessing modern technology, has created a huge
pornographic industry engaged in the voyeurism and subsequent
exploitation of the wish we all of us have—to participate and to
witness parental coitus. The actors putting on tape a show of fucking
are but surrogates for our own fathers and mothers, and the sexual
excitation experienced by today's armchair voyeurs comes from a
recall, imagined or real, of the sight of what Freud called "the primal
scene", one that falls into the category of what he named "the primal
fantasies": "Among the store of fantasies of all neurotics, and probably of all human beings, this scene is seldom absent."[14] No study
can be made of the exceptional voyeurism which we are attributing
to Defoe without an endeavour to assess the consequences of his
particular fantasy of the primal scene. The voyeurist fantasy of the
primal scene is, so psychoanalysts instruct us, from our earliest
years, from our pre-Oedipal infantile experience: "The understanding and interest which the child brings to the parental coitus are
based on the child's own pre-Oedipal physical experiences with the
mother and its resultant desires."[15] The oral pleasure of the suckling
babe is associated with, and enhanced by, the sighting of nipple
and breast; when the babe moves on to the anal phase, it is the
sight of his creations, of his faeces, which adds to the coprophilic
yearnings which societal prohibitions must needs deny him; a little
later, as he enters the genital phase, his exhibitionism will invite
the world to join him in celebrating a full frontal display of his
genitals. Always, in each phase of our development, the eye has a
constituent role in the excitation of the erotogenic zones which are
predestined to play so determinant a part in the shaping of our adult
character.

   The special privilege of erotogenicity accorded, however, to certain bodily zones—the breast, the anus, the genitals—which induce
sexual excitations does not result in the exclusion of its property

from other bodily organs.[16] Every man who has been given the glad eye by a flirtatious woman knows of the erotic quality possessed by the eye. It has often been said that the eyes are the windows to the soul, but the poetry of such an attribution must not persuade us to judge, acknowledging less noble qualities. With unblinking eyes we display our hostilities when facing our enemy; eyes can flash, laugh, banish, pierce, be meditative, sleepy, dry or wet; the eyes register and carry our deepest emotions. Only the unimaginative would believe the eyes are the province solely of the ophthalmologist.[17] The eye is indeed the reservoir from which we draw sustenance to arouse our sexual fantasies, not least those that surround the primal scene; and in our mind's eye we conjure up in misshapen dreams pictorial representations of the taboo, the deviant and the prohibited.

From birth onwards, and perhaps even before in the foetus, the eye participates in all the vicissitudes the infant experiences in his pre-Oedipal life; but the eye's gaze must shift, not remain fixated, as the infant moves from one stage of his libidinal development to the next; the eyes must keep up with the weaning, not remain attached to the sight of the nipple or bottle; and then they must renounce the pleasures of gazing at the shit wondrously produced so that the perilous journey can be made into the Oedipal situation where the full and discomforting recognition must be accorded to the mother and father.

The journey is fraught with hazards, for the eye is a conservative organ, and enjoys lingering, always reluctant to give up the pleasures that the initial sightings have brought. The ubiquity of the thrill and frisson of the viewing of the primal scene is chasteningly attested to by present-day sales of pornographic videos, but how early in the infant's life the fantasy comes into play is problematic; and whether the primal scene is a memory of an actual experienced event, or is pure fantasy, is a problem much debated between Freud and Jung.[18] Freud has suggested that it is not a retrospective fantasy but may be a true reality, perhaps prompted by clues coming from noises or sight of animal coitus. Colourfully, one clinician has said that the infant's fantasy begins as soon as the door of the parents' bedroom is closed. However, whatever may be the point at which the fantasy is conjured up, what cannot be gainsaid is that it is woven into the eroticism which is endowed by the eye as the infant moves on from one developmental stage to another. With the eyes so sexually charged, it is unsurprising that embarrassed mothers in each generation warn their little ones that it is rude to stare. If young Daniel received such an admonition from an unempathic mother, it is likely to have been expressed not gently but abruptly, as a reprimand rather than as instruction; the avid sharp sightings of the great and extraordinarily persistent adult observer may well be circumlocutions of the initial prohibitions, a sly defiance, a regaining of the voyeuristic pleasure that too prematurely was snatched away from him as an infant.

But with Defoe we must be ever wary; these circumlocutions could be decoys, distracting us from discovering his utmost secrets. So engaging are his peregrinations that, having canvassed the notion that his sight-seeing journey is a postponed subversion of the strict mother's prohibition, we are loath, lest it be an act of spoliation, to pursue yet further our interrogations. If, however, we yield to that temptation, then Defoe will indeed have succeeded in his distractions, for although the thwarting by a peremptory martinet mother of the infant's desire to gaze can indeed leave the lustful eye so dissatisfied that in adult life an inordinate wish to look and find what was denied can prevail, nevertheless voyeurism has other components that are particularly revelatory in Defoe's case, and need scrutiny.

There is no shortage of clinical material to help us explore the aetiology of voyeurism; and as in my young days, when daily I encountered in court the pathetic procession of voyeur and exhibitionist defendants, today such offences constitute one-third of all sexual offences committed, becoming the most commonly perpetrated sexual offence, more widespread than buggery, gross indecency with a child, infant incest, procurement or rape. I soon learned from my voyeur clients that, as they peered at open-air lovers, the vantage points they chose, the bushes and undergrowth concealing their presence, were chosen not only to escape detection by the police; they were, too, carefully chosen so that as the pervert gazed fixedly at the love-making, he would not be de-masked himself, for every voyeur precariously wears a mask and fears that if it slips, if looking is not firmly in place, then far worse anti-social conduct may be the outcome. A dangerous doing will replace seeing; looking and showing belong to a dualism in the same way that sadism and masochism coexist; "commonly" the experienced clinician dealing with voyeurs and flashers tells us that "the voyeur has unconscious exhibitionist wishes".[19] Voyeurism holds in check the exhibitionist mode of expression; fences are drawn around a static viewing zone as a defence against the assault of exhibitionism which, if acted out, could have disastrous personal and social results. Compulsive looking, a disturbance found in many neurotics, although not amounting to a fully developed voyeuristic perversion, can also have bizarre consequences; the case histories are replete with tales of men and women, so fearful that their sightings will be overwhelmed by their desire to exhibit themselves, that they will not venture out into the streets.[20] Others will travel only in the seat-belted car, for being thus immobilised, they are inhibited from responding to a provocative sight by an unseemly display of exhibitionism; it is, of course, an established fact that a considerable number of accidents occur because drivers cannot take their gaze away from a passing attractive woman, and those are the occasions where voyeurism is indeed fatal.

We well know, however, from our indebtedness to Defoe, who, in *The Storm, Journal of the Plague Year* and the *Tour*, allowed no detail to escape his attention, that compulsive voyeurism can be transmuted so that it can illuminate our world, giving us a vision hitherto unseen by our dull accustomed eyes. Yet our gratitude must not lead us to avoid making the uncomfortable diagnosis that compulsive viewing is essentially a pathological condition and that the more persistent and elaborate are its manifestations, the more certain we can be that it is acting as a defence mechanism, a bulwark against a threatening exhibitionism. A serious and rigorous attempt to explore that vicissitudes of Defoe's pre-Oedipal life and relate these to his work must include the questioning of the nature and source of such exaggerated exhibitionism, from which, it is proposed, his voyeurism and much of his creative writing were distilled.

★　★　★　★　★　★　★　★　★　★

For Freud, exhibitionism forms an important part of ordinary childhood development; but as he revealed in his *magnum opus, The Interpretation of Dreams*, we certainly do not leave it behind when we grow up. In adulthood, nudity and genital exposure, our dreams reveal, remain our secret nostalgic desires to return to the bliss of those moments when, born naked, our rudimentary genitalia would have been displayed for all to see. Freud indeed listed exhibitionism in the very first category of what he described as "Typical Dreams". When I was defending flashers the magistrates had before them not only evidence of the accused's behaviour but also evidence of their own dreams and mine of the previous night; more fortunate than the hapless wretch in the dock, we had early upbringing, socialisation and acculturation that enabled us to jettison, or at least smother them before we sat down to breakfast. But woe betide those of us who, possessed of the hubris of those exhibitionist dreams, believe these can be totally banished in our waking hours. Exhibitionism is one of what Freud called the "component drives"; out of control, it can take us to disaster.[21]

How fierce or how governable that drive is in an adult is dependent above all else on whether as a babe he has the benefit of a facilitating and enabling environment;[22] in the beginning he is the centre of the world, indeed there is no world, only "me". How the mortification of that limitless narcissism comes about, whether it comes about as part of a transaction with a mother who brings the gifts of loving care in exchange for the renunciation by the babe of his solipsism, or whether the acknowledgement of the exterior world is brought about coercion, by peremptory infringements of a less than good enough mother, will determine the quantitative level of an adult's exhibitionism. The babe, denied sufficient admiration of his narcissistic displays by a churlish mother, will forever feel robbed; in adult life he will demand reparation and attempt by one means or another to obtain attention from the world; the deeper the initial wounds to his narcissism, the more extravagant may be his attention-seeking behaviour; he may become a bad actor, a Blair-like politician or a television "celebrity"; and, at the very worst, the unassuaged babe still searching for corroborative acknowledgement will, as an adult, publicly display his penis and end up in court.

But Defoe, as we have seen, was wiser; he renounced some of the pleasures of exhibitionism for the secondary and safer delights of voyeurism; he looked but did not crudely display for that could have provoked fatal retaliatory responses. But the smouldering gaze was possessed of no gentle mien; it was charged with all the energy of the suppressed exhibitionism. If his mother had given the response to the babe, clamouring for attention, and had received reassuring, approving, admiring smiles, it would have been otherwise; and he would have tempered, and not so feared, his exhibitionism.

His initial disadvantage was to be our advantage; posterity was bequeathed the legacy of the works by the great and inimitable Observer of eighteenth-century Britain.

Nevertheless, it would be an inadequate reading of his works simply to pronounce them as rare exotica, plants which grew and flourished in the soil of his parched exhibitionism; the subsoil itself at least needs scrutiny. Even although we can never reach bedrock, we can dig deeper. The origin of Defoe's creativity is beyond our reach but the psychical mechanisms of its development can be observed. We shall never find the holy grail but we can approach the periphery of its domain; each step we take backwards, deciphering on our way the footsteps once made by Defoe as he advanced to his destiny, can bring us rewards which enrich our reading of his works.

But always in our attempt to make an investigative journey into Defoe's pre-Oedipal hinterland, we should be mindful of the many anxieties overcasting that territory, for it is here where, in fact or in fantasy, the primal scene has ever been avidly witnessed by the babe. Melanie Klein emphasised that child's feeling of exclusion in relation to the parental couple.[23] As the child wishes for an exclusive and possessive relationship with the desired parent, there is intense envy of the rival parent who seems to possess the exclusive and possessive relationship denied to the child. The child wishes to spoil and destroy the conjugal bliss of the parental couple. Intruding upon the parents' privacy in witnessing the primal scene is a manner of overcoming the sense of exclusion. Yet violating the sanctity of the parents' sexual exclusivity is forbidden. Thus, whatever voyeuristic and spoiling desires are gratified in witnessing the primal scene are also guilt-ridden and generate an anxious need for punishment.[24] These powerful emotions create a conflict between wishing to observe the parents' sexual relationship and wishing to turn away in denial of its reality. Looking is motivated by wishing to be voyeuristically aroused by intruding upon the privacy and exclusivity of the parents' sexual relationship. Looking away is motivated by a wish to evade the sense of exclusion, envy, humiliating betrayal and, above all, the fear of punishment for making forbidden observations.[25]

The punishment feared is castration, and that fear is never totally extirpated, but the strength of such a continuing castration anxiety depends upon how threatening the infant feels his upbringing to be, how much love has tempered his fear of what he interprets as threats coming from society; the notion that the anatomical differences between boys and girls arise because the girl's "penis", as a punishment, has been cut off[26] is not easily abandoned and, with Defoe, the constant sighting of the vaginas of his two little sisters could have been regarded as a corroborative warning signal; with an unempathic mother, as Defoe's mother certainly appears to have been, the boy can be left feeling he is under constant threat from an inhospitable and hostile environment.[27] The phallus is an essential component of the male self-image; but if it becomes regarded as a dangerous provocation, as an invitation to self-destruction, in desperation, as a survival stratagem, the infant will never dare to flaunt it; even worse, he may give it up entirely and opt for the safety of femininity. The emergence in adulthood of this symptom is commonplace among exhibitionists and voyeurs brought before the courts for making public nuisances of themselves. Ismond Rosen, who, more than anyone in Britain, had a wide experience of treating such offenders, has told us:

> The patterns of identification with the parents are usually disturbed in the exhibitionist and voyeur. There is a strong tendency towards a feminine identification, which is revealed in some cases by the additional symptoms of transvestism, or dressing-up in feminine apparel. Exhibitionism or voyeurism is used by the individual to defend himself against these feelings of femininity. In addition, the sexual identification with the mother (the boy taking the negative Oedipal role in feeling that he wants to take Mother's sexual role with the Father) results in passive homosexual wishes being aroused. These passive homosexual wishes are also defended against by the act of exhibitionism. The voyeur's need to defend himself against these passive homosexual wishes is increased because his capacity for empathy is usually a strong one, and intense curiosity about parental intercourse includes the wish to experience the sexual roles of both partners.[28]

The passive homosexuality and the primal scene curiosity, which Rosen found lurking behind the display of the exhibitionist and voyeur, has been remarked upon by a wide range of clinicians. In the United States the psychoanalyst Charles Socarides, becoming aware of the presence of homosexual wishes and tendencies in his exhibitionist patients, concluded that the exhibitionistic perversion functioned in large measure as a means of achieving a deeper sense of masculinity in a male who struggles with his own sense of sexual identity.[29] Similarly, the Hungarian-born Sandor Lorand, noting in his exhibitionist patients the lack of confidence in their heterosexuality, has pointed out that exhibitionism reinforces one's belief in the potency and security of the penis; by unveiling it to unsuspecting bystanders, the perpetrator can elicit a reaction in his victim, emphasising that the penis does still exist and that it must be very powerful indeed.[30] The insightful therapist Brett Kahr is indeed not lacking in authority when, in his recent book on exhibitionism, he asserts that exhibitionism protects the patient against homosexuality and functions as a defence against castration anxiety, and as a means of reinforcing masculine potency.[31]

All the specifics these clinicians have found as they have explored the aetiology of their voyeuristic and exhibitionist patients are, it is reasonable to surmise, of the same kind that would have afflicted Defoe in his pre-Oedipal months; they are both intimations and explications of the obstacles which so fatefully hindered him when he conspicuously failed to negotiate, as we have repeatedly emphasised, his admission to, and subsequent relinquishment of, his complete Oedipal phase. Attempting to monitor the strivings of Defoe in his pre-Oedipal months, identifying nascent and anticipatory traits found there, and suggesting that they are striated in all his monumental works, is no exercise in nihilistic deconstruction; awareness of the details embedded in the works enlivens, not deadens, our appreciation of their architecture.

Inevitably there will be those, ever desperate for "facts", who will resist any hermeneutic hypothesis and will claim that too little is known of Defoe's mother to posit a specific concatenation between her temperament and Defoe's works. Those, however, who are more sympathetic to the arts of divination will find that the restless, almost frenzied, jactitations which gripped Defoe almost to the very end of his days corroborate the suggestion that in his mother's arms he had never found quietude. Freed as he was in his older years from the obligations of his journalism, Defoe might have been able in retirement to nurse his ailing body and wander contemplatively in the garden of the house he had acquired. But as Novak has commented, "Such an ending was hardly compatible with his restless spirit."[32] Provocative pamphlets and litigation continued to engage him and only when his body could no longer sustain his relentless aggressivity did he give in, and die.

In his lifestyle Defoe displayed many of the symptoms that can arise in adult behaviour when the man, as a babe, lacks the tender and good care which allows a fusion of his aggression and his eroticism. The paediatrician Donald Winnicott elegantly taught us that the motility that exists in the intra-uterine life, as the babe kicks in the womb, and that exists when a babe of a few weeks thrashes away with his arms, is the precursor to the aggression that has to be positively organised in the child if he is to become an integrated person.[33] For some, the environmental chance which enables the babe to ensure a successful integration of personality is denied. They become not the healthy adults whose behaviour is positive and whose aggression is meant but, at worst, the sick whose aggression is not meant, who are like the babe who kicks in the womb or thrashes away with his arms, and upon whom we project the notion that they mean to kick out or mean to act, when in fact we have no right to make such assumptions. They are, in short, the men who have not lived their earliest lives constantly discovering and re-discovering the environment by using their motility as they snuggle and struggle within their mother's arms; they have not enjoyed that primal erotic experience within which they can fuse that aggression and love. For them contact with the environment has not been an experience of the individual; lacking sufficient loving care, they lacked a series of individual experiences helping them on their way to integration and have suffered only an environment which was felt as an impingement.

The tragedy of men who have suffered such an early fate is that as adults they must constantly expose themselves to opposition that is vigorous, if not dangerous, because only in aggressive reactions to impingement can they feel real. Such persons may have erotic experiences but only if seduced, and since they do not enjoy in the act a fusion of their aggression and their eroticism, the erotic experience does not feel real; for they are doomed to have a personality which has developed falsely as a series of reactions to impingement, and their only hope of possessing a total sense of feeling real is by provoking situations which arouse resistance and opposition. The violent gangsters and rapists whom I defended in the courts were such men; each of them was an exotic illustration of the consequences of being the child of an uncaring mother. It is, however, a syndrome in milder form that I have found, in my political life, frequently extends to men who, although not the children of the disastrous mothers who breed criminals, have experienced a dutiful but essentially affectionless upbringing. They are a type of men who in politics delight in being in permanent opposition, and are afraid they will dissolve if they accept the responsibility of government; a handful of such men can be an incubus upon mainstream political parties since such character types persistently concoct extravagant policies which are guaranteed to enrage large sections of the community and keep their political party out of office for ever.

Yet, though torments may be inflicted on the individual, insensitive mothering may sometimes result not in iconoclasm but in extraordinary societal gains, and such was certainly the case with Defoe. His resentments against the earliest impingements of the brusque mother endured unto his death. He was ever engaged on retaliatory attacks, ever seeking out targets, abuses, wrongs and pretensions, against which he would hurl his aggression; if sometimes the targets were undeserved victims, for the most part his onslaughts were well directed and often accompanied by reparative prescriptions which he claimed would remedy the evils he was identifying.

If, given the irascibility so frequently shown by the notoriously quarrelsome man, I nevertheless make this positive assessment of the social consequences of his nursing, it is, I concede, partly because I am prejudiced in his favour. Every authentic biography is autobiography; the biographer's analysis of his subject should lead to self-analysis and, with this in mind, and in this context, I should as an admission make mention of my own mother. She was an exceptionally pretty woman known in her circle for her beauty and tactlessness; over-confident of her appearance, she never depended on or developed charm; the consequence was a total absence of tact. One does not need to be an etymologist to link tact and tactile; the same deficiency which she displayed in her social relations would have been evident in her handling of me when I was a babe and her inept impingements doubtless have provoked similar retaliatory and aggressive responses as I am attributing to Defoe. My possession of a warm, hands-on affectionate father has perhaps mitigated some of the undirected aggression released by clumsy nursing; but when I find myself still campaigning, and endeavouring to put the world to rights, I believe not a little of my continued zeal has its source in the maladroit handling of my tantrums eighty-nine years ago. If Defoe, as is suggested, as a babe experienced the environment as more hostile than benevolent, then as he grew up this was to be corroborated, not vitiated. The Dissenters were outsiders, never belonging to the compact majority, at odds with the Establishment, and even when Defoe was to work for the powerful, he was barred by temperament, class, education and religious affiliation from ever becoming an insider. Perhaps if he had been able to struggle into the welcoming arms of an affectionate mother it would have been otherwise; then he would have had a sense of belonging. He would have been a happier man and we would never have had the astonishing polemical critiques of his, and sometimes our, society.

Notes

1. Freud, S., *The Economic Problems of Masochism*, SE, Volume 19.
2. Furbank, P. N., Introduction to *Tour thro' the Whole Island of Great Britain*, Yale University Press, 1991.
3. Defoe, D., *Tour thro' the Whole Island of Great Britain*.
4. Ibid.
5. Ibid.
6. Taylor, D. J., Coetzee's Nobel, *Guardian Review*, 13 December 2003.
7. Von Domarus, E., Zur Theories es Schizophrenen Denkesens, in *Zeitschrift für Neurologie und Psychiatre*, 1927.
8. Berrios, G., *The History of Mental Symptoms*, Cambridge University Press, 1996.
9. Coetzee, J. M., Man and his man, Nobel Prize acceptance lecture, 9 December 2003.
10. Coetzee, J. M., *Foe*, Penguin Books, 1987.
11. Furbank, Introduction to *Tour thro' the Whole Island of Great Britain*.
12. See Chapter 3.
13. Coopersmith, J., Pornography, technology and progress, *Icon, Journal of the International Committee for the History of Technology*, 4 (1988).
14. Freud, S., A Case of Paranoia Running Counter to the Psychoanalytic Theory of the Disease, SE, Volume 14, p. 269.

15. Brunswick, R. M., The pre-Oedipal phase of the libido development, *Psychoanalytic Reader*, 1950.

16. Freud, S., *An Outline of Psychoanalysis*, SE, Volume 23.

17. Groddeck, G., Vision, the world of the eye, in *Pscychoanalytische Schriften zur Psychosomatik*, Wiesbaden, 1970.

18. Laplanche, J. and Pontalis, J. B., *The Language of Psychoanalysis*, Hogarth Press, 1973, p. 355.

19. Rosen, I., Looking and showing, in R. Slovenko (ed.), *Sexual Behavior and the Law*, Charles C. Thomas, 1965.

20. Ibid.

21. Freud, S., *The Interpretation of Dreams*, SE, Volume 5; Freud, S., *Three Essays on the Theory of Sexuality*, SE, Volume 2.

22. Winnicott, D. W., The maturational processes and the facilitant environment, in *Studies in the Theory of Emotional Development*, Hogarth Press, 1965; Winnicott, D. W., *The Family and Individual Development*, Tavistock Publications, 1965.

23. Klein, M., Early stages of the Oedipus conflict, in *Contribution to Psychoanalysis, 1921–1945*, Hogarth Press, 1948; Klein, M., The Oedipus complex in the light of early anxiety, in *The Writings of Melanie Klein, Volume 1*, Hogarth Press, 1948.

24. Freud, S., *Some Character-types Met with Psychoanalytical Work*, SE, Volume 14.

25. Josephs, L., The observing ego as voyeur, *International Journal of Psychoanalysis*, 84 (August 2003).

26. Freud, S., *Essays on the Sexual Theories of Children*, SE, Volume 9.

27. Abse, L., *Fellatio, Masochism, Politics and Love*, Robson Books, 2002.

28. Rosen, I., Looking and showing.

29. Socarides, C. W., The demonified mother: a study of voyeurism and sexual sadism, *International Review of Psychoanalysis*, 1 (1974).

30. Lorand, S., The psychology of nudism, *Psychoanalytical Review*, 20 (1933).

31. Kahr, B., *Exhibitionism*, Icon Books, 2001.

32. Novak, M. E., *Daniel Defoe: Master of Fictions*, Oxford University Press, 2001.

33. Winnicott, D. W., Through paediatrics to psycho-analysis, in *Collected Papers*, Tavistock Press, 1958.

CHAPTER NINE

The spy

I n 1688, when James II quit England, the principle of the inviol-
ability of the divinely ordained hereditary monarchy went with
him; but the Glorious Revolution brought no consensus clearly
defining the nature of the future constitutional governance of the
land. Society was being called upon to renounce its infantilism, to
give up dependency and belief in the faultless father-ruler, one
whose words were God's; maturity demands a relinquishment of
the idealisation of the parent and recognition of his blemishes and
inadequacies, and growing up can be as painful for a society as for
an individual.

Inevitably the acceptance of a secular solution to the constitutional crisis occasioned by the arrival of William and Mary was for
some intolerable. The Archbishop of Canterbury of the day, marked
as was his disapproval of James, nevertheless refused to sign an oath
of allegiance to the newcomers; his response echoed a large body of
opinion resenting the interlopers whose credentials, given English–
Dutch commercial rivalry, were in any event highly suspect. Even
among those who thought they were being rescued from a reign
that would have become as unremittingly anti-Protestant as was
that of Bloody Mary, there were misgivings; disposal of natural

God-given parents is one matter, welcoming strange step-parents is quite another. They are surrogates who in political life, as in fairy stories, can so often become hate figures. No wonder that at one stage before the century ended, William even contemplated abdicating.

There was no unanimity in place; partisan political controversy abounded. Factions representing vested interests describing themselves or being described as the Country Party, the Tories, Jacobites or Classical Republicans waged their internecine wars. Into that turmoil, with relish, Defoe plunged and already, early in 1689, he set out his stall and published his first full-length political pamphlet, *Reflections, upon the Late Great Revolution*. It was to be the first of many such forays and was ultimately to lead to the publication in 1697 of his first book, *An Essay upon Projects*. Over the last decade of the century, and later, he consistently publicised and developed his agenda.

He was a defender of the Government, insisting upon the legality of the replacement of James II by William of Orange—but no less insistently he declared that the relationship between the monarch and his subjects was to be essentially secular. The king is an executive who contrives to act as the "Chief Magistrate", and as long as the ruler and his heirs obey this "Original Contract" he and his family may stay in office, his power coming from the consent of the people. He presented William as a willing partner to such a contract, a man who was a true Protestant hero in the fight against the aggression of Louis XIV and the Catholic Church; those "Trimmers" lacking enthusiasm for that cause were traitors.

Defoe wanted his monarch to be free to act as leader in military engagements both abroad and at home, putting into effect a programme of toleration and progress: toleration of the Dissenters that would extend to allow them to serve in all aspects of government, progress in following an expansive economic policy that would employ the labouring poor and find new markets abroad while encouraging trade within England. "In the name of such potential good, Defoe was willing to sacrifice much in the way of checks and balances on executive power."[1]

Confident in his belief that William would keep his side of the "contract", Defoe never ceased to lavish the most extravagant praise on his hero. When William died, he pronounced: "I take all occasions to do for the expressing the Honour I ever preserved for the Immortal and Glorious Memory of the Greatest and Best of Princes." During the King's life, as on his death, Defoe presented himself as the most obsequious of subjects. His critics have ever continued to mock his untempered self-abasement and to claim that Defoe's fierce pro-William pamphlets were obeisances prompted not by conviction but by venality.

It is undoubtedly true that his propagandising was tainted by self-interest, by the hope that patronage would bring personal advancement and the reward of government orders for his commercial undertakings, but such velleities were coincidental and do not vitiate the strength of the convictions, nor adequately explain the stamina he showed in his pursuit of William's political opponents. The vitality of his polemics, the Socratic skills of his rhetoric, as he challenged all who would subvert William, do, however, contain a concealed sub-text. It was with the 1688 Glorious Revolution in mind that, a half-century ago, the historian Sir Louis Namier gave us a clue, helping us to uncover and decipher that sub-text:

> One inevitable result of heightened psychological awareness is, however, a change of attitude towards so-called political ideas. To treat them as the offspring of pure reason would be to assign to them a parentage about as mythological as that of Pallas Athene. What matters most is the underlying emotions, the music, to which ideas are the mere libretto, often of a very inferior quality; and once the emotions have ebbed, the ideas . . . become doctrine or . . . . clichés.[2]

Defoe's political ideas cannot be treated as mere clichés, although sometimes in his borrowings they occasionally are, but what is certain is that the music of which Namier speaks was played loud and clear when in his librettos Defoe recited his paeans to the king.

In the particular socially resonating conditions of post-1688 England, Defoe was able, with exquisite ease, to act out, with considerable political effect, his earliest unresolved Oedipal problems. The personal became the public; his private wrestlings and buried emotions became enmeshed in the public domain. The times advantaged him; serendipity gave him the political stage on which he could first rehearse and then display his talents as the great pamphleteer, and in the grand debate on Authority, where it lay and how and if it could be or should be contained, in a marvellous abreaction, he swore his allegiance to his father-king.

Such support was welcome to the King's circle, for the pamphlet in those days was an important weapon in the political armoury; an arresting pamphlet, written with verve in a vigorous laudatory or vitriolic style, could be a significant influence on public opinion. For Defoe, such pamphleteering, acting as a catharsis, relieved his personal tensions; as he praised William and mocked his enemies, Defoe could, with social propriety, use language charged with the unspent incestuous homosexual passions of his earliest childhood.

His fierce partisanship on William's behalf was far more than an expression of political prejudice; it was a reminiscence. It brought the Master, as he described William, closer and closer to him; unconsciously it evoked his first emotional strivings, his buried desire as a babe, never relinquished, to be taken and abused by his Dissenting father; his services to the Protestant king were proffered not as mere genuflections but as prostrations. The joy and zest of his political trafficking came to him not only from the jousting in the war of pamphlets with William's adversaries, but even more from the intimacy with William that came from such campaigning. Defoe's triumph was that William yielded to his seductions, put him on the secret service payroll, accepted his suggestion to create a spy-ring to identify and invigilate the King's enemies, and used him as a speech-writer. Perhaps Defoe later exaggerated the reciprocity that came into existence between the two, but in fact and in fantasy Defoe felt he had achieved with William the fusion that had been his primal desire to achieve with his natural father.

To be near the King excited him; proximity itself set him alight. He was one of those who rode to greet William at Brixham in November 1688 and joined the Earl of Peterborough's Royal Regiment of Volunteer Horse, one of the few open to Dissenters, which, in the Lord Mayor's Show staged by the City the following year to honour William and Mary, enabled him to be part of the monarchs' escort cum guard of honour on duty on this occasion. He remained with the regiment for some years, was regularly in attendance upon the King and discharged various court duties. His devotion was total. When, in his pamphleteering, he would sing William's praise, there was ever a trill in the voice; a feminine voice emerged, a beguiling tune sung by a castrato, not by a bass.

His service to William brought other fraught delights, one laced with the *frisson* that temptation always brings; the compulsive observer now had a licence to revel in his illicit indulgences, to dissimulate and in this guise to gaze at the forbidden and, with the most noble of motives and his surrogate father's full approval, pleasure himself; the voyeur Defoe was let loose into a society where spying was endemic and where every rival power group was intent on finding a bedroom door ajar so that the infidelities of coupling betrayers could be minutely observed. The secret regressive wish to view and participate in the primal scene was, in the immediate post-1688 years, socially sanctioned.

There were in effect three courts: that of William, that of James in France at St Germain and that of James's estranged daughter Princess Anne, later to be Queen Anne, at Berkeley House in London. In France, where some 50,000 Stuart supporters were in self-imposed or compulsory exile, conspiracy and plans for invasion to regain the throne for James proliferated. Meanwhile, Princess Anne, choked with hatred for her brother-in-law William, was subtly and with guile endeavouring to subvert him in order to regain her priority as successor and erase the "abdication" that had been enforced upon her. An ecology was in place where intrigue, double-dealing and the informer could abundantly flourish. Defoe was in his element.

Beyond, however, knowing he was in William's pay, we know few of the details of the clandestine services Defoe rendered to his master—but we know well the nature of the terrifying agenda to which he would have been working, and that he was later to set out openly, after William had died and when he had transferred his own allegiance and obeisances to his new powerful patron, Robert Harley, the Earl of Oxford. To maintain power and to govern successfully, he counselled that it was essential to create a spy state. No Cold War warrior in our twentieth century exceeded the zeal with which Defoe advocated the use of espionage, moles and secret agents to defeat opposition to the ruler. Defoe put forward what he called "a Scheme of General Intelligence", a system of spies and agents who would send a constant supply of information. More, an agency should be set up to handle the information, but it should be made to appear just another harmless government office; the machinery was to work in so cunning a way that even office clerks would not know what was actually happening. By these means,

Defoe argued, "openly . . . a Correspondence may be Effectually Settled with every part of England, and all the World beside".

Defoe expanded upon this advice in a document called "Maxims and Instructions for Ministers of State", written some time in 1704; in this Defoe was at his most Machiavellian. Here he suggested that the real key to ruling would lie in the organisation and processing of information coming in from all parts of England and from abroad so that a ruler would have a clear idea of conflicts and change within the various parties at home and in foreign governments. Secret agents should be placed in Paris, Rouen, Toulouse, Brest and Dunkirk to report on happenings; a mixture of diplomacy, spies and force was the best way to work in dealing with foreign affairs, while at home "Dissimulation" was the best technique to retain popularity:

> Tho this Part of Conduct is called Dissimulation, I am Content it shall be Call'd what They will, But as a lye Does Not Consist in the Indirect Positioning of Words, but in the Design by False Speaking to Deceive and Injure my Neighbour, So Dissembling does Not Consist in putting a Different Face Upon Our Actions, but in the further Applying That Concealment to the Prejudice of the Person . . .

The aim of such deception, Defoe argued, was "the Reall happyness of us all"; he then quoted St Paul, "Becoming all Things to all Men, that he might Gain Some", and concluded, with breathtaking insouciance, "This Hypocrise is a Virtue, and by this Conduct . . . you shall be Faithfull and Usefull to the Soveraign and Belov'd by The People."

This is not the voice of a scrupulous Dissenting moralist; abandoning himself to the masochistic delights that submission to the leader brought him, revelling in the thrills of a licensed voyeurism, enjoying spying for its own sake, quoting scripture, like the devil, for his own purposes, the extravagances of his language and propositions betray their orgiastic origins; given absolution by a Protestant king, all the constraints and ethics of his strict upbringing were set aside and, uninhibited, as a heretic, Defoe defended and acted on gnostic principles to defeat the Catholic Stewart opponents daring to usurp his belovèd William. Far more as an Antinomonian than as a troubled Nonconformist, he hid his private sensuous games behind the Manichean ideology claiming Satan to be co-equal with God, a doctrine that ever lends itself so easily to the dangerous rule that all means justify the ends, that by holy blasphemy, the Kingdom may be reached. Defoe always believed in keeping on good terms with Satan; indeed, twenty-two years later, ruminating on evil in his intriguing work *The Political History of the Devil*, he doubted that the devil should be regarded as a mere metaphor; rather, he regarded him as a living force whose friendship should be cultivated and whose advice was often worth following; certainly he was acting upon it in his devilish, amoral *Maxims*.

Long before I was to encounter spies operating in and out of the House of Commons, I had learned at the knee of my Talmudic grandfather the validity behind Defoe's claim that a spy will bring his nation and himself to the Promised Land only by abandoning the usual norms; the conscripted spy, lacking the dynamic of the hidden sexually charged motivation, will be handicapped by propriety and realism and his negativism will lower, not boost, the morale of his paymasters and their followers; that is the exegesis to be placed on the biblical story of the spies sent by Moses to probe the defences of the land flowing with milk and honey; only the reckless, enthusiastic Caleb, and Joshua, lit up by their roles, were permitted to enter the Holy Land; all the other compulsorily recruited spies were, for their defeatism, condemned by God to perish in the wilderness.[3]

To succeed, the man who is moved to choose espionage as a career, as Defoe did, must be possessed by revenge; only the avenger, smarting under a sense of betrayal, is suitable material to qualify as spy or whistle-blower. The insistence in Christian civilisations upon the virgin birth stands witness to the deep sense of betrayal felt by every man; each resents his own conception. The denial in the Christ myth of the intervention of the human father reveals the true agony of every son; and Judas, the betrayer, is the scapegoat for the parents who dared to love exclusively. The injunction of the Catholic Church, still not completely eroded, that love-making must only be for procreation, is the penalty the sons of God have imposed upon their parents, forbidding them to revel without thought of children. Within a Christian culture, haunted by the betrayal theme, particularly at times when threats emerge of organised violence against the state, as in our times and as in Defoe's, the role of the spy, the voyeur, who fulfils the babe's wish to view and discover the secrets of the coupling authorities, can assume a particular and sinister, loved and hated, significance. Always, in any age, the Judas will find ideology justifying his betrayal. What Defoe found in his anti-Catholicism was in the next century to be found by many alienated Englishmen, the Napoleonites, in their eulogising of Napoleon and their loathing of the British Government,[4] and in the twentieth century compulsive traitors were afforded exquisite opportunities to have ready-made apologias as they joined the ranks of idealistic British communists and fellow-travellers, like my young self, whose hatred of Nazism had blinded them to the vileness of the Stalinist regime.

Nowadays, with God and faith dead, with ideology a pejorative noun, neither Christian myths nor passionate political commitment are available to help us to act out, or to work through, our vengeful feelings which parental exclusion inevitably prompts. It was otherwise in Defoe's day, for then politics were never secular; religion and politics were one, and all the manifestoes of all the partisans were scriptural. The Gospels, now unread, were known, and when Christ on the cross accused God the Father of betraying Him, He spoke for Everyman; the cock—an uncomfortably explicit sexual symbol—crows thrice to herald Peter's foreshadowed betrayal of Christ and is one of the most significant leitmotifs of the New Testament and, in Defoe's time, would have been heard and understood by all. Within such a facilitating cultural environment, if we did not know our Defoe, we would have expected his anger to be held and contained; but such was his primal rage against the parental dyad that it could not be quenched; the ultimate wish, the desire to betray the betrayer, could not be dared but, at one remove, it could be attempted. As a spy, affecting his false loyalties, wearing his masks, parricide could be practised vicariously; the victim would in real life be another's father but this was only second-best; in the unconscious the murdered man would be his begetter. Only by delving into Defoe's undeclared and complex motivations can we begin to understand how the man, blessed with such extraordinary talents and creativity, would squander so many years of his life in England and Scotland, at the behest of his paymasters, in the demeaning roles of informer and spy.

Yet all the symptoms that Defoe displayed in the spy syndrome which so possessed him are wearisomely familiar. The rationale he gave justifying the conduct which many regard as ignoble, and which was to earn him a reputation as a political turncoat, may be unusually sophisticated, but the virus that Defoe carried was commonplace, one that infects all compulsive traitors. By a curious combination of circumstances in my political and professional life, I have been compelled to ponder on the psychopathology of a number of major spies, either because I have met them or because their activities have impinged upon a field of endeavour, such as the repeal of homosexual law, in which I have been involved. Their case histories were so repetitive, so explicit and indeed so monotonous that I concluded that they would never have been allowed to enter and penetrate our security services—which contained many of high intelligence—if it were not that too many of those manning the services, and screening new entries, tend to bury their unconscious motivations which have caused them to choose their odd career. To weed out their enemies would require a self-scrutiny which they cannot face; if they understood themselves, they would be more likely to understand and identify those who seek to subvert.

The distinctive feature of all the traitors who crossed my path was the experience in their childhood of painful episodes of grievous loss, not unlike that suffered by Defoe in his boyhood. Defoe, I believe, responded in the same unforgiving manner, and was just as eager as they were to inflict punishment upon any proxy or surrogate of the fateful avenger who, in their imaginings, they would conjure up as being responsible for their sufferings.

Few hard facts are available of Defoe's boyhood but it is known that his mother died when he was about eleven years old; all children irrationally experience a death of a parent as a desertion; Defoe's feeling of betrayal by his mother, given the ambivalences upon which we have already remarked in his early nursing, is likely to have been more intense than most. And, a few years later, in Defoe's puberty, at a time when the slumbering Oedipal passions would, as is biologically determined, re-awaken, Defoe's father remarried. The intense and morbid relationship which we have postulated as existing between him and his father, the lack of freedom from his negative Oedipus complex, would ensure that he felt he had been cheated of the exclusive relationship for which he pined; and the action of a hard stepmother by immediately bundling him off to boarding school[5] must surely have left him feeling that treachery had precipitated his banishment. Those who regard this scenario, which attempts to illuminate some of Defoe's adult spying proclivities, as too conjectural, may perhaps be less sceptical if, in our efforts to unmask Defoe as a spy *extraordinaire*, we temporarily leave the seventeenth century and engage with some of the spies operating in the second half of the twentieth century. This may prove to be no anachronistic diversion. Their motivations and biographies, often fresh and accessible to us, may, on scrutiny, assist us in the almost impossible task of understanding and re-creating one of the most bewildering chapters of Defoe's varied life.

★   ★   ★   ★   ★   ★   ★   ★   ★   ★

After every spy scandal or intelligence failure, as in 2004, almost routinely, a Government Commission or enquiry is set up, charged with the task of finding out what went wrong and advising how future blunders may be avoided. In 1981 when Thatcher announced in the Commons yet another Commission, I insisted, not for the first or last time, on the continuing need to examine in depth, with professional aid, the motivations of those being recruited by our intelligence services. I pressed the Prime Minister in these words:

> Is there not a clear need to strengthen still further the rigours of the Security Service Selection Board which was introduced in 1977, so that the motivation of candidates is probed in depth? The dangers are increasing. We face dangers in admitting those whose private heterosexual infidelities bear witness to their incapacity for loyalty, or those whose disturbed homosexuality—following a long line of spies from Marlowe, to Casement, to Burgess and Blunt—means that they are compulsively disloyal. Surely it is time that we sophisticated our procedures and brought in psychoanalysts and psychiatrists to be attached to the Board, so that we do not use out-of-date, old-fashioned, rule-of-thumb methods of selection. If the Prime Minister is looking to the future as she says, surely it is time that we made certain that our selection procedures are worthy of the twentieth century not the nineteenth century.[6]

The Prime Minister replied:

> That is exactly what the terms of reference will enable the Commission to do, among other things. The terms of reference are: "To review the security procedures and practices currently followed in the public

service and to consider what, if any, changes are required." What the Honourable Gentleman said will be within the terms of reference.

Within the terms of reference it undoubtedly was, but Commissions—as the truncated reports which they issue so often illustrate—prefer to sail in shallower waters, and one wonders whether the lessons to be gained by a close study of the early lives of those who have betrayed the nation have been learned.

The notorious intelligence failures exposed by the blunders of the Iraq War are certainly not reassuring; more, one questions whether, in making assessments of our relationship with Russia, the Foreign Office fully understands and takes into account the significance of dealing with a head of state who was the world's most successful master-spy; Putin's attempts to join the KGB at the age of sixteen and, when temporarily rebuffed, again at the age of twenty-three—this time more successfully—reveal an enthusiasm for rule by spying that has in no way diminished over time. His Kremlin enforcers are increasingly composed of officials who have served in the KGB or its successor, the FSB, or in the military. The proportion of such people among federal officials was under 5 per cent in Gorbachev's time; in 2004 it was 58 per cent.[7]

It is certainly to be hoped that, in the current atmosphere of fear, and with the security services for the first time publicly inviting applications to serve in intelligence, the hundreds of would-be recruits are being far more insightfully screened than in the past; it is a past which, particularly in these fraught times, cries out to us to be alert to the early family history of any volunteer eager to embark upon a career as a clandestine informant. Failure to focus on such beginnings has repeatedly led to national security disasters. One of the most notorious instances of such many failures was the naive recruitment of the double, perhaps treble, agent George Blake who inflicted more damage on the British security services than any other man in the twentieth century. He caused the death of scores of British agents on Soviet territories and the Lord Chief Justice inflicted upon him a sentence of forty-two years, the longest determinate sentence ever meted out in recent legal history. His escape after a short period in prison, with considerable resources and ultimately with Soviet aid, scandalised the nation.

It required no special prescience to identify Blake as far too vulnerable a man to be employed in our intelligence services. His whole early life was punctuated by events calculated to make him, at least unconsciously, yearn for revenge upon Britain. His father Behar, an Egyptian Jew holding a British passport and living in Holland, was an ostentatious British patriot who probably acted as a British intelligence agent in the First World War. In honour of George V, young Blake was burdened by his Christian name and, like everything else that was to associate him with his determinedly British father, it was to bring him little but misfortune. His father was poisoned by German phosgene gas in the First World War and died when George was only thirteen. Children irrationally interpret the death of a parent as a desertion; George's father's death also meant that the boy was summarily wrenched away from his mother (a Lutheran Protestant), from his sister, from his possible ambition to be a priest and from his settled home. For Behar had left a fiat, submitted to by his wife, that on his death his son had to be sent to an uncle in Egypt. It needs no special imagination to relate to the feelings of the young adolescent who found that the consequence of his Egyptian father's love for Britain was to make him an orphan, exiled to a strange land.

Worse was to follow. When eventually George Blake returned to Holland, the tenuous British connection was to precipitate the break-up of the family home, with the Dutch mother and daughter compelled to flee to Britain, and with the British George arrested by the Gestapo. When the young man did finally succeed in making his getaway, he came to a Britain where his foreign descent barred him from ever feeling fully accepted. Certainly holding a British passport was not a blessing but a curse for George Blake. With a father who had betrayed him by his choice of nationality, by his unnecessary death condemning him to exile, and whose allegiances had provoked his son's arrest in Holland and alienation in Britain, it would indeed be astonishing if the son's deep resentment was not to be worked out against his father's first love. Only our secret service could have been so accommodating as to provide full facilities for George Blake to attack his father's land and so to commit posthumous parricide. Yet the scantiest psychiatric screening by the intelligence service would have saved Blake from himself and scores of our agents from falling into Russian hands.

There are many in the spy industry anxious to protect their

territory and they dismiss any psychologising of the spy's condition; they do not wish to de-romanticise the glamorous characters who people their television dramas and their books, for they know their viewers and readers wish to be told tales of heroes and resourceful bold villains, not of maimed, immature men, nearly all of whom suffer lonely exiled lives. They would affirm that the facts about Blake are quite simple: Blake was a committed communist from his youth and acted throughout in accordance with his principles.[8] They choose to believe that Blake was no exception to the general rule that professional spies select their roles out of ideological passion; they justify that opinion by asserting that Blake, as a youngster in Cairo, was influenced by his cousin, a founder member of the Egyptian Communist Party. It is probable that Blake did once say that early in his life he thought of "becoming a Roman Catholic priest but chose the alternative faith of the communist world"; but they fail to grasp that the oscillation of the young Blake between the infallibility of religious authoritarianism and a party of anti-clerical atheists presaged the future switch of loyalties which made him the supreme double agent. The ambiguities of his youthful commitments were reflections of the struggle waged within his psyche, conflicts which were never to be resolved—but which were acted upon throughout his life. The man who truly understood Blake was his fellow-prisoner, a psychopath who had attempted murder and who masterminded the spy's escape and later joined him in Moscow, and who said of Blake: "He is a born traitor. Blake does not betray for ideals; he betrays because he *needs* to betray. If Blake had been born a Russian he would have betrayed the KGB to the British. That's how he's made."[9]

The same behaviour patterns to be observed in Blake were presented to me when I met the spy Peter Kroger in prison, where he was serving a twenty-year sentence after his raided house had revealed a treasure trove of Soviet-made espionage paraphernalia: a short wave transmitter, false passports and concealed bundles of a variety of currencies. In gaol he had insulated himself from his severe surroundings and from his long sentence by play-acting a part in a debased Dostoevsky story. It was an easy role for him to assume. He was a half-educated man with embarrassing literary pretensions and a self-conscious love of books and, despite the absurd press glamorisation of this spy—as of every spy—the only identity he was capable of attaining was that of a second-rate hero in a shabby novel. The stilted literary language and the vulgar brummagen of sentiment in which he artificially described to me his predicament trivialised the real tragedy of his position. Yet, from the interstices of the droll and over-gentle lines he had assigned to himself, there welled up a great hatred of authority.

He shared, with all the murderers and violent robbers by whom he was surrounded, a hatred and fear of all the parent-surrogates—from the Home Secretary to the prison governor responsible for containing him in the maximum security block. He was clearly at home with all these rejected men and, with barely concealed conceit, used his slightly superior intelligence to act as priest-confessor to them and become a presiding chairman between the rival gang groupings within the security block. The game became him. He could empathise with his outcast prison colleagues and at the same time play the father: simultaneously he was betrayer and betrayed, and although the fear of dying in the prison sometimes overwhelmed him, the satisfaction to be obtained from his fantasy as a gaoled romantic hero shored him up.

Kroger bristled as I sought unobtrusively to move to a discussion on his relationship with his parents. His defences were alerted and determinedly he redirected the conversation and discussed his wife Helen, telling me of his love for her in embarrassingly novelettish terms. She had been separately jailed and I found his opportuning, asking me to intervene and obtain for him the right to meet her periodically, couched in adolescent terms. He addressed me not as man to man; he seemed to be more concerned to assert his rights under the prison regulations and persuade me of the tyranny of the authorities than to meet his woman. The shadow of assertive antagonistic parents, thwarting his claims, enshrouded him.

Kroger's fellow-spy, the Russian masquerading as Gordon Lonsdale, has given us even more explicit documentation of his motivation. Whatever ambiguity there may be about his birthplace, it is established that Lonsdale's parents' marriage broke up and the deserted mother, living in Russia, unable or unwilling to keep the twelve-year-old boy, sent him far away to a state institution school. Lonsdale has explained the position in a letter discovered in Kroger's bungalow: "I did not wish it and I did not seek it; but it turned out to be. I have thought very much about it—why all this? The answer is it all started in 1932 when mother decided to send me to the nether regions. At that time she could not imagine all the consequences of this step. I do not blame her." His protest that his mother did not bear any responsibility may be too much, but the significant lack of acquittal of his deserting, betraying father cannot be denied; in all his life he worked out his revenge by creating a life totally dedicated to betrayal.

Sometimes these unhappy men, who, as Lonsdale poignantly declared, do not freely seek their fate, are propelled a little off the more usual spy trail. There is a character type that originates in a childhood picture of the father as a figure of almost unlimited power who sets a problem in loyalty because the child does not know how to dispose of the hostility which grows up together with his strong feelings of love. This ambivalence is sometimes imperfectly resolved by distinguishing between a good father who is loved and a bad father who is repressed and displaced. In adult life, the less integrated may recreate a representative of the good father as the head of the country, and the bad figure as the world outside. Out of such material can spring blind patriotism and great hatred of alien authorities. But sometimes the primal loyalty of the child to a father who was himself an outsider causes a reversal in the pattern.[10]

Kim Philby was the son of such an outsider. His singular father, St John Philby, had played the part of an Arabist *éminence grise* to the oil chiefs of the desert, receiving much honour outside Britain but little or none within, and his resentment of such lack of recognition consumed him. I was reminded of St John Philby when I encountered the notorious Soviet spy Colonel Wennerstron, who was incarcerated in horrifying conditions in an ancient wing of a Swedish gaol; smarting from inadequate recognition by his own mother country, he, in droll mode, had been ready to betray in return for the Soviet Union secretly promoting him to be a Russian general and thus enabling him to gain, in fantasy, the narcissistic corroboration denied to him in the arms of his mother. St John Philby's hostility to his fatherland was much less concealed; his hatred was so fierce that it was safer in 1940, during the Second World War, to imprison him. It was incredible folly on the part of the security services to have elevated to a key position the fractured son of such a man and so give that son full opportunity to act out his unresolved Oedipal problems.

In Kim Philby's case, the original love bond had prompted an alliance between the son and his father in the wilderness. In his alienation from Britain the fractured son was following his father's example. When Kim Philby said "To betray, you must first belong", he was announcing the fact that he was always estranged from Britain; his communism was but a vehicle for his hate. In Britain he found only his bad father; Russia was his good father and it was his bad father who was, deservedly in his eyes, to be punished by him. For his wretched work he was to receive full praise from his good father and he was buried in Moscow in 1988 amidst paeans of appreciation from the Kremlin. Those in our security services who were so blind as to let him wreak his vengeance would, before he was lowered into his honoured grave, have been deserving bearers of his coffin.

Philby, of course, had conquered them with his extraordinary charm, an essentially feminine quality, to which those in our security services responsible for his advancement yielded so bounteously. Men who never accept their homosexual component, and are for ever rigorously repressing it, are particularly vulnerable to charm of Philby's order. In such company they can release an imperfectly repressed element in their nature in socially acceptable form. How dangerous and how extravagant and blinding such repression can be is only too obviously revealed in the ease with which the most blatant and disturbed homosexuals have, to their discomfort and the nation's, been granted clearance by our security invigilators.

The spy Vassall provides an obvious example of the self-deceit of those who direct our intelligence services. An agent for the Russians for seven years, he was positively vetted by the security service before being sent to Moscow and again positively vetted before being attached to the Naval Intelligence Division. Yet he was as obvious a passive homosexual as I have ever encountered. A few minutes' conversation with such a man, and an awareness of his style of speech, manner and posture, would surely have alerted any worldly person, unless of course the interviewer was so anxiously trying to obscure his own homosexual component that he was oblivious to its appearance in anyone else.

The worthy judges and lawyers who conducted the Vassall inquiry and came to the conclusion that no one could be held responsible for failing to detect Vassall's homosexuality as a security risk and, further, that the senior members of our Moscow embassy could not be blamed for failing to notice his effeminacy were, however, bound to record that the more robust members of the junior embassy staff referred to Vassall among themselves as "Vera". And whatever assessments our ambassadors, Under-Secretaries of State for Scotland and security chiefs made, I have no doubt he would have been so described by any group of factory workers within my former constituency if he had spent ten minutes with them.

Those who have come to terms with their own homosexual component, possessed as it is by every man and woman, are not terrified to see and empathise with a man whose homosexuality has overwhelmed him and left him emasculated. For many years the wretched Vassall languished in his cell after being thrust into roles by men of superior rank and intelligence that, given his character, provoked his nemesis. The over-civilised Radcliffe Tribunal acquitted his superiors of responsibility for the resulting breaches of security but I doubt that any of his superiors were entirely without responsibility for this miserable man having found himself in a maximum security prison.

There was within the Radcliffe Report, as in the later Diplock Security Commission Report, an assumption that the real danger to our national security came from a homosexual's vulnerability to exposure and prosecution, not from his homosexuality. Indeed, the Diplock Commission justified its policy of barring anyone discovered by positive vetting to be homosexual from the diplomatic services—and from any government or civil service post which might involve an overseas posting—by explaining that "adult homosexual relationships between consenting male adults are still offences against the criminal law of foreign States to which persons serving in the diplomatic service are liable to be posted, and these include the USSR and other States in the Soviet bloc."[11] This was an extraordinarily jejeune view; the antics of heterosexuals were used as blackmail by the Russians with equal effect as they used the conduct of homosexuals. The Commissioners in 1982 appeared to be unable to face the real problem, which is only too clearly spelt out in the spy stories strewn across British history.

From James I—of whom it was said he gave his money to his favourites and the secrets of state to everyone—down to the Cold War spies, treachery is uncomfortably linked with disturbed homosexuals who are unable to come to terms with their sexual destiny. This is a harsh judgement, but from Elizabethan times the names of notorious homosexual traitors and spies have rung out. Vassall, Burgess and Blunt are but the end of a long line stretching back to Lord Henry Howard, Francis Bacon, Christopher Marlowe and Antonio Pérez. In the past century two of the most notorious traitors, the Austrian Colonel Redl and the tragic Roger Casement, were compulsive and bizarre homosexuals. This correspondence between irreconciled homosexuality and treachery is not surprising. In so many cases a contributory cause of homosexuality is a hostile father, or one who is felt to be hostile, who takes away the manhood of the son. It would be more surprising if such an emasculated son did *not* grow up feeling compelled to seek revenge upon the state, the symbol of all authoritarian and interfering paternalistic qualities.

So obvious was Vassall's frailty that to fail to keep him away from security matters was inexcusable. But an intelligence service with a serious and sophisticated capacity to invigilate those they recruited would have also disqualified Anthony Blunt—and that was not only because of his past public commitment to Marxism or because of his homosexuality, activities which were also recklessly ignored. There were other factors which could have placed informed recruiters on enquiry, for the reputation which was later to lead Blunt to become the Keeper of the Queen's Pictures had become well established before he had been recruited. Art critic to *The Spectator*, lecturer at the Warburg Institute, Reader in the History of Art at the University of London and Deputy Director of the Courtauld Institute of Art were all part of his CV by the time, in his early thirties, he entered the secret service. As his revelatory and sparkling books show, he had the gift of vision and a penetrating mind; he was, in short, the supreme voyeur. But our security services were not alert enough, when faced with such a disturbed homosexual, to recall the warning jingles: "I spy, I spy with my little eye" and " 'Will you walk into my parlour?' said a spider to a fly: 'Tis the prettiest little parlour that ever you did spy.' " We can learn much from our nursery rhymes if we recall them in adulthood: they have endured because of the truth they tell. The spy, it can be learned, enjoys the considerable pleasure of the eye. Scoptophilia, the eroticisation of the wish to look, can become compulsive and dangerous. The early urge to look in a babe will persist in a most dangerous form in adult life if it has been frustrated and denied adequate expression because of the lack of response by a nursing mother. If the babe never receives the needed corroboration of his vigour and healthy narcissism, if his earliest exhibitionism is too severely mortified, if he never sees himself as a gleam in his mother's eye because there is no gleam, then the unspent scoptophilia can morbidly persist into adult life.[12] Blunt's scoptophilia clearly persisted; its singular libidinal vitality made him a good art critic but it also made him a compulsive spying viewer.

Clinicians long ago pointed out that the scoptophilic impulse regularly includes an element of sadism.[13] Highly developed voyeuristic perversions do not always act as a sufficient guard to protect the afflicted men from the sadistic urges welling up inside them. Blunt's sadism was certainly not adequately held back by his scoptophilic guards; it burst out in a determined and prolonged assault on the nation's security; his massive intellectual ability gave him the capacity to rationalise his behaviour as a political commitment, but the source of his treachery lay not in his Marxism but in his perversions. There is no dichotomy between the man as a great art critic and as a traitor.

Similarly, the scoptophilia that afflicted my parliamentary colleague Tom Driberg, Lord Bradwell, one-time Chairman of the Labour Party, was the common factor in his practice of a superb espionage tease and his journalism. His voyeurism, as that of Defoe, was transmitted into his writing; in pre-war days, in his William Hickey column in the *Daily Express*, his sightings were avidly read by millions. Unfortunately this did not leave his voyeurism satiated; so compelling was his need to look that he was forever wanting to gaze at, fondle and suck other men's penises. If it were not that, like Defoe in his time, he had had a powerful protective patron, the first Baron Beaverbrook, his cock-sucking escapades would have led to public scandal and imprisonment.

I found Tom Driberg one of the most delightful of my Commons colleagues. His wit and erudition enlivened for me many a dreary hour in the Commons Smoking Room as, during all-night sittings, we awaited the division bell to release us from our captivity. After his death a whole gaggle of spy-writers heaped their obloquy upon him, extravagantly claiming that, as an MI5 agent, he had spied on the Communist Party and on his own parliamentary colleagues.

They alleged our secret services used him as a means of colluding with Burgess in Moscow. Their paranoiac elaborations abounded and Driberg was said to be a double agent.[14]

Notoriously, indeed deliciously, indiscreet, he was an odd choice for MI5. I believe it is far more likely that he hooked MI5 into recruiting *him*. All his life he walked on a tightrope and gained his thrills by a never-ending series of public and private adventures, courageously and foolhardily oscillating from one role to another almost every day of his life. Distinguished journalist, grammarian and churchman, he would be as punctilious about ecclesiastical ritual or a semi-colon as he was obsessional in his trawl of the "cottages" of Britain—his fastidiousness was never extended to the unkempt, delinquent youngsters who, in his prowlings, he compulsively pursued. Driberg doubtless played the part of a spy with superb skill. The MI5 officers who ineptly recruited him would never have been able to use Tom; Tom would have had an especial pleasure in making fools of them. And, knowing him, I have no doubt he would have told his credulous controllers Bible stories they would never have heard before; it must have been a glorious send-up. Surely such a debunker of the secret service myth deserved the peerage bestowed upon him.

He was too self-aware, possessed of too much insight into his own condition, to be blindly propelled into high treason. Born to a sixty-five-year-old authoritarian father and a doting, suffocating mother in her thirties, he was acutely conscious that his bizarre needs arose from the dissonances in a childhood within a near-dysfunctional family. In his posthumously published and truncated autobiography he tells of his never-exorcised nightly dreams of his mother, and acknowledges his "obsessive filial relationship of the kind from which Freud constructed his theory of the Oedipus Complex". Tom may have fooled others but he had the courage not to fool himself. He certainly cannot be categorised among those disturbed self-justifying homosexuals like Blunt and Burgess—who belonged to a long and dishonourable tradition of treachery. They were among the Judases foretold in the Christ story; their saint was the Judas who kissed and embraced Christ as a preliminary to betraying Him.

During the Cold War it was in the United States of America that there emerged, among devotees of the Judas cult, a most sophisticated practitioner: the egregious disturbed homosexual Whittaker

Chambers; he was the accusing informant who precipitated what has often been called the "Spy Trial of the Twentieth Century", the arraignment for espionage of the brilliant Alger Hiss, Roosevelt's adviser in 1945 at Yalta, Secretary to the nascent United Nations and a top official of the US State Department with an impeccable record of public service. Chambers was a serial betrayer. He ratted on his original avowed Quakerism and joined the Communist Party, ultimately becoming the editor of the American *Daily Worker* until, to savage it, he quit the Party in 1938. For years he had been an enthusiastic spy for the Soviet Union but later, during the McCarthy era, he turned on his erstwhile paymasters and spectacularly denounced Hiss as a Soviet agent. His behaviour was a classic illustration of the betrayer of the betrayer, for although Hiss protested his innocence, and although the prosecution failed to prove the espionage alleged, he was found guilty on a charge of perjury and imprisoned for forty-four months. In London some time after his release, Hiss, for reasons I did not initially grasp, manoeuvred a meeting with me. I found myself and my wife attending a small dinner party at which he and his wife were the only other guests. He wanted to talk—and he did, until the early hours of the morning. He had charm and a formidable intelligence, and no doubt his prison years had replenished his wide reading; on that evening he drew on all three of these personal resources. The trial and question of his guilt were, in our dialogue, only elliptic referents, never explicitly reviewed, but his erudition and wry humour were fully on display, with purpose; I was to be dazzled into a belief of his innocence; a hypnotic trance can be induced by a skilled manipulator as effectively over a Kensington dinner table as in a psychiatrist's consulting room.

I was on guard. My own heavy flirtations with Marxism during my late teens equipped me to recognise instantly interpretations which, however elaborated, still carried both the illusions and the insights of Marxist theory; and as our talk wandered widely there were occasions, such as when we discussed the inimitable Nietzsche, when there was, although not avowed, a Marxist cast to his intriguing judgements on the literary figures and philosophers we were presuming to assess.

Yet, even while we engaged in our courteous verbal duels, my underlying thoughts were focused elsewhere; the pavane we were enacting was an unconvincing superficial rendering. Freud has remarked: "He who has eyes to see and ears to hear may convince himself that no mortal can keep a secret. If his lips are silent, he chatters with his fingertips; betrayal oozes out of him at every pore." The eyes are not the only windows of the soul. Our frowns, ticks and facial contortions are all part of the repertoire of emotions which are revealed, not concealed, in our body language. Even as our hand-writing is a seismograph tapping out the secrets of our psyche, so the twitches that involuntarily form upon our faces are loquacious messengers and even the masters of histrionics, politicians and spies, cannot always dissimulate and mask their guilts and conflicts.

For me, Hiss's mien that evening was a corroboration of what was, and remains, unproven: his guilt. It would have been cruel to have broken the taboo I imposed on myself and to have, even by a hint, turned our conversation to his childhood; his wounds still bled; and since I could not affect a belief in his innocence, I could not help to stem them. The clinical picture of his earliest years was too depressingly similar to that of other spies I had met to have been coincidental. When he was three years of age, during the peak period of the Oedipal experience when the infant is most vulnerable, his father died; that would have been felt as a desertion, as is wont when a child loses a parent, but in Hiss's case there were especial reasons why he felt his father had betrayed and abandoned him; the death was not involuntary; the father had chosen to die; he had committed suicide, and the shot resounded throughout Hiss's adult life. Believing himself to be an innocent victim undeserving of any punishment for his justifiable attempted parricide, he would never accept the correctness of a verdict that sent him to prison. From the moment he was released he, unremittingly, deployed all his extra-ordinary intellectual skills in fighting to erase the court's verdict. He had his successes—the American Bar reinstated him—but he never received the pardon he was seeking. His meeting with me, as no doubt with many other opinion-formers, was part of his ceaseless campaign to create a public opinion that would support his demand. Still protesting his innocence, in 1996, at the age of ninety-two, he died a convicted perjurer.

There was a certain grandeur in the hubris and fall of Hiss; his story has indeed all the pathos of a Greek tragedy; that, however, could not be said of some of the other spies who have crossed my path. They were essentially frightened men; fear lacks nobility, and fear is the precipitate that often turns men into informants. The venal and squalid Will Owen, one-time member for Morpeth, was such a creature. In 1970, although acquitted by a credulous jury of spying, he was compelled to admit he had received payments from the Czechs. After his consequent resignation from the House, he came to me complaining that, despite his acquittal, the security service was harassing him—obviously wishing him to "sing"—and he asked me to protect him. I knew the man to be a cunning rascal; on one occasion, having won in the annual parliamentary ballot the right of priority to introduce a Bill, and knowing that I wanted to put through a reforming measure, he offered to *sell* me his place! Still, he knew that whatever distaste I had for him I would, as a lawyer, acknowledge the legitimacy of his complaint as an "innocent" man. My subsequent intervention led to the request that I help to persuade him to talk and I cooperated, although I found the role of intermediary unpleasant. Owen ultimately agreed, provided I obtained immunity for him and that I sat in with him during the interrogations—requests which the security service willingly granted. The following sessions gave me full opportunity to understand the unconscious motivations which had driven him into his shabby role.

Owen was a textbook example of those who resort to a defence mechanism well explained in psychoanalysis—the overcoming of fear by the stratagem of unconsciously identifying with the frightening aggressor. Anna Freud, in a seminal book on the syndrome, used as simple illustrations of the phenomenon children who used the mechanism to overcome anxiety.[15] A child who was always making uncontrollable grimaces in class and who, when reproved, would react with abnormal behaviour was in fact found to be making grimaces which were simply a caricature of his teacher; when the boy feared a scolding he tried to mask his anxiety by involuntarily imitating the feared teacher. Similarly, a little girl found to be making all sorts of singular gestures in the dark was seeking to overcome her dread of seeing ghosts, and her magic gestures, representing the gestures she imagined ghosts would make, were helping her to surmount her anxiety: she became the ghost she feared would otherwise meet her.

The defence mechanism is not only to be found in children's idiosyncratic behaviour or, indeed, in their games where they impersonate a dreaded object and, by the metamorphosis, quench their fear; nor is it only to be found in primitive tribes who use the technique to evoke and exorcise spirits in their religious ceremonies. The defence mechanism ploy was to be seen in its most florid form in Will Owen. He, the son of a miner, was the oldest of ten children who came from a poverty-stricken household where love, like money, was thinly spread. He felt keenly the displacement he had endured as a succession of new brothers and sisters arrived and his cloying, sentimental recollections of his mother did not disguise from me the wrath he felt against her; he could not forgive his submitting, ever love-making mother. Owen, in fantasy, allied himself with the Russian conquering enemy, thus identifying himself with the all-powerful father he hated and feared. He fitted exquisitely into the picture of a traitor presented to us by Ernest Jones, who wrote: "Treachery, by allying oneself with the conquering enemy, would seem to be an attempt sadistically to overcome the incest taboo by raping the Mother instead of loving her. Perhaps that is why it is generally regarded as the most outrageous and unnatural of crimes, since it combines disloyalty to both parents."[16] Certainly Owen, with his fumblings, did his clumsy puny best to rape his motherland.

Often, by chance, during the Cold War period I stumbled across other agents far less dreary than Owen, some British, some Russian, some known traitors, some undiscovered; but as far as it was known to me, the early personal histories of these enthusiastic informants were in so many respects indistinguishable one from another. The traumas and consequences of their sad or unempathic childhoods matched, and the culture of the Cold War had afforded them an opportunity to act out their dilemmas under the cover of ideological commitment. When fanatical, political or religious doctrines abound, the spy flourishes. Defoe lived in such a time, in a period which he saw as "an Age of Blood and Deceit, of Contradiction and Paradox".[17] The times chimed with his emotional needs and wresting advantage out of disadvantage, the handicap we have postulated of his stuttering Oedipal woes, equipped him to become one of the most significant spies in British history.

* * * * * * * * * *

In 1702 William III, following a horse-riding fall, unexpectedly died. His many domestic enemies rejoiced; they toasted the mole which precipitated the accident and lauded the horse, Sorrel, on which the king had been riding; but Defoe was bereft. He felt, and was indeed, abandoned. Thirteen years later he was still recalling the loss of his master, speaking of "The Immortal and Glorious Memory of the Greatest and Best of Princes, and who it was my honour and advantage to call Master as well as Sovereign, whose Goodness to me I never forgot, neither can forget; and whose Memory I never patiently heard abused, nor ever can do so . . ."

For Defoe, William of Orange had long been the living embodiment of the Glorious Revolution, the man who wished to bring clearly stated private rights and liberties to every Englishman, toleration for Dissenters, a firmly established Protestant succession forever and an extirpation of Scottish Jacobinism ensuring that Catholic France would never have a base in a Britain which, unified with Scotland under a Protestant sovereign, would become Great Britain. But the bond between Defoe and William was not only the result of the congruence between their religious and political commitments. Nor, although it strengthened that bond, was it dependent upon the way Defoe's fluency made up for the lack of communicative skills of the inarticulate sovereign. Even Macaulay, who made William his hero in his *History of England* and stressed his stamina, courage and statesmanship, had to concede the lack of charm possessed by the bleak, humourless Dutchman. Of his manner at Court, Macaulay wrote:

> He seldom came forth from his closet; and when he appeared in the public rooms, he stood among the crowd of courtiers and ladies, stern and abstracted, making no jest and smiling at none. His freezing look, his silence, the dry and concise answers he uttered when he could keep silent no longer, disgusted noblemen and gentlemen who had been accustomed to be slapped on the back by their royal masters, called "Jack" or "Harry", congratulated about race cups or rallied about actresses.[18]

For such a taciturn man, Defoe's skills as an eloquent and aggressive pamphleteering spin doctor were invaluable; the King had a perfect speech-writer and in turn Defoe, as his catamite, could enjoy boundless submission without the fear that his Master, bound by his "Original Contract", would abuse his domination. This was a relationship not founded on mere convenience, nor, for Defoe, only on shared religious and political convictions; without any penalty, with royal immunity guaranteed, Defoe had been able to wallow in guiltless masochism and, as a bonus, revel, as a spy and informer, in the delights of his voyeurism. This was the bliss that Defoe lost when Sorrel threw the Master and left Defoe friendless and so poignantly and utterly alone.

The paediatrician Donald Winnicott has taught us that the capacity to be alone in adult life originates in the infant's experience of being alone in the presence of his mother. If the child's immediate needs—such as contact, food and warmth—have been satisfied and there is no further need for the mother to be concerned with providing anything, nor any need for the baby to be looking immediately to the mother for everything, then at such moments there is a blissful stillness. This relatedness between mother and child is the basis of a capacity to be alone. The paradox, Winnicott indicated, is that "the capacity to be alone is based on the experience of being alone in the presence of someone, and without a sufficiency of this experience the capacity to be alone cannot be developed". This was a capacity never bestowed upon Defoe by a remote mother.

Few have more lacked that capacity to be alone than Defoe. He was a man who ever yearned to be free of the emotional dependency which unconsciously bound him throughout his life to his father.

By finding prominent father surrogates he strove to distance himself from the fatal Oedipal affliction which so oppressed him. If his mother had been otherwise, he, with her aid, would have been emancipated from that early obsession; but it was not to be. Never endowed by his mother with that capacity to be alone, he could not endure a lonely walk through life; a solitary walk without a patron as companion was for him almost unendurable; although his most profound wish was to be unencumbered, he feared what he most desired. Yet that buried desire, to be able to walk tall, in his own footsteps, with no helping hand, to gain the emotional independence his faulty maturing had denied him, was in reality never to be fulfilled; that was to be his pain but our gain. It was seventeen years after William's death before Defoe could bring himself to share with us his marvellous fantasy of self-sufficiency, the condition denied to him in real life. It was in his most imaginative work, *Robinson Crusoe*, that he conjured up the remote island where, in solitude, liberated from the demands of parents and the world, and with no strangling relationships, he was the self-dependent hero beholden to no one.

It was a courageous, not a pusillanimous, fantasy; dreams of a languorous desert island, with nature the abundant prodigal provider, are Garden of Eden dreams, wish-fulfilments of the pre-natal, of the attainment of the perfect symbiosis, of the desire to return to the security of the womb of the "good mother"; that regressive fantasy of merging was no part of Defoe's imaginings. On the contrary, his was a defiant assertion of separateness; his bare inhospitable island, thousands of miles from anywhere, was no delightful off-shore isle in sight of land; he was alone, resourceful, the sole creator of his world, commanding, not yielding to, niggardly nature to whom he owed no debts. Defoe, in *Robinson Crusoe*, lived out the paligenetic myth which historically has possessed so many peoples, the myth of self-creation, of being born again undefiled by any tainted conception, a man indebted to no father or mother, a man who has achieved the total ablation of his parents, a man who alone, like God, can bestride the world.

But at the time of William's death the conjuring up of such a compensatory blasphemous fable to alleviate, by total denial of dependency, the pain of his loss and fear of loneliness was evidently not within his personal resource. The options available to him as responses to his abandonment were limited: either to despair or to rage against all and sundry whom he could blame for having conspired with fate to end the life of his master and his works. Defoe made his choice; he refused to mourn silently; he attacked violently, wildly. It was a catastrophic choice; it was to bring him to the brink of execution by mob violence. A rational response by Defoe to William's death would have required an acknowledgement that the King's death was bound to occasion considerable political change; but Defoe was in denial; he probably did not grasp "emotionally that a relatively peaceful revolution such as that of 1688 might be followed by a period of reaction and that Anne would allow, if not encourage, turning back the clock on the many reforms of the Glorious Revolution".[19] Defoe could not face the reality of the changing zeitgeist. His assessment that Anne would slavishly follow William's example was wishful thinking; she was certainly to be no strong patron upon which he could unfailingly rely. Anne was a Stuart, a daughter of James II and sister to the Pretender, a High

Church Anglican and a Tory.[20] By the time she came to the throne she was worn out by the pain and sorrow of bearing and then losing fifteen children, as well as by fits of gout and dropsy. Her husband, Prince George of Denmark, was a dullard and a drunkard. Anne too consoled herself with the brandy bottle.

That Defoe, usually possessed by an acute political sensibility, refused to see the obvious, that the tectonic plates were shifting, that the times required him to exercise caution, that the days when no matter how restlessly and provocatively he wrote William would protect him were over, indicates how powerful were the unconscious forces at work and, in the event, almost swept him into the abyss; he could not accept that William was dead and he would not therefore mourn him. A genuine acknowledgement of the reality would have meant, for Defoe, accepting that he had been cruelly abandoned to the loneliness he was not equipped to tolerate; that he had been punished by his surrogate father.

A fear of that punishment mobilised all his defences, for the terrible fear that now assailed him was not of abandonment; it was of castration. His repressed fear of being castrated—a fear that haunts all men and was bound to be especially present in a man who had never worked through his negative oedipal complex and still, unconsciously, lusted for his father—on William's death surfaced. We find Freud, in the writings of his last decade, increasingly instructing us that castration anxieties loom compulsively as determinants governing responses to dangerous situations, to threats of separation, loss of love and death; castration anxiety, he found, could swallow up and overwhelm other anxieties.[21] Through William's death, Defoe felt he was being cut off; he made an attempt to escape the ultimate punishment by unconsciously denying the death, and yet, cunningly, creating a situation in which he would receive the punishment he felt he deserved, albeit one less dire than castration.

The dynamic behind this elaborate circumvention, which took the form of publishing outrageous and provocative pamphlets which were bound to occasion a punitive response, is a familiar one to forensic psychiatrists,[22] and is one I frequently saw at work when professionally defending criminals. There is a class of criminals who are criminals through a sense of guilt. When one of these men consulted me professionally he did not really want to be acquitted. On the contrary, when I succeeded in persuading the court that a case was not proved beyond reasonable doubt, I sensed the resentment of my client as he muttered surly and ungracious thanks. I had many grateful letters from men whom I defended but whom the courts had sentenced to long terms of imprisonment, thanking me for having fought on their behalf, but I had none from those who were acquitted. In truth there are many criminals who are neurotically burdened with a sense of guilt for childhood crimes they have committed only within their earliest infantile or oedipal fantasies of possessing and slaying their parents; they stagger inexorably, like doomed characters in Greek myths, towards the punishment which they demand as a right. Lacking the imagination of a Lawrence of Arabia to justify the flagellations for which they ache and which alone can bring relief, albeit temporarily, they commit the most petty and stupid of crimes to ensure that the blows of society will fall upon them. At times to guarantee that their claims to punishment should not be overlooked, they all but leave their visiting cards behind when they commit their offences. Some immediately rush up to the police to enjoy the agony of confession, a few even selecting and insisting upon seeing a particular officer in whose presence they wish to conduct their self-abasement. The majority, on being challenged, regularly offer an incriminating statement which they sign and later repudiate, often suggesting that they have been threatened or beaten into submission by the police. The hapless and embarrassed policeman has in fact rarely yielded in this way to their masochism and in the witness box tries in vain to step out of the fantasy world which the determined victim, with exquisite delight, has projected upon him. The charade continues to the very end of the trial and the plea of "not guilty" persists even after conviction—for this is the only way in which the last remnants of self-respect can be maintained. But the defending solicitor who cheats the accused out of his punishment is not loved. It is true that the accused requires someone to present the denial of his guilt with fervour, so that the shameful need for punishment can remain secret; for such a man to be acquitted is a most terrible denouement.

Defoe was playing a similar game to these criminals when, in the aftermath of William's death, he published pamphlets, professing they were innocent of any mischief or subversion, but thus, unconsciously, provided himself with a guarantee that he would be prosecuted and convicted and thus given the desired opportunity to expiate his sin. The skills available to him to perform his task were extraordinary; this was the man capable, for years, of producing single-handedly his thrice-weekly journal *The Review*, in which he showed himself to be the principal pathfinder and pace-setter in what is now generally regarded as the "Golden Age" of journalism;[23] he was the first master, if not the inventor, of almost every one of the contents of modern newspapers, including the leader, investigative reporting, foreign news analysis, the agony aunt, the gossip column and the candid obituary. With all these resources available to him, he savagely and libellously assailed all those whom he saw as departing from or compromising the Protestant principles of the Glorious Revolution; with his vitriolic pen he unnerved the shifty, milk-and-water Dissenter leaders and simultaneously enraged the Anglican Establishment. He ensured that his potential dissenting allies were estranged and that the Tory High Churchmen were left choked with anger. He was determined to fight a lone and friendless battle; unconsciously he was inviting retaliation; he was determined to be a victim, and he succeeded.

By so ostentatiously and ineptly at this inauspicious time affirming in his publications his unwavering attachment to William's principles and his contempt for all backsliders, he was, on one level, unconsciously, denying that the King, by dying, was betraying and punishing him; in his fantasies, the bond between his master, a decorous political bond, one permitted, not tabooed, was firmly in place; he was not to be punished for the Great Sin, the love that could not speak its name; he would ward off the terrible punishment that would follow if that excessive primal desire was revealed; punishment would be deflected by provoking William's enemies, who would then find him guilty of a lesser crime and administer severe but lesser punishment; he would be punished for his principles, not his guilty yearnings. The provocative pamphlets which rocked England at the time were replete with over-determined assaults which must be understood, at least in part, as obsessive and cryptic responses to Defoe's buried guilt.

Those responses, intemperate poems, articles and pamphlets were indeed inflammatory. He affected to be concerned only with the principles, or lack of them, held by leading Dissenters or Churchmen, whom he claimed were yielding to the temptations of Jacobinism;

but his passionate polemics were in fact calculatingly personalised. His relish in depicting the vices of the men he attacked, his deliberate selection as his targets of the most well known public figures, testify that he was motivated by more than moral indignation; he was being driven by his unconscious need to goad the powerful to take revenge upon him.

The flashpoint came with the publication of *The Shortest Way with the Dissenters*, a work which I often recalled when, in the Palace of Westminster during my parliamentary days, I would cross New Palace Yard where, by Resolution passed by a furious House of Commons, the booklet was burned by the Public Executioner. The anonymous pamphlet purported to be the work of a fundamentalist High Church Tory and, initially, was read as such and not perceived to be a bitter satire on the bigotry of the High Churchmen who were for ever assailing Dissenters. Many approved the viciousness of their attacks; in Oxford and Cambridge *The Shortest Way* was placed next to the Bible on many a college table. It reads as an ebullient, ferocious diatribe against all who would tolerate any compromise with the Nonconformists; if the Queen and moderate Tories in Parliament were insufficiently vigorous in protecting the Church from their subversive activities, then the Church itself should act without restraint against these snakes and toads: "It is cruelty to kill a snake or a toad in cold blood, but the poison of their nature makes it a charity to our neighbours to destroy these creatures."

When it was revealed that the pamphlet, which was so enthusiastically received or condoned by many across the Establishment, was in fact a parody written by Defoe, the anger of the fooled was boundless. At a time when Britain and France were at war, and domestic incitement to civil strife between rival factions was most unwelcome, the Government responded vigorously to the clamour that the miscreant be punished. Defoe took to his heels but failed to evade arrest. He was charged and ultimately brought to trial before a court of law where not a few of those judging him had been mercilessly lampooned in some of Defoe's earlier pamphlets. He was sentenced harshly to endure three days in the pillory, a substantial fine and "to remain in prison 'til all be performed"—a vaguer, more sinister term than the usual "at the Queen's pleasure". Defoe was also bound under heavy surety for seven years' good behaviour, so that for many years thereafter he would often be in danger of arrest because of complaints from such diverse people as the Russian ambassador, an admiral, a judge and a Devon magistrate who objected to something Defoe had either written or said.

Defoe was indeed receiving the punishment he had courted; and although he was, much later, to claim that his surprising plea of guilty to the charges was a misjudgement on his part and made only to gain leniency, it is far more likely that unconsciously he, as ever, wanted to be purged of sins far removed from political travail; his public confession of guilt displaced and relieved him of the oppressiveness his inner infantile sins bore down upon him.

The ambivalences in his acknowledgement of culpability to the prejudiced court could not for long be hidden by Defoe. Subliminally, what he had pleaded guilty to was his earliest infantile fantasies; but at a conscious level he well knew that he had, by publishing his satire, committed no offence except that of making the Establishment politicians and bigoted High Churchmen utterly ridiculous. Cast into Newgate Prison to await the ordeal of the pillory, he could no longer suppress his anger at the injustice he was suffering. Courageously and recklessly he wrote and had distributed his *Hymn to the Pillory*, an indictment of his tormentors who, he declared, were really the ones who should be put into the pillory. His pen and daring saved him from physical injury and, perhaps, death.

Only a few weeks before he wrote his *Hymn*—a work more of doggerel than poetry—another pamphleteer in the stocks had been savagely stoned by the mob. Yet Defoe had the guts and guile to have printed and distributed his devastating lampoon on his judges even when his incarceration was leading to his financial ruin, to the collapse of his brickyard business in Tilbury, and when he had no means of helping his pregnant wife and children. His courage was amply rewarded; on the three days that he stood with his head and hands in their wooden cases, he was surrounded by cheering supporters and was pelted with flowers. The people of London evidently admired the man who had so impertinently cheeked the high and mighty and especially the judges and aldermen of the City.

Defoe had triumphed over the pillory while still facing an as yet undetermined sentence in Newgate Prison: "an emblem of hell itself, and a kind of entrance to it". In prison, Defoe languished; all his pleas for release fell upon deaf ears. Some of the verse he composed in Newgate shows Defoe, in a deep depression, contemplating hanging himself; he could not maintain his bravado and defiance. But he was not completely abandoned. His condition was not going unobserved; an old political enemy, one-time Speaker of the Commons, Robert Harley, and now becoming powerful as Secretary of State, the man who had helped in initiating the fateful proceedings against Defoe, was keeping him well in his sights. Harley knew that Defoe was too gifted a man to be wasted, and was set to turn Defoe and make him his own propagandist and spy even as William had done. Harley gave Defoe the treatment that was given in the twentieth century by Stalin, who threw political suspects suddenly into the hell of the Lubyanka gaol and ensured that the terror and shock they suffered would soften them up sufficiently to make the confessions required by his secret police. In a calculating and dilatory manner, Harley dangled the possibility but not the certainty that a pliant Defoe might regain his freedom; he kept Defoe in suspense for months. Defoe succumbed to the treatment; through Harley's eventual intervention he obtained, on Harley's terms, his release, and Harley got his man.

Harley, however, knew he had at his disposal no mere hireling. As Speaker of the House of Commons, this subtle politician had excelled because of his understanding and sound judgement of people's characters; he well knew that in Defoe he had not merely a man content to do his bidding but someone of inveterate independence and with a capacity to divine and, through his pamphlets, manipulate public opinion; and Harley had grasped that the changing times demanded that successful governance could only be achieved by taking into account and shaping that opinion. As the historian George M. Trevelyan has explicated, when describing the coming together of the two men,

> Perhaps because he himself was so little of an orator in Parliament, Harley realised sooner than any of his colleagues or rivals the relation of public opinion to political power in post-Revolution England. It was not only the Queen but her subjects whom he approached by the backstairs. He found the observer-agent he wanted in Daniel Defoe, a man of shifting and secret ways like himself, of moderate views and kindly nature like himself, like himself of Puritan upbringing, but with a style of writing as lucid and telling as Harley's was slovenly and confused . . . and Harley now employed him to travel round

England and report. Moving about under an assumed name, he communicated with the Secretary of State by stealth. Defoe was still so unpopular with all parties in Church and State that Harley dared not own him in public. Moreover, both men loved mystery for its own sake. Defoe became Harley's Man Friday, and remained so for long years to come, through many changes of men and measures.[24]

In Defoe's day, and indeed ever since, many excoriated him as a hired pen, a turncoat who for purse and status prostituted his talents and sold his soul when he bedded down with Harley. In fact it would be nearer the truth to say that Defoe had entered into a marriage made in heaven.

Defoe should not be measured by using as a yardstick present-day shoddy spin doctors like those employed by Blair; such a proleptic approach could not only be challenged as anachronistic, it would fail to convey the full significance of the role played by Defoe, who, as psephologist, economic adviser and journalist, ever revelling in his subtle espionage, advanced the goal both he and Harley shared. Whatever the political differences that had initially brought them into conflict, both men were determined to protect the Protestant succession, both scorned little Englanders, both had a vision of a burgeoning Empire governed by a Great Britain; the alliance between Defoe and the moderate man who in his earlier days came from a Nonconformist background did not constitute, on Defoe's part, the *volte-face* which some have attributed. Above all, there was a concordance between Defoe's emotional needs and the tasks Harley soon assigned to him.

Of those tasks there was none more congenial to Defoe than to act, at Harley's command, as a secret agent in Scotland. On his deathbed Defoe's belovèd William had urged the English Parliament to press for a union with Scotland; now his new surrogate father, Harley, was charging him to assist the fulfilment of William's wish and, more, to give that assistance in a manner that so exquisitely became Defoe's temperament. Defoe was ordered by Harley to go to Scotland and to conceal his work there for the government. He told Defoe that he should let it be known that he went to Scotland "upon your own business and out of love of the country . . ." On the highest level, he was being given social sanction to indulge, as a spy, his voyeurism; his deceits, impersonations and lies were legitimated.

In a letter to Harley Defoe confirmed the tasks of his mission. These were first to identify the parties opposed to the Union and then to undermine them; to dispose people to Union through conversation; to answer, through pamphlets and *The Review*, "any objections, libels or reflections on the Union"; and to dissipate fears about secret designs against the Kirk, the established Presbyterian Church of Scotland. The statement thus presented is cool, seemingly detached; but how emotionally charged, how exciting and thrilling Defoe was to find his assignment is revealed when we see him boastfully displaying an exhibitionism he could not contain, soon reporting to Harley his successes as a confidence trickster:

> I have compassed my first and main step happily enough, in that I am perfectly unsuspected as corresponding with anybody in England. I converse with a Presbyterian, Episcopal-Dissenter, Papist and Non-Juror, and I hope with equal circumspection . . . I have faithful emissaries in every company and I talk to everybody in their own way. To the merchants I am about to settle here in trade, building ships, et cetera. With the lawyers I want to purchase a house and land to bring my family and live upon it (God knows where the money is to pay for it). Today I am going into partnership with a Member of Parliament in a glasshouse, tomorrow with another in a saltwork. With the Glasgow mutineers I am to be a fish merchant, with the Aberdeen men, a woolen and with the Perth and Western men a linen manufacturer . . . Again, I am in the morning at the Committee of Parliament, in the afternoon in the Assembly of the Kirk, I am privy to all their folly, I wish I could not call it knavery, and am entirely confided in.

Incorrigible as ever, to enhance the delights which he, as do all con-men, enjoyed by deceiving his dupes, he masked his espionage and increased his credibility with his victims by returning to his old indulgence, to what he, significantly, described as his "whore"—trade. Undeterred by the results of his previous commercial undertakings, and affecting an expertise in wine, he went into the business of wine wholesaler specialising in canary and claret. Fancying himself an expert too in horseflesh, he became a horse-dealer; more, he joined with a Scottish master weaver in the manufacture of tablecloths, claiming to employ a hundred poor families in Edinburgh. In

140 THE BI-SEXUALITY OF DANIEL DEFOE

those early years of his sojourn in Scotland, Defoe was certainly on a trip; his addiction, as spy and dubious businessman, to the thrills of risk-taking was never more overt.

The fastidious may look with distaste at Defoe's swaggering during this period of his life; and the squeamish may find the life of lies he was enjoying unforgivable. Yet, at the end of the day, even when the dangers in politics of amoral means corrupting noble ends are acknowledged, it surely cannot be disputed that Britain is indebted to Defoe as a supreme practitioner of murky politics.

He was operating at a time when, in England and in Scotland, there were diverse and unusually squalid, for parochial reasons, powerful vested interests eager to wreck any efforts to unite the two countries. Defoe, by his undercover manipulations and manoeuvres, as well as by his didactic persuasions which contemporaneously he was publishing in his *Review*, played a considerable part in defeating those saboteurs and in bringing about the Act of Union in 1707; that Act brought to an end the excesses of the feuds and wars that had bedevilled relations between the two countries and, to the benefit of the people of both lands, heralded a long and enduring peace which today we take for granted.

When, in 1709, Defoe published his *History of the Union of Great Britain*, dedicated to Anne, the Queen thanked him as she gave him her hand to kiss. We too should give the rascal our thanks even as, wryly, we are aware that it is only by a hair's breadth that his perversions, his voyeurism, his lust for father figures, found benign expression in the public domain of the politics of eighteenth-century Britain rather than in the humiliating behaviour of a wretched compulsive pervert.

Notes

1. Novak, M. E., *Daniel Defoe: Master of Fictions*, Oxford University Press, 2001.
2. Namier, L., *Personality and Powers*, Hamish Hamilton, 1955.
3. Numbers 12: 12–14: 22; Brichto, S., *Moses*, Sinclair-Stevenson, 2003.
4. Lean, T., *The Napoleonite*, Oxford University Press, 1970.
5. Bastien, L., *Defoe's Early Life*, Macmillan, 1981.

6. Hansard, 26 March 1981. See also Abse, L., *Margaret, Daughter of Beatrice*, Jonathan Cape, 1989.

7. Sakwa, R., *Putin, Russia's Choice*, Taylor & Francis, 2004.

8. Knightley, P., *The Second Oldest Profession*, Deutsch, 1986.

9. Bourke, S., *The Springing of Blake*, Cassell, 1970.

10. Abse, L., *Private Member*, Macdonald, 1973.

11. Statement on the Recommendations of the Security Commission, May 1982.

12. Kohut, H. and Wolf, E., The disorders of the self and the treatment, *International Journal of Psychoanalysis*, 59 (1959), 414–25.

13. Fenichel, O., The scoptophilic instinct and identification, *International Journal of Psychoanalysis*, 18 (1937).

14. Pincher, C., *Too Secret, Too Long*, Sidgwick & Jackson, 1984.

15. Freud, A., *The Ego and the Mechanisms of Defence*, Hogarth Press, 1939.

16. Jones, E., The psychology of Quislingism, *International Journal of Psychoanalysis* (January 1941).

17. Novak, M. E., *Daniel Defoe: Master of Fictions*, Oxford University Press, 2001.

18. Macaulay, T. B., *History of England*, 1848–55.

19. Novak, *Daniel Defoe: Master of Fictions*.

20. West, R., *The Life and Strange Surprising Adventures of Daniel Defoe*, Harpers, 1997.

21. Ward, I., *Castration*, Icon Books, 2003.

22. Zilboorg, G., *The Psychology of the Criminal Act and Punishment*, Hogarth Press, 1955.

23. West, *The Life and Strange Surprising Adventures of Daniel Defoe*.

24. Trevelyan, G. M., *England under Queen Anne*, Longmans, Green, 1934.

CHAPTER TEN

Coprophilia and creativity

F ollowing the success of *Robinson Crusoe*, in 1719 Defoe's novella *The King of Pirates* was published. At a time when piracy
was rife in the South Seas and a notorious pirate, Captain
Avery, was a name well known to Defoe's contemporaries, Defoe, in
this story, endows this ready-made character with mythic dimen-
sions. He takes him from ocean to ocean in never-ending and, against
all odds, improbably successful pillaging expeditions, stripping
scores of ships of their cargoes of gold, silver and precious jewels.

The gains are always lovingly, sensuously, measured by Defoe:
"the value of 16,000 pieces-of-eight in gold of Chile, as good as any
in the world"; he lingers over his compilations, loath to leave these
delights of avarice. The repetitive recitals of Avery's stolen wealth
ever excite Defoe, even as they were intended to titillate his acquisitive readers in the nascent capitalist world of the early eighteenth
century; this absurd tale is pornography without sex.

There are apologists who would defend the work. Some excuse it
as an understandable pot-boiler hurriedly conceived to exploit the
popularity of *Robinson Crusoe*. Others would claim that its super-
ficiality, its lack of depth in any characterisation and its presentation
of tiresome litanies of compass details to lend credibility to the

pirates' voyages are all blemishes that can be forgiven if we treat the work as simply a proleptic sketch, an anticipation of his future fictions like *The Life, Adventures and Pyracies of the Famous Captain Singleton*.

But there are some who would champion, not defend, the work; and none do this more vigorously than the distinguished novelist and biographer Peter Ackroyd, who sees it as "a tract for the burgeoning new empire being created by Defoe's contemporaries" and would persuade us that it "is a tale of acquisitiveness in which a nation, as well as an individual, is the true subject".[1] Less persuasively, he invites us to award Defoe yet another accolade: "if Defoe can claim the palm as the first of the English novelists, then *The King of Pirates* can be confirmed as one of the very earliest 'adventure novels' in the language".

I do not share Ackroyd's enthusiasm. It is so lacking in Defoe's usual sophistication that one wonders indeed if it is a work that, for commercial gain, has been butchered by booksellers or other interlopers, and that we should therefore regard it as only a caricature of the original work. The book is certainly not an "adventure" for adults. It is essentially a puerile tale eminently suitable for a pre-pubescent boy. Defoe himself, through Avery, heatedly repudiates any suggestion that it is otherwise; genital sex was in no circumstances permitted to intrude into this anal fantasy of ever-accumulating boundless stolen wealth. When, in the tale, Avery captures a ship carrying the Great Mogul's daughter, he insists it is the booty not the woman that he covets, that those who have suggested he was motivated by lust, not greed, traduce him:

> The account given of Captain Avery's taking the Great Mogul's daughter, ravishing and murdering her, and all the ladies of her retinue, is so differently related here, and so extravagantly related before, that it cannot but be a satisfaction to the most unconcerned reader to find such a horrible piece of villainy, as the other was supposed to be, not to have been committed in the world.

> On the contrary, we find here that, except plundering the Princess of her jewels and money to a prodigious value—a thing which, falling into the hands of freebooters, everyone that has the misfortune to fall into such hands would expect—that, excepting this, the lady was used with all the decency and humanity, and perhaps with more than

ever women, falling among pirates, had found before, especially
considering that, by report, she was a most beautiful and agreeable
person herself, as were also several of those about her.[2]

Thus, explicitly, Defoe relegates genitality to acquisitiveness; this
novella is indeed a celebration of anality. By prioritising anality,
unmortified, raw, never sublimated, the telling lacks aesthetic merit;
the distinction between life-denying pornography and erotica which
so often enhances artistic productions is here well illustrated. In
many of his writings—as in his *Giving Alms No Charity* (1703), *An
Essay upon Publick Credit* (1710), *An Essay upon the Trade to Africa*
(1711), *An Essay on the South Sea Trade with an Enquiry into the
Grounds and Reasons of the Present Dislike and Complaint against the
Settlement of a South-Sea Company* (1712), *An Essay on the Treaty of
Commerce with France* (1716), *An Essay upon Loans* and *Every-Body's
Business, Is No-Body's Business: Or, Private Abuses, Publick Grievances
Exemplified in the Pride, Insolence, and Exorbitant Wages of our Women-
Servants, Footmen, &* (1725)—Defoe's prurient interest in money
(ever unconsciously a faecal equivalent) is presented in refined,
intellectualised and often elegant and constructive forms; in *The
King of Pirates* there is no such transmutation of Defoe's coprophiliac
yearnings.

Coprophilia—the clinical term given to the pleasure of touch-
ing, looking at and eating faeces—was always a temptation for
Defoe. Sometimes, ingeniously, he did find means of yielding to
his desire in ways that did not invite disapprobation. His handling of clay, freeing it from excessive soil to manufacture bricks
and pantiles in the works he established in Tilbury, no doubt,
brought him displaced illicit pleasures as well as one of his rare
commercial successes. But in *The King of Pirates* his coprophilia
emerges unashamed.

The slobbering of Captain Avery, as he salivates while counting,
hoarding and fondling his stolen gold, disgusts, for it advertises far
too blatantly the perverse desire to play with the obvious equivalent
of excrement, golden eggs, golden coinage and golden nuggets. Yet,
trivial and deviant though the tale may be, and truncated and distorted by clumsy hacks as it surely is, nevertheless it does perhaps
deserve inclusion within the canon of Defoe's writings, for it
uncovers a major source of the man's creativity; it moves us to delve

into Defoe's shit. That may seem a bizarre and repellent probe, but it is there, amidst the detritus, that we may glean some of the elements that constitute Defoe's genius. The smell of ordure always clings to creativity. Thus it was at the beginning and so it will be to the end. God, the Creator, is our precedent; out of a clod of earth, of excrement, of clay, upon which He breathed was Man created. With God as our exemplar we do not need to be squeamish; when God breathed, the spirit of the Lord lingered upon the anus.

★   ★   ★   ★   ★   ★   ★   ★   ★   ★   ★

The anal reverie that so starkly, so undisguised, is presented to us in *The King of Pirates* is no mere self-indulgent aside; however various may be his works, Defoe's autobiographical protagonists almost invariably advertise their unabashed love of wealth; contrariwise, simultaneously, they acknowledge their lack of enthusiasm to consummate their desires in heterosexual acts. Treasure, money and jewels are lauded rhapsodically, but towards genital sex, diffidence and ambivalence are always essayed.

In his tale *Memoirs of a Cavalier*, one suspects in self-mockery, Defoe is providing us, by way of his hero's behaviour, with a clinical picture of the emotional arrest occasioned when anality will not yield to the seductions of the genital: "At a certain town in Italy, which shall be nameless, . . . I was prevailed upon rather than tempted, *a la courtezan*," the Cavalier tells us. On entering her apartment, he is so overcome by the opulence of the jewellery, silver plate and furniture, that he takes her at first for a lady of quality, "but when after some conversation that she was really nothing but a courtezan, in English, a common street whore, a punk of the trade, I was amazed, and my inclination to her person began to cool". He is charmed by her conversation, but:

> when the vicious part came on the stage, I blessed to relate the confusion I was in, and when she made a certain motion by which I understood she might be made use of, either as a lady, or as—, I was quite thunderstruck, all the vicious part of my thoughts vanished, the place filled me with horror, and I was all over disorder, and distraction. I began however to recollect where I was, and that in this country there were people not to be affronted; and though she easily saw the disorder I was in, she turned it off with amiable dexterity, began to talk again a la gallant, received me as a visitant, offered me sweetmeats and wine. Here I began to be in more confusion than

before, for I concluded she would neither offer me meat or drink now
without poison and I was very shy of tasting her treat.

The brave young Cavalier made his retreat. The lady's jewellery,
her silver plate, her adornments, the opulence of her home, the
young man found most desirable—but not the woman. This woman,
whom Defoe lasciviously but fearfully dared to depict offering the
attractions and repellents of anal sex, was particularly dangerous
territory. The Cavalier preferred the battlefield where he took his
pleasures in the loot from the enemy dead, wounded and prisoners:
"a bundle of some linen, thirteen or fourteen pieces of plate, and in a
small cup three rings, a fine necklace of pearls, and the value of one
hundred Rix-dollars in money". Rather the comparative safety of
the anal zone which yielded defined faecal equivalents than risk the
hazards and mysteries of a genital world.

Even in his recounting of his erotic dreams Defoe would skirt, not
enter, that world. His voyeurism found great satisfaction in conjuring up visions of compliant naked women, but they were women
upon whom he would only gaze, always stopping short of dreaming
of a cumulative fuck. In his intriguing *The Political History of the
Devil: As Well Ancient as Modern* he tells of a man, obviously himself,
tempted by Satan:

> I know a person who the Devil so haunted with naked women, fine
> beautiful ladies in bed with him, and ladies of his acquaintance too,
> offering their favours to him, and all in his sleep; so that he seldom
> slept without some such entertainment; the particulars are too gross
> for my story, but he gave me several long accounts of his Nights
> Amours, and being a man of virtuous life and good morals it was the
> greatest surprise imaginable; for you cannot doubt that the cunning
> Devil made everything he acted to the life with him, and in a manner
> most wicked; he owned with grief to me, that the very first attempt
> the Devil made upon him, was with a very beautiful lady of his
> acquaintance who he had been something freer than ordinary with in
> their common conversation. This lady he brought to him in a Posture
> for Wickedness, and wrought up his inclinations so high in his sleep
> that he, as he thought, actually was about to debauch her, she not at
> all resisting; but that he waked in the very moment, to his particular
> satisfaction.

We now have an advantage of a better acquaintance with the
Devil, one not open to Defoe when he, in his *Political History of the*

Devil, scrutinised Satan. A hundred years ago Freud, in his essay *Character and Anal Eroticism*,[3] explained to us that "the Devil is certainly nothing else than the personification of the repressed unconscious instinctual life". The evil-smelling Devil smeared with detritus, which we have conjured up, is one upon whom we can project our own varied coprophiliac yearnings: "We know", Freud comments, "that the gold the Devil gives his paramours turns into excrement after his departure", and he goes on to remind us that:

> according to ancient Babylonian doctrine, gold is the "faeces of Hell" . . . wherever archaic modes of thought have predominated or per-sist—in the ancient civilisations, in myths, fairy-tales and supersti-tions, in unconscious freightings, in dreams and in neuroses—money is brought into the most intimate relationship with dirt.

It was this excremental vision of the Devil that haunted Defoe; in his dreams the Devil taunts him with a tempting display of naked women, but it is only a devil's tease. Mired in filth, Defoe is stuck; he struggles to free himself and move on, away from anality, to reach the shores of genitality but, even as he approaches, he becomes fearful of what may lie there; terrified, he escapes. He wakes up.

This retreat from the road to genitality, this incapacity to erase the anality so deeply embossed on so many of Defoe's works and character traits, relates back to those dissatisfactions he experienced as a babe during his oral phase, which, we have suggested, account for his preoccupation with cannibalism.[4] The ontogenetic approach to human personality, the description of adult character in terms of childhood experience, one of the basic principles of psychoanalysis, is sometimes, for schematic purposes, misleadingly presented as if the libidinal development of the babe passes through separate and distinctive oral, anal and phallic phases; but in fact there is no "pure" culture to be found in the character make-up of an adult. Where there is marked oral dissatisfaction, as demonstrably was the case with Defoe, clinical experience would teach that an admixture of traits subsequently occurred; the frustrated babe whose sucking impulses have been left unsatisfied will desperately aim to obtain satisfaction at the anal level.

Defoe could never give up that quest; balked at the breast, he rested his hopes for satiation in the sensuous delights of defecation. If those hopes had been fulfilled, if without reproof the pleasures of sphincter control and relief could have been enjoyed, if his gaze had been able to linger upon the golden eggs he had produced, thus satisfied, he could have moved on, but that was not to be; for the mother who is pre-emptory when the child wants satisfaction at the breast is the same severe unemphathic mother who denies her child the pride in his first creation, his faeces.

When the infant is far too brusquely compelled to relinquish the phase in which the anus and defecation are the major sources of sensual pleasure and form the centre of his self-awareness, then the child, denied adequate acknowledgement of his proud assertive anal-phase self, will all his life unconsciously deploy stratagems which defy the parental imperative.

Many and various were the circumlocutions practised by Defoe, in defiance of the original imperious parental command, to regain the coprophiliac joys insensitively denied to him in infancy. Sometimes this resulted only in trivial daydreaming, in the fantasies of his Captain Avery of secretly handling piles of illicit wealth; but there are other occasions when we witness a certain grandeur in his elliptical stratagems; he commands our respect as he engages in intellectual wrestling matches with his metamorphosed turd, the Devil. In all those strivings, the objective, to our benefit, is sometimes marvellously achieved; what essentially Defoe is endeavouring to obtain is compensation. In his infantile anal phase he was, one suspects, given insufficient, if any, compensation to make up for the parsimony of the grudging breast. In his creative works, we are seeing a superstructure built upon the ruins of an oral eroticism whose development had miscarried.

The pronounced anal traits, so openly displayed or transmuted, that we find in Defoe's work point to the clumsiness of a martinet mother lacking sufficient affect, of the resistance such a mother would have provoked by over-strict toilet training. The central position occupied by the training of our excretory functions during our early years may be modified but can never be excluded from the rest of our lives. The shit we create, which in turn has created sensations for us, is a plastic source of fantasy and the very first object in which our relationship to others is concretised; to expel or to hold back, to give or not to give, to assent or to disobey, the seemingly trivial contest of wills forges a link, a meaningful nexus between those involved, as Elvio Fachinelli, the Italian psychoanalyst, emphasised:

> Within the nexus, a significant relationship of mutual tension and desire is gradually developed between the child and his mother. Moved by love for her and by the fear of losing her, by the pleasure of gratifying his desire or the pleasure of being compensated for not doing so, the child slowly renounces total control over his new-found power and agrees to produce the golden eggs only when and where she commands. But in order to re-exert some authority over her in turn, to win her recognition and some revenge for all the wrongs inflicted on him, he learns at the same time to postpone, to disappoint her, to make her wait.[5]

Yet with sensitivity and love, a happy armistice can be achieved. The baby gives his great gift, the precursor of all gifts, and the mother's former prohibitions are now felt as wondrous approvals. I believe no such peace treaty was ever signed between Defoe and his mother. The rumblings of the war continued throughout his life; unconsciously he strove to regain his denied earliest sphincter thrills and his thwarted coprophilia by sharing vicariously the uninhibited lustful greed and avariciousness of so many of those peopling his stories.

By thus relating Defoe's early coprophiliac yearnings to his works, we are following a well worn path. The enigmatic relationship between perversion and creativity has been continuously explored since Freud's message: that, in effect, the artist and the pervert emerge from the self-same ecology. Freud mocks those who recoil from acknowledging their association:

> We must learn to speak without indignation of what we call the sexual perversions—instances in which the sexual function has extended its limits in respect either to the parts of the body concerned or to the sexual object chosen. The uncertainty in regard to the boundaries of what is called normal sexual life, when we take different races and different epochs into account, should in itself be enough to cool the zealous ardour . . . The sexual life of each one of us extends to a slight degree—now in this direction, now in that—beyond the narrow lines imposed as the standard of normality. The perversions are neither

bestial nor degenerate in the emotional sense of the word. There are a development of germs all of which are contained in the undifferentiated sexual disposition of the child, and which are being suppressed or by being diverted to higher, asexual aims—by being sublimated— are destined to provide the energy for a great number of our cultural achievements.[6]

It has to be acknowledged that the existence of what Donald Winnicott described as "primary creativity" has a source apparently unrelated to perversion, for Winnicott posits that when the nursling has an inkling—because of the temporary absence or withdrawal of his care-taker—that he and his source of life are not one, the babe then seeks to *re-create*, in hallucinatory fashion, the lost fusion with the maternal universe.[7] But whatever may have been the initial precipitate, the abundant clinical evidence of all those psychoanalysts treating artists and writers suffering a blockage reveals that the libidinal foundation in all creative expression is invariably infiltrated with pre-genital drives. The distinguished French analyst Joyce McDougall has emphasised the role anality plays in that creative expression:

> Although oral, anal, and phallic drives all contribute to creative production, the anal component holds a place of pre-eminence, since it is the source of the first "interchanges" between the infant and the external world. The initial "creation" the infant offers to the first caretaker is the faecal object, with all the erotic and aggressive meanings invariably associated with anal activity and faecal fantasy. Thus this unconscious libidinal origin plays a vital role for the creative person in every domain.[8]

And certainly, as so many of Defoe's works demonstrate, for him it indeed played a vital role. But there are oft-times imperfections in his creations; so strong was the pull of his wish to enjoy untrammelled, directly, his coprophilia, that he found it difficult to renounce its pleasures, to direct it, as Freud has put it, to "higher asexual aims". Sublimation, it has been said, is "a vicissitude of the pre-genital instinct as opposed to the direct relief in a perverse act".[9] But the line between perversion and sublimation is perilously close and there are many occasions when we find Defoe with one foot over that line; his incessant vivid depictions and condemnations of vice tell us only too explicitly his perverse attraction to what he affects to deplore.

Yet, fortunately for us and posterity, many are the occasions when he forfeited his right to play with his shit; in exchange, he plays with his imagination; the resultant fiction and faction are delights which he has shared with us; we should not begrudge him his lapses; he surely is entitled to his occasional onanistic diversions and we should therefore be ready to overlook his childish *King of Pirates* and, in similar generous mood, we should be grateful to Alice, his mother. Without her strictures Daniel Defoe would certainly be unknown to us.

Notes

1. Ackroyd, P., Foreword to *The King of Pirates*, Hesperus Press, 2002.
2. Defoe, D., *The King of Pirates; Being an Account of the Famous Enterprises of Captain Avery, the Mock King of Madasgascar*, 1719.
3. Freud, S., *Selected Works*, SE, Volume 9, p. 174.
4. See Chapter 5.
5. Fachinelli, E, *Anal Money-time*, Allen Lane, 1974.
6. Freud, S., *Fragment of an Analysis of a Case of Hysteria*, SE, Volume 7.
7. Winnicott, D. W., *Playing and Reality*, Basic Books, 1971.
8. McDougall, J., *The Many Faces of Eros*, Free Association Books, 1995.
9. Chasseguete-Smirgel, J., *Creativity and Perversion*, Free Association Books, 1985.

CHAPTER ELEVEN

Captain Singleton: the ablation of Alice Defoe

D aniel Defoe, the master of literary disguise, who even died in hiding, sets us a puzzle from the outset by leaving no firm evidence of when and where he was born, or what his family background was. An army of scholars, after patient research, have acknowledged that the paucity of extant documentary material has left them baffled; all admit that they are unable to give us a definitive and comprehensive account of the man's origins; and, in particular, as we have earlier remarked,[1] almost nothing that can be cited as an unassailable fact is known of the person who in his life, as in all our lives, played so significant a role: the mother.

To remedy the glaring omissions, all the biographers have intensively trawled his works seeking to discover within them hidden autobiographical material; none has undertaken this task more diligently than Louis Bastian,[2] who honestly acknowledges the danger that such methodology can sometimes lead to what begins as a surmise ending up as a firm statement. Such a charge of unsupported speculation no doubt can, and will, be legitimately directed against this essay where so much that is presented is predicated upon the assertion that Alice Foe was an unempathic mother. It is therefore serendipitous that, seen through psychoanalytical lens, there is at least one work of Defoe that wards off that charge and provides us with the evidence that will perhaps persuade the sceptics that the profound dissonances we have catalogued between the babe Daniel and his mother did in fact exist. It is in an unlikely work, in Defoe's *The Life, Adventures, and Pyracies, of the Famous Captain Singleton*, that the veil behind which the fierce battles were fought between the infant and the insufficiently responsive mother is unexpectedly drawn aside.

Captain Singleton was published a year after Defoe's *King of Pirates* and has a long sub-title listing the travels of Captain Singleton in Africa and the West and East Indies. The novel is in many respects a formulaic rendering of the improbable adventures of the Captain, with the "hero" afflicted with the same addiction to the acquisition of wealth by robbing and piracy as was Captain Avery in the *King of Pirates*. Defoe the journalist was giving the public what it wanted: an opportunity without risk of punishment to delight in the anti-social activities of a pirate, Captain Bob Singleton; like a Robin Hood, a Dick Turpin or a train robber, Bob was one of those villains whose daring and pillage of the envied and undeserving rich can sometimes command admiration. And, ever a superb press reporter, Defoe picked up the vibes of the times; piracy, for good reasons, was in fashion.

During the decade covering the period when the novel was written, 600 pirates were hanged and many met their death in prison. Thousands of ships were being captured or pillaged; a rising world trading system and European empire-building overseas were being threatened by these outlaws. Indeed, one distinguished historian depicts pirates as primitive class warriors and interprets their actions as the terror of weak proletarians against too-strong adversaries, capitalism and the growing nation-state.[3] Defoe, in his piracy novels, was enlisting as readers the many secret sympathisers who in fantasy sailed in a ship carrying the flag of the skull and crossbones.

Defoe tells the tale well. Edward Garnett has pronounced that "The style is so perfect that there is not a single ineffective passage, or indeed a weak sentence, to be found in the book."[4] This may be an extravagant assessment but certainly the claim Ackroyd made for *The King of Pirates* as one of the earliest adventure stories in the English language can unequivocally be applied to *Captain Singleton*, which is a far more sophisticated work than the earlier novella, is often told with an engaging wit and is deliciously sardonic in its depiction of the invented characters. We do indeed find here what Ackroyd has described as Defoe's invention of "the poetry of fact".

But there is one most significant lacuna common to both works: the shutters are firmly closed, denying us sight of the origins of both of Defoe's "heroes". He is not willing to permit us to pry into his own origins by revealing those of either Captain Avery or Captain Singleton; the notice "Keep Out" is firmly staked at the commencement of each work. Captain Avery tells us:

> I shall not trouble my friends with anything of my original and first introduction into the world. . . . In the present account I have taken no notice of my birth, infancy, youth or any of that part which, as it was the most useless part of my years to myself so it is the most useless to any that shall read this work to know, being altogether barren of anything remarkable in itself, or instructing to others.

Defoe's refusal to reveal the origins of Bob Singleton is far less peremptory. Singleton first agrees that it is most appropriate for people whose lives have been remarkable "to insist much upon their originals, give full account of their families, and the histories of their ancestors". Having thus raised our expectations and disarmed us of any accusation of concealment, he tells us he too would like to tell us all but, he mourns, he suffers from a severe disability: he knows nothing of his mother or father or of his earliest years; he was stolen, he believes, when he was about two years old, and used, when forlornly displayed, to arouse pity for a beggar, and then was sold on to a gypsy. He had never learned anything of his forebears or earliest years; it was not his fault nor that of his parents that he had been involuntarily abandoned but the consequence was that he did not know even when or where he was born. His background is blank; it is ignorance not discourtesy that causes him not to observe the usual conventions of an autobiographer recalling his past.

This apologia for Bob's reticence is not as subtle or as convincing as Defoe may have thought. In his day the myth of the foundling hero embedded in the culture of so many different civilisations and in so many similar forms was still unchallenged. Today, deconstructed, gutted of its original vigour, it adds another abandoned foundling to the series which begins with Sargon, the founder of

Babylon, and continues with Moses, Cyrus, Romulus, Oedipus, Paris, Hercules and so many others whose origins are suspect. We have unravelled the riddle set by this passion to suppress knowledge of original parentage, the desire to confabulate records of the erring heroes' births, the wish to erase biological parents from the biography of the babes.[5]

There are many variants of this myth but all tell of a foundling, and most tell of how, having been abandoned by the mother, the babe is taken over by humble foster-parents only to discover, as an adult, that he is really the son of aristocratic or royal parents. The adoptive parents are far too low in status, far too deficient, to have sired such a wondrous son. Defoe acted out a fragment of this fairy-tale, this "Family Romance", as Freud names it, when he, dissatisfied with his origins, changed his real name from "Foe" to "Defoe", seeking to dupe his world into believing he was of Norman lineage and, forsooth, a kinsman of the hero Sir Walter Raleigh.

The name change was more than an act of social pretentiousness; it was a belated attempt at repudiation, at the age of thirty-five, of his parents. As Freud has written, "The liberation of an individual, as he grows up, from the authority of his parents is one of the most necessary though one of the most painful results brought about the course of his development."[6] Defoe's name change can be seen as an extravagant gesture made by him in his attempt to achieve liberation.

In *Captain Singleton*, vicariously, Defoe dares to go further. By making the Captain, in effect, an orphan, free of all early parental influences, he gave him a blanket immunity able, without culpability, to be thoroughly anti-social:

> for I had no sense of virtue or religion upon me. I had never heard much of either . . .; nay, I was preparing and growing up apace to be as wicked as anybody could be, or perhaps ever was. Fate certainly directed my beginning, knowing that I had work which I had to do in the world, which nothing but one hardened against all sense of honesty or religion would go through . . .[7]

Defoe was permitting his creature to defy every tenet of his parents' principled religiosity; he was being outrageously provocative. Freud has explicated the reasons for such provocations:

A feeling of being slighted is obviously what constitutes the subject matter of such provocation. There are only too many occasions on which a child is slighted, or feels he has been slighted, on which he feels he is not receiving the whole of his parents' love, and, most of all, on which he feels regret at having to share it with brothers and sisters. His sense that his own affection is not being fully reciprocated then finds a vent in the idea . . . of being a step-child or an adopted child.[8]

Such a denial by a child of his own parentage is a retaliatory response. The motivations behind Defoe's onslaught, "revenge and retaliation", were those which Freud found in his neurotic patients immersed in the "Family Romance Tragedy".[9] In Defoe's case motivation included revenge against the grudging mother who had denied him sufficient love, retaliation against the father who had chosen his wife over him. In fantasy, through Bob, Defoe obliterated his parents; and so deep were the wounds he felt he suffered that he was unremitting. In the family romance myth the story usually ends in reconciliation, in the abandoned foundling being acknowledged and rediscovered by his royal parents; but there is no such happy ending in *Captain Singleton*. Towards the end of the novel his parents are eliminated; Bob remains without known parents; they are never to return, never to be forgiven.

More, the determination to expunge the parents, to transgress against and to defy the ethics which Defoe's parents upheld, is shamelessly pursued; the vigour and élan which carry the novel so racily along are, to our surprise, free from the ceaseless penitential abasements that we have come to expect from Defoe. Captain Singleton seems to plunder and pillage without guilt, to amass his ill-gotten wealth in the manner of a conscienceless psychopath.

Only as the novel comes nearer to its conclusion does Defoe falter; he shows the ancestral voices warning Singleton to think of the punishments awaiting him in the afterlife. Yet still he will not be intimidated. Told that it would be better that death was thought on before it came, Singleton makes the riposte: " 'Thought on!' says I; 'What signifies thinking of it? To think of death is to die, and to be always thinking of it is to be all one's life long a-dying. It is time enough to think of it when it comes.' " But considerable as must have been the unconscious rages and resentment Defoe felt against his parents, it was not possible for him, through *Singleton*, to maintain such insouciance. Man is born of woman; erasing the mother, becoming an autochthonous Adam, is a dangerous fantasy bringing with it the attendant doubts of those who dare, in imagination, to commit matricide and patricide. Bob's attempt to deny his biological past was doomed; he was bound to suffer for such hubris; punishment for his heinous offences was unavoidable; he punished himself; he fell into a depression. All was ashes in his mouth: "I grew very sad. As to the wealth I had, which was immensely great, it was all like dirt under my feet; I had no bearing for it; no peace in the possession of it, no great concern about me for the leaving of it." To attain redemption, to relieve himself of the burdens now oppressing him, his only recourse was repentance, to acknowledge his grievous errors, to reinstate the parental images and to submit to their moral authority. But Defoe would not allow his alter ego to be so defeated; he was not to be allowed to grant victory to the parents. With ingenious but not altogether convincing casuistry, Defoe guides Bob to the belief that his way to repentance was totally barred; repentance, salvation, requires restitution; and since that was impossible, for who the true owners were of the property he had acquired through his piracy could never be ascertained, with no hope of reformation therefore open to him, Captain Bob was in despair. He contemplated suicide:

> no joy of the wealth I have got. I looked upon it all as stolen, and so indeed the greatest part of it was. I looked upon it as a hoard of other men's goods, which I had robbed the innocent owners of, and which I ought, in a word, to be hanged for here and done for hereafter. And now, indeed, I began sincerely to hate myself for a dog; a wretch that had been a thief and a murderer; a wretch that was in a condition which nobody was ever in; for I had robbed, and though I had the wealth by me, yet it was impossible I should ever make any restitution; and upon this account it ran in my head that I could never repent, for that repentance could not be sincere without restitution, and therefore must of necessity be done. There was no room for me to escape. I went about with my heart full of these thoughts, little better than a distracted fellow; in short, running headlong into the dreadfulness of despair, and premeditating nothing but how to rid myself out of the world; and, indeed, the Devil, if such things are of the Devil's immediate doing, followed his work very close with me, and

nothing lay upon my mind for several days but to shoot myself into the head with my pistol.[10]

But though Defoe took himself and Singleton to the very brink, he nevertheless successfully resisted the tug of his masochism. He did not allow the Captain to blow his brains out. He provided him with the proposition that if he listened to the devil and killed himself, hell would be his certain fate; he would be damned; but if he remained alive there was at least a possibility that God in His mercy would grant him redemption. And thus buoyed up, Bob, with his wealth intact and his former ways forsaken, is left by Defoe to go on his way, marry a good woman and, above all else, still, as a foundling, triumph over his disadvantages and live happily without parents.

★   ★   ★   ★   ★   ★   ★   ★   ★   ★

The phenomenon, reflected in this novel, of the ablation of parents, of the desire to suppress a biological past and an insistence upon being self-made with no umbilical link to a mother's womb, is well known to psychoanalysts; and nowhere has such denial of one's ontology been more elegantly delineated and the public and private consequences more thoroughly explored than in Charles Rycroft's psychoanalytical essay *Ablation of the Parental Images or The Illusion of Having Created Oneself.*

Rycroft shared with me the privilege of belonging to the Savile Club, and a meal there with him oft-times gave me the considerable benefits of his insight. He was an unusual psychoanalyst, son of a baronet, an enthusiastic fox-hunter like his master of foxhounds father, initially an early communist fellow-traveller like so many of my duped generation, a Cambridge product who was a historian before he turned to medicine and psychoanalysis. He was too civilised an Englishman to endure the intemperate quarrels of the rival groupings within the psychoanalytical world usually conducted by continental Jews scarred by their undeserved exile. Long before I met Rycroft he had undemonstratively withdrawn from membership of the established psychoanalytical institutions and gone his independent way. Rycroft found that his experience, so deftly set out in his essay, enabled him to pinpoint and explain the traits which are so characteristic of ablators. When we extrapolate from Rycroft's case histories we find we are unwittingly making a chastening enumeration of Defoe's positive and negative attributes. Rycroft wrote:

The purpose of this essay is not to discuss the causes but the effects of ablation of the parental images and to suggest that these may be paradoxical; that a person for whom it is not totally catastrophic, ablation of the parental images may be at one and the same time imaginatively liberating in a way that can be creative and also productive of an element of falsity and dishonesty of character which throws suspicion on the value of their creativity. . . . The creativeness, the falsity and the dishonesty all derive from the same source. If the natural parents are disowned, the patient acquires an illusion of choice about precisely those aspects of himself that are given and unalterable: his parentage, his identity, his physical and mental constitutional endowment. If his parents are psychologically dead to him, he can choose other parents and therefore his identity. Or he can deny that he ever had any parents and claim to be self-made in the most abysmal sense imaginable. . . . This process of re-creation of the self can be regarded as imaginative and creative, but it is also false, since it can only be squared with the dreary truth by suppression of some facts, by distortion of others and by subordination of memory to mythotoeisis.[11]

Sometimes indeed, when reading Rycroft, it is difficult to believe we are reading a case history of one of his patients; rather, we muse, we are being presented with a blurred profile of Defoe himself. The profile is not a carbon copy of those patients whom Rycroft diagnosed as suffering from "character disorders" but it is sufficiently decipherable for us to be surprised by the similarities, sometimes dramatic, between Defoe and those seeking relief on the couch. They dream of betraying parents by way of ablation; the horror of the crime is concealed in ablationary mode. They wipe out the parents; they end allegiance to the biological parent and choose another; these are dreams telling of betrayal. Thus interpreted, they certainly illuminate for us the source of Defoe's puzzling passion for espionage:

This underlying sense of betraying something, even and indeed especially when they feel that they are being creative, explains, I think, why such people not infrequently dream about espionage and double agents, since the world of espionage is one in which every action is ambiguous, in which physical courage may be linked with moral cowardice and in which the hero and the traitor may be one and the same person.[12]

Such was the vengefulness possessing Defoe that the mere dreaming of the betrayal he wished to effect was, for him, an inadequate abreaction; the retaliatory responses against the grudging mother were to be acted out in real life; only by actually becoming a master of espionage could he find some relief. Whether Alice Foe deserved such responses to her maternal inadequacies may be doubted, but that there was a failure of communication between mother and son cannot be gainsaid. In ablating his parental imagoes we find Defoe behaving in a similar manner to those of Rycroft's patients who so determinedly attempted to expel all parental images from their psyches:

> One must, I think, presume that as children such patients . . . suffered some emotional catastrophe, some gross breach in communication with their parents, which they dealt with by withdrawing all interest from their parents and by divesting their images of all meaning. . . . I have the impression that as children these patients were not deprived but humiliated. They were not underfed or underprotected or exposed to long periods of separation from their parents but were either totally misunderstood, so that their assets and potentialities were entirely unrecognised, or were treated as things, as possessions of the parents, who felt it unnecessary to be either considerate or truthful to them. They come from families in which toys are thrown away without the children's permission being asked and in which the parents make it clear that the home belongs to them and that the children are there on sufferance.[13]

It may be that Defoe's home was not as bleak as those depicted within the households of Rycroft's patients but if from the beginning, when a babe, his mother failed to communicate to him the feeling that he was cherished and wanted, then subsequent events could have corroborated that feeling of being unwanted. Irrationally, as so often occurs with the death of a mother, a young child feels that she has, by leaving him, rejected him; and when his father soon re-married and the stepmother speedily packed him off to boarding school, he inevitably would have felt he was being treated as an encumbrance.

The infantile catastrophes suffered by Rycroft's patients were probably more severe than that endured by young Defoe but the syndrome of the "false self" which can follow as a consequence of feelings of early rejection was certainly not absent in Defoe's adult life. As Rycroft tells us,

> The patients I am describing seem to me to have recovered from their infantile catastrophe by constructing a mythical "false self" which is conceived to owe its origins to some source other than their own actual physical parents. As a result, they are not consciously ambivalent towards their parents—though one must presume that they once were—but have disowned them . . . and have ablated their images.[14]

The nomenclature games Defoe played throughout his life spell out his profound dissatisfaction with his own self; even as chronic criminal impostors assume a multiplicity of false identities, so did Defoe. Foe became Defoe. His pamphlets and treatises were written under so many different names that confused biographers continue to quarrel over the authenticity of their attribution; as a spy he was ever operating under different names, and as a fraudulent debtor he evaded his creditors by abandoning his birth-name for some fanciful invention.

The need to live out his life in disguise, to present to the world a false self and never to reveal his vulnerable authentic self oft-times provoked discreditable consequences; but in *Captain Singleton* we enjoy the benefits of his creative deceits. Almost all of Defoe's novels are written in the first person singular; with Bob Singleton as his false self and raconteur, Defoe, the foundling, can let his transgressive imagination soar, commit appalling crimes without retribution. This is a work of triumphant defiance, the severe moralistic parental injunctions mocked and Alice Foe eliminated.

A babe, Kohut has taught us,[15] needs an approving mirror for his initial healthy exhibitionism; denied this by an unresponsive and negative mother, lacking such necessary corroboration, the infant's psychic core can sustain irrevocable injury. The self-esteem not granted to him in the cradle can result in a narcissistic rage that continues to roar in adulthood. Defoe's ablation of his mother is surely a clinical manifestation of such a condition; unforgiving, he retaliates against the curmudgeonly mother; he wipes her out.

We should perhaps be more generous, more forgiving. If Alice had been capable of giving more to her son, we would have had less. Daniel Defoe would have been a happier man and we, most certainly, would not have had the delight of knowing of the wicked escapades of that engaging villain Captain Bob Singleton.

Notes

1. See Chapter 4, p. 47.
2. Bastian, L., *Defoe's Early Life*, Barnes & Noble Books, 1981.
3. Rediker, M., *Villains of All Nations*, Beisl, 2004.
4. Garnett, E., Introduction to *Captain Singleton*, J. M. Dent & Sons, 1941.
5. Rank, O., *The Myth of the Birth of the Hero*, Nervous and Mental Diseases Publishing Company, 1914. Freud, S., *Mosses and Monotheism*, 1938.
6. Freud, S., *Family Romances Essays*, SE, Volume 19.
7. Defoe, D., *The Life, Adventures and Piracies of the Famous Captain Singleton*, 1720.
8. Freud, S., *Family Romances Essays*.
9. Ibid.
10. Defoe, *Captain Singleton*.
11. Rycroft, C., The ablation of the parental images, in *Psychoanalysis and Beyond*, Chatto & Windus, 1985; Pearson, J., *Analyst of the Imagination: The Life and Work of Charles Rycroft*, Karnac Books, 2004.
12. Rycroft, The ablation of the parental images.
13. Ibid.
14. Ibid.
15. Kohut, H., *The Restoration of the Self*, International University Press, 1977.

CHAPTER TWELVE

The birth traumas of Sheppard, Wild and Defoe

No biographer of Defoe can approach his task without humility, for he is writing of his master. Defoe was the presiding restless genius of the young aggressive genre emerging in early eighteenth-century England which liberated the biography, setting it free to tell a new kind of human story. In his commanding introductory essay to Defoe's synoptic biographies of John Sheppard and Jonathan Wild, Richard Holmes tells us how primitive literary forms—folk tales, ballads, journalism, "True Confessions" and pious sermons—were consumed by this innovative genre and, thus absorbed, yielded a recounting of the human condition with greater depth, historical accuracy and, at the same time, freely, sometimes wantonly and disreputably, sometimes generously, told us of its joys and tragedies.[1] Such emancipated studies were Defoe's narratives of Sheppard, the handsome, thieving, young, eighteenth-century Houdini-like escape artist who three times broke out of his cell in Newgate's death row, and Wild, the infamous Thief Taker General who, amidst scenes of mayhem at Tyburn, was himself hanged for his clandestine racketeering.

When the sixty-four-year-old Defoe wrote these two predictably popular biographies, he was under no financial pressures to produce any lurid pot-boilers, and indeed no critic could so describe these little gems, which are far more than mere reportage. With *Crusoe* and *Moll Flanders* completed and successfully marketed, and with *Roxana* just published, and having signed a four-year contract with a consortium of publishers eager to publish what was to be his famous *Tour* of Britain, he had established himself in a handsome Queen Anne house with a substantial acreage and was commuting to the City, where he had set up a business merchandising luxury foods. Meanwhile, he must have been carrying in his mind the contents of his weighty work *The Compleat English Tradesman*, which, within a year, was to be released. Amidst all this frenetic activity, one asks what prompted Defoe to burden himself with writing the biographies of Sheppard, a wretched petty thief, and Wild, a disgraced bent copper.

It has been suggested that the tabloid journalist in Defoe found the tales of the thief's escapades, and the unmasking of London's chief detective, irresistible news stories, and that he was engaged in an exploitative exercise of the prevailing widespread public alarm at the growth of gang criminality which had just led to the so-called Black Act of 1723, which increased the number of capital offences to more than two hundred, an Act that imposed the death sentence on anyone found stealing a silver spoon from a private house or a shilling's worth of lace from a shop.

P. D. James, one of today's most deft and successful detective novelists, takes the view that the successful pursuit by the detective of the criminal, and the consequent punishment of the villain, brings to a bewildered society a welcome affirmation and reassurance that we do live "in a morally comprehensive universe"[2] and that problems can be resolved. No doubt some may claim that Defoe, in publishing these two biographies, was, with guile, deliberately taking advantage of this societal need. Others have attributed more creditable motivations to Defoe. They see the two biographies as interrelated, that Defoe is depicting an intense clash of personalities and life-principles, the incorrigible young escapist pitted against the grim relentless thief-taker: "It could be seen as a duel between crime and justice, the rebellion and authority, youth and age or freedom and oppression".[3] Such perspectives are attractive but strained, since in fact Defoe in his Wild cameo makes only passing mention of the thief-taker's pursuit of Sheppard.

What, however, is common to both works is the fascination Defoe displays with the techniques and stratagems used by the protagonists to escape from the consequences of their defiant transgressions. The climax of the Sheppard biography is a recital of the breathtaking escape upwards, first through a chimney, then through six massively bolted doors and finally to freedom achieved by leaping over the rooftops of Newgate; Defoe lingers over every detail of Sheppard's obstacle course, recounts the ingenious methods used by him to defy all locks and bolts, with the whole adventure taking more than nine hours, and in total darkness. It is a thrilling tale, Defoe conveying all his own excitement in the telling, and, throughout, ensuring every reader would enjoy the same fraught thrills as he and Sheppard experienced as the escape trembled on the edge of success or failure.

The same focus on the mechanisms used to escape the entrapment of the law prevails in the Wild biography. The first half is almost entirely spent in carefully analysing and praising Jonathan Wild's brilliant methods of fencing stolen property without being ensnared by legal prohibitions. Defoe, disapproving but revelling withal in the cunning of the sleuth, invites us to share in the accompanying joys of the rogue's slipperiness: "It must be allowed to Jonathan's fame, that as he steered among rocks and shoals, so he was a bold pilot; he ventured in and always got out in a manner equally surprising; no man ever did the like before."[4] The anti-heroes of each biography were, in their several ways, supreme escapologists. The innumerable modern escapees like those detailed in films such as *The Great Escape, Papillon* and, my favourite because it is set in the time and place where, in Vienna, I impatiently awaited my demobilisation, *The Third Man*, containing the sequence of the Harry Lime chase through the sewers of the city, all tell us how irresistible, as tense voyeurs, we find the thrills of the *frisson* that an escape tale engenders. These are akin to the thrills with which Defoe in his biography so empathised and which were those experienced by Sheppard and Wild as they engaged in their criminal activities. Sheppard, breaking in and out of the most heavily guarded premises, is seen revelling in his triumphant overcoming of all obstacles; that, and not the often piffling value of the items stolen, brought him his delights. And we see Wild, a supreme conman who could find a far greater reward in his successful deception of his victims than from the material gains they brought him.

Both men's behaviour was compulsive; after each escape, Sheppard would again commit an offence which attracted capital punishment; he could not be deterred. When Parliament, in 1724, passed an Act specifically aimed at closing the legal loopholes which were being exploited, Wild continuously sought to evade the injunctions until, finally caught, he went to the gallows.

I frequently discerned in some of my criminal clients this syndrome, the compulsive need to challenge the law for its own sake, to break and enter premises not primarily to steal but to demonstrate their prowess. An exotic example came to my attention when a prolonged series of burglaries took place in a wealthy suburb of Cardiff. The thief would gain his unlawful entry often by most hazardous means, through seemingly inaccessible apertures, and then leave, taking little of value but only a token to ensure his visit was noted. I was therefore startled to find a man whom I well knew socially coming to me professionally, complaining that he was being questioned about the burglaries by the police. Possessing a Cambridge double first and a distinguished war record, and holding very successfully a high-ranking post in a public utility, he was indeed an unlikely cat burglar. He gave me his story to prove his non-involvement; there was a flaw in his ingenious explanations, and I pointed this out to him. He went away and came back with another tale, the original lacunae well concealed. I knew then that he was guilty but my professional duty was to defend, not judge, him so when he was committed for trial I did not, of course, in any way intimate my doubts to the defence counsel, a barrister who was later to become Lord Chancellor. The presiding Recorder, a future Deputy Speaker of the House of Commons, with my client word-perfect in the witness box, was willingly persuaded that he was innocent and in this far too cosy court of law, in his summing-up he practically directed the jury to acquit my client. But the shrewd Welsh working-class jury was unimpressed by the galaxy of Oxbridge forensic talents being deployed and, within less than an hour, returned a verdict of guilty.

This unfortunate man, during the War, had been able, as a daring commando, to act out his compulsions in thrilling experiences that served his country and earned him his medals. Constrained in peacetime, he had been left to create his own anti-social opportunities in order to assuage his deep-seated emotional need. In his case, his anti-social behaviour was trivial; in some cases, as in sexual offences, anti-social behaviour can be very serious. The dedicated psychiatrist Mervyn Glasser, who at London's Portman Clinic treated so many criminals, has written:

> Careful exploration of the dynamics of the offence will reveal that the pleasure comes as much, if not more, from the excitement of defying the prohibitions, as from the sexual acts themselves. Criminals know this "dicing with death" thrill very well, even having a term for it, namely, the "adrenalin factor".[5]

That "adrenalin factor", the pleasurable thrills which many a burglar enjoys as he breaks and enters, often culminates, his objective achieved and his tensions relieved, in a tumescence or defecation in the premises to which he has gained entry; thus, temporarily, his anxiety is stilled. The motivation of his burglary is not primarily to plunder but to deal with an anxiety which is overwhelming him; that is the true purpose of the crime; it has a function; and, aware of this purpose, some psychoanalysts have named the delights accompanying deviant behaviour as "functional pleasures".[6]

To understand the nature of the anxieties which propel the Sheppards of this world into their crimes, and to divine why, by proxy, Defoe rid himself of some of his anxieties in writing of Sheppard, by sharing them with the burglar, and, indeed, for us to gain insight into why we too respond to such a telling and find pleasurable tension in the recounting of the suspense of an escape tale, we need to probe much further. What is prompting the anxiety which acts as such an extraordinary precipitate?

★   ★   ★   ★   ★   ★   ★   ★   ★   ★

For all of us there is one travail, replete with anxiety, that is inescapable; being born is the trauma we all are fated to endure. Freud considered that it was the act of being born, when the biological helplessness of the infant is proclaimed, when the inner world of the womb is replaced by an unknown external environment, when the organism is flooded by amounts of excitation beyond its capacity to master, that induces what Freud named as "primary anxiety";[7] this is the common root of all the anxieties that afflict us later in life.[8]

Painful or traumatic events have to be endured by most over their life-cycle; these are the times when the primary anxiety of the birth trauma is ever evoked. The ability to contain the panic and fear that arises is dependent upon the severity of the initial trauma—whether it was a difficult birth and perhaps because of the size of the baby—and the quality of the caring reassurance that the totally disorientated babe needs.

John Sheppard was fated to have an anxious personality by the mischances of his arrival in the world; he strove to exorcise the anxiety that continued to envelop him by symbolically re-enacting the birth scene as he demonstrated his ability fearlessly and enjoyably to break out from the most cramped spaces; his repetition of his escapes is akin to that of the child who, to diminish the fears aroused by a game or frightening fairy-story, enjoys the endless repetition of the same game or the same story, which has to be told in exactly the same words.[9] And the symbolic re-enactment of Sheppard's birth is, some would say, less anti-social than the fantasies of re-birth of born-again fundamentalists, like George W. Bush, who seek relief from their personal anxieties by unloading it upon the children of Iraq.

All of us seek to repress the painful memory of the trauma of our birth but still reverberations from the primal trauma resound within our psyche to the end of our days. Somehow or other, to reduce the anxieties which the buried memories occasion, we strive to discharge the emotional burden which we find so threatening; then, to use the psychoanalyst's vocabulary, we abreact. The nature of those abreactions can vary widely; it can find expression in a Sheppard's escapology or a Bush's bombing, but it can find more innocent and sometimes most creative forms. When the child plays hide and seek, he is making playful use of the tragic motif, slipping in and out of the womb-like hidden place and thus gaining tempered thrills in a pleasurable manner that advantageously denies the reality of any initial trauma. The early psychoanalyst, Otto Rank, in his influential work *The Trauma of Birth*, claims that:

> Psychoanalysis has been able to show how, from the child's game, the higher and the highest pleasure-giving unrealities, namely, fantasy and art, emerge. Even in the highest forms of these pretended realities, as, for example, in the Greek tragedies, we are in a position to enjoy anxiety and horror because, in the meaning of Aristotle's catharsis, we abreact the primal affects.[10]

And certainly, in Defoe's two biographies of the escapologists—

works that are no mean flat recordings of the events which brought them to the gallows—the embellishments and extravagances Defoe interlaces with the facts create a "pretended" reality which, by the telling, enables him and us to distance and yet to enjoy the tremors of the birth trauma.

Nowadays there are some who, far from dismissing as hyperbole Rank's 1929 thesis of the importance of the birth trauma in determining our psychic life, insist that even before birth the embryo suffers never-to-be-forgotten trauma-inducing shocks. The psycho-historian Lloyd DeMause, in order to advance his view of the importance of the psychological imprinting that he contends takes place in foetal life, has assembled an intimidating collection of obstetric and clinical evidence relating to the role of the placenta.[11] It would seem that during the second trimester, while the amniotic sac is rather roomy, the foetus is able to float peacefully, kick vigorously, turn somersaults, urinate, suck its fingers and toes, grab its umbilicus, become excited by sudden noise, calm down when the mother talks quietly and rock back to sleep as she walks about; but a change of scene in the foetal drama comes about during the third trimester when, as its length and weight increase, the foetus becomes distressed. The crucial problem of the foetus in this newly cramped womb lies in its outgrowing the ability of its placenta to feed it, provide it with oxygen and clean its blood of carbon dioxide and waste. DeMause postulates that when the blood coming to the foetus from the placenta is bright red and full of nutrients and oxygen, the foetus feels good, but when the blood becomes dark and polluted with carbon dioxide and waste, the foetus feels bad; the foetus therefore has to contend with a placenta that is not only nutritious but can be poisonous. On such an interpretation, even before our actual birth, we are all fated to be traumatised. It is as screaming, wailing neophytes that we are initiated into the external world.

The biological determinants may be intractable but how we are then received will decide whether or not the load of anxieties we are carrying is to be lightened. A warm mothering mother, with soothing affection, lullaby and love, may quell the terrors of a baby so painfully expelled into a new and seemingly total hostile world; enfolded and cradled within a mother's arms, held securely in a softly lit room, feeling the heat of the mother's body, rocked gently to and fro, the baby slackens its screamings as the sensitive holding mother evokes for her child the reminiscence of his earliest intra-uterine state. No such mimetic exercise, bringing much-needed solace, will be performed by an unempathic mother deficient in communication skills; for her child no lost Eden is recaptured. Given Alice Defoe's temperament, Daniel would have been denied the blessings of the analgesic which may have relieved him of some of the anguish of his birth trauma anxiety.

When, by writing his Sheppard and Wild books, Defoe turned aside from his engagement with his weighty literary novels, he was doing more than titillating a public appetite for tales of crime; he was exploiting to the full the unusual opportunity given by the public interest in the escapologists; by vicariously participating in their re-enactment of their birthings, he too could dissipate some of the anxiety arising from his own birth trauma. And we also, in our defeatist anxiety-ridden world, responding to the resonances within Defoe's artful story-telling, learn that Man, ignoble though he may be and futile though may be his defiance, can courageously challenge biology and refuse to accept that destiny is irrevocably determined at birth.

Notes

1. Holmes, R., Introduction to *Defoe on Sheppard and Wild*, Harper Perennial, 2004.
2. Quoted in *The Sunday Times*, 12 September 2004.
3. Holmes, Introduction to *Defoe on Sheppard and Wild*.
4. Defoe, D., *Defoe on Sheppard and Wild*, Harper Perennial, 2004.
5. Glasser, M., Some aspects of the role of aggression, in E. Rosen (ed.), *The Perversions, Essays in Sexual Deviation*, Oxford University Press, 1979.
6. Fenichel, O., *The Psychoanalytical Theory of Neurosis*, Routledge & Kegan Paul, 1971.
7. Freud, S., *Beyond the Pleasure Principle*, SE, Volume 18.
8. Fenichel, *The Psychoanalytical Theory of Neurosis*.
9. Spitz, R., in *Imago* (*Journal of Pyscho-Analysis*), 23 (1937).
10. Rank, O., *The Trauma of Birth*, Kegan Paul, 1929.
11. DeMause, L., *Foundations of Psycho-history*, Creative Roots, 1982.

CHAPTER THIRTEEN

The preacher

A t the age of sixteen Defoe was placed by his father in a Dissenters' academy. The intention was that he should take the necessary five-year course that would qualify him to become a minister. After three years' study he dropped out. The circumstances which brought about this defiance of his father are to be found within a thinly concealed autobiographical sketch, ostensibly of a student at a university, written by Defoe forty years later. This student was:

> a young gentleman . . . eminent for learning and virtue, of prompt parts and great proficiency, insomuch that he was taken great notice of . . . and everyone promised fair in their thoughts for him, that he would be a great man; but whether from his own earnest desire of more knowledge or the opinion of his own great capacity . . . this gentleman, falling upon the study of divinity, grew so opinionated, so very positive and dogmatic in his notice of religious things . . . that his tutor saw plainly that he had little more than notions in all his religious pretensions to knowledge, and concluded that he would either grow enthusiastic or obstinately profane and atheistic. So it was that he and others who fell under his influence really reasoned themselves out of all religion whatsoever . . . pretending that those

things really were not, of which they could not define how and what they were, they proceeded to deny the existence of their Maker, the certainty of a future state, a resurrection, a judgement, a heaven or a hell. Indeed, he gave out that he could frame a new gospel, and a much better system of religion than that which they called Christian; and that if he would trouble himself to go about it, he would not fail to draw in as great a part of the world to run after him as he had after any other.[1]

Treating this sketch as giving us a picture of the young Daniel, some suggest that this tells us of a spiritual crisis;[2] that the rebellious attack of the "student" upon Christianity reveals a crisis of faith which precipitated Defoe's abandonment of his intention to become a Dissenter minister. The full truth is surely more prosaic. Rebellion accompanied by vapourings about the purpose of life and the existence of God is endemic to the adolescent condition; philosophising and the questioning of religious doctrine is a commonplace infatuation of so many an intelligent youngster going through a delayed adolescence, assailed by new and, to him, frightening sexual awakenings; religious or ideological expositions are used to smother emotions which threaten his autonomy. Byron, of such a youngster, once ironically remarked:

In thoughts like these true wisdom may discern
Longings sublime, and aspirations high,
Which some are born with, but for the most part learn
To plague themselves withal, they know not why;
'Twas strange that one so young should thus concern
His brain about the action of the sky;
If you think 'twas philosophy that this did,
I can't help thinking puberty assisted.

Defoe himself, a few years after his temporary defection from God's battalions, acknowledged, in retrospect, the role his personal passions had played in his heavy teenage flirtations:

Fatall and accurst desyres,
That burst from Thence with too Uncertain Fires.[3]

As Defoe moved into adulthood, the threatening fires were

dampened but never totally extinguished; they smouldered all his life, and his religious tracts are replete with fears that they could flare up again and consume him. Of the ages of man, adolescence and old age are the most difficult; the difference between the two is that one grows out of adolescence. In Defoe's case, however, there were especial reasons why he could never completely expunge from his biographies the consequences of his daring adolescent reconnoitres with the faithless; the ideational content of his turbulent adolescence was indeed more than a teenage effervescence. His pubertal hormones clearly played a significant part in determining that content but the persistence in his adult life, within all his religious expositions, of an undercurrent—one never wholly under his control—of subversive anti-God satanic doctrine means we should not regard Defoe's flight from his religious studies as irrelevant, as merely a gesture of a bewildered youth; it is more meaningful. If we treat it lightly we certainly shall never understand what his biographer, Bastien, accurately describes as the "very strength of his horror of atheism in later years".

Adolescence, the period in Defoe's life when we learn of his religious struggles and doubts, is, psychoanalysis postulates, the second, not the first, phase in the evolution of our sexuality, for our psychosexual development is diaphasic. Defoe, when he quit the academy, was still in his teens and wrestling with threatening and seductive intimations that all of us meet in the second phase. After we have, successfully or inadequately, at about five years of age, passed through our Oedipal phase, there comes about a period of emotional quiescence, a "latent phase" as it has been described. This takes place between the dramas and turmoils of earliest childhood and adolescence; the onset of puberty heralds the end of that hiatus; and, with its closure, there comes about what has been described as "a surge in the libidinal pressures"[4] which we witness in the storms and stresses of the adolescent. The harmonic charge destroys our repressive barriers that in the latency period held back any recall of the terrors and anxieties of our earliest years, which, with the barriers down, out of control, now invade the psyche of the adolescent: "Puberty is a 'repetition' of the infantile sexual period, and only rarely are conflicts encountered in puberty that have not had the forerunners of infantile sexuality."[5] The earliest conflicts of Defoe's infantile sexuality certainly resound in his adolescence; his adolescent theological musings are, we feel, epiphenomena, a reflection in particular of the unresolved Oedipal strivings upon which we have placed so much emphasis.[6] The betrayal by the father in choosing not him but his wife as his lover is avenged as, conflating God and the father, Defoe, in his "student" guise, wipes out God the Father and denies the very existence of the Maker.

But young Daniel could not for long sustain this rebellious repudiation; soon the inexorable recapitulation of the vicissitudes of his oedipal phase was at work; he could not tolerate the permanent loss of his belovèd father by whom he desperately wished to be possessed; by the time he was twenty-one, he capitulated to his desires. In chastened mood he wrote the first of the second poems which he called "Meditations"; there one finds him in full flight from the land of the profane; he was returning to his fatherland, fleeing

> From a false Confidence
> And all the Aery joys that Flows from Thence
> From all my Brain begotten Faith
> From all my Doubt
> And all my Foolish Thoughts about
> What Heaven Sayeth,
> From all my growth in Morralls Schoole,
> With which I mock't my Maker, and my Soule.

The penitent prodigal son has returned to be embraced by a forgiving father. From then on he was for ever to proclaim his allegiance to God, to preach the Word in the most strident and militant manner; above all else, he would ceaselessly excoriate the doubters and atheists who had led him into temptation. Even as Paul, after his conversion on the road to Damascus, excoriated stubborn Jewry, in no less extravagant language did Defoe condemn the atheist and the papist; the atheist for his irreverence, for daring to make a jest of God the Father, the other for thwarting, by insisting upon a priestly intermediary, man's desire for a direct and intimate relationship with the Creator. Wryly he was to remark: "the pulpit is none of my office. It was my disaster first to be set apart for, and then to be set apart from, the honour of that sacred employ." But if he had failed his father in not becoming a Dissenting minister, his religious expositions, pamphlets and books were certainly an ample, indeed, excessive, reparation. He was the defender of the true faith, and his certainty in his cause had all the absolutism that can only come from over-compensated doubt; to him there was no ecumenical compromise, no way to heaven except by his route. As an upholder of the gospel of love, all his life Defoe preached against the unbelievers with an inspired hate. Inevitably, as an artist in estrangement, his tirades ensured he recruited perhaps more enemies than converts. He behaved in like manner to those politicians I have described as hav-ing a special and abrasive talent for unnecessarily antagonising their supporters and inflaming their enemies; their handicap as propa-gandists I have emphasised earlier in this essay;[7] it has its source in the lack of encouragement they received as babes from a brusque mother whose negative responses had prevented them from ever enjoying the primal erotic experience within which they could fuse their aggression and love; their earliest experience of the outer world was as an impingement, not a loving embrace; in adult life they could only feel truly alive when they had reactivated those impingements; provocations arousing resistance and opposition ensured that they would gain from the counter-attacks confirmation of their own existence.

Nowhere more than in his religious writings do we find Daniel, son of the austere Alice, exhibiting the symptoms of this syndrome. Defoe may have described his early poems as "Meditations" but their noisy clamour disqualifies them being so entitled; and as he began as a young man, so he continued; there is no tranquillity in the man; by his intemperate, sometimes vicious, attacks on the irreligious, and on those who would not share his particular religious convictions, he gains a corroboration of his identity. Still-ness was dangerous; it could lead him to his dissolution. His Christianity was not one of "Gentle Jesus, meek and mild" or of "the Lamb"; with the zeal of an early Jewish prophet, he inveighed against the irresolute and what he regarded as pagan infiltration; he used his pen even as Christ used words to lash the money-grubbers defiling the Temple.

Defoe was, of course, goaded into making such aggressive res-ponses. He was fighting courageously against the Zeitgeist, against the forces bringing about the collapse of moral Puritanism.[8] A hun-dred years later, looking back, the MP-playwright Richard Brinsley Sheridan was to comment on the extreme volatility of the English character as revealed in the continuing transformation of personal conduct Defoe was witnessing: "In Oliver Cromwell's time they were all precise canting creatures. And no sooner did Charles II come over than they turned gay rakes and libertines."

But the changes which Sheridan was noting did not arise only from the local circumstances in England. Defoe was battling against a profound change taking place throughout European cultures. The process which was to cause God to be absent from man's consciousness began in the sixteenth century; it was to prove irreversible; its climax was perhaps reached in Nietzsche's declaration in his *Thus Spake Zarathustra* of 1885: "God is dead". The advent of a scientific methodology meant that gradually a new way of looking at man was emerging; the old certainty that man was made in the image of God was being challenged; the model of man was not God; a questionable but assertive theorising was being widely canvassed, advancing a view that the mind of man had an autonomy; that the mind of man was governed or possessed not by God but by the autonomous self-contained functionality of a machine.[9]

To the adult Defoe that notion was an affront to God and to the dignity of man; the fiercest of his attacks, in a tone so offensive to modern sensibility, upon those who denied his religious orthodoxy, must be understood as coming from a man who found himself simultaneously waging war on many fronts. He was first at war with himself; the doubts of his youth had to be quashed; he had to fight too not only the advancing secularism but also, as he saw it, the ever-present danger of the infiltration into the Established Church of popery, which could result in the undermining of the 1701 Settlement and in a foreign policy accommodative to the Catholic powers of Europe. More, he loathed the frivolity of the landed class whose indolence was a transgression of the Protestant work ethic; as we have seen, for Defoe the moral virtue of hard work was a fundamental tenet of his Puritan creed, blessing from God giving the nation a way to find happiness. Only in the context of all these considerations can we fully evaluate the significance of the religious writings of this embattled man.

In the most revealing and important of these religious contributions, *Religious Courtship*,[10] Defoe, with considerable artifice, encompassed all these themes; in this lengthy work the attentive reader will find an affirmation of his own faith and a disarming polemic against those indifferent to religion, against the destructive influences of popery and Quakerism, against love and passion being given priority over religious commitment and against the indulgence in banal pursuits by a leisured aristocracy. It is an uncomfortable work, intolerant of tolerance, one likely to be read with full approval today only by the bigots within Bush's fundamentalist constituency and those dwelling in the darkest alleys of Paisley's Belfast. It is a work which twentieth-century biographers and essayists understandably prefer either to ignore or implicitly to belittle; such a devaluation, however, fails to acknowledge the extraordinary religious dynamism within the work. It is that dynamic which in all his writings spurred Defoe to be ever the preacher, optimistically proclaiming that heaven can be created on earth if man would only remedy the blemishes and resist the evils in society—evils, of course, which Defoe took great delight in depicting.

Virginia Woolf,[11] when she found that a monument erected to Defoe was inscribed as being to the memory of the author of *Robinson Crusoe*, wrote indignantly that by their omission his other works, such as *Roxana, Moll Flanders* and *Captain Singleton*, were being slighted; but she made no mention of his *Religious Courtship*. That work, important as it is in the Defoe canon, would certainly not have fitted in with Bloomsbury preoccupations; it would indeed have been a severe reprimand to that group's carelessness with marriage vows. But even sympathetic biographers lacking Virginia Woolf's prejudices distance themselves from its explosive and challenging content. Novak pronounces that it shows Defoe: "in his narrowest state of mind" and would relegate it as being a "transitional work more novel than conduct book".[12] That is surely a misreading, for it implies, erroneously, that it is inchoate when in fact it is a mature and complete compendium of Defoe's religious views. Discomfiting they may be, and perhaps offensive to the genteel who believe strongly held religious convictions are bad manners. Today's suburban etiquette may rule that religious differences are mere shibboleths and that only the uncouth and narrow-minded would air them in company; but to accept such protocol when assessing Defoe's religious assertions and then to conclude that he was appallingly narrow-minded is both anachronistic and undeserved.

Few men indeed may be found to possess wider horizons. In his *Scots Poem* we wonder at Defoe's global vision:

I'd gladly breathe my Air on Foreign Shores:
Trade with rude Indians, and sun-burnt Mores.
I'd speak Chinese, I'd prattle African.
And briskly cross, the first Meridan.
I'd cast the line, and turn the Caps about.
I'd rove, and sail the Earth's greatest Circle out.
I'd fearless, venture to the Darien Coast;
Strive to retrieve the former Bliss we lost,
Yea, I would view Terra Incognita.
And climb the Mountains of America.[13]

And, to ensure his freedom from parochialism and narrow-mindedness should be emblazoned, he signed this poem, in capital letters, "A NATIVE OF THE UNIVERSE". I suspect that the derogation of *Religious Education* by twentieth-century critics comes from a failure of nerve, a fear of confronting this unfamiliar presentation of a cosmopolitan man holding, in so unabashed and passionate a manner, a particular and exclusive religious conviction.

Even Richard West, one of his most generous biographers, attempts to demean the work by describing it as a "moral tract",[14] appearing to believe it is only to be distinguished from other "pious tracts" because Defoe "had an ear for the language of ordinary sinners". Such appreciations of the work are inadequate. This is no slight and quirky pamphlet or tract; it is a principled, 150,000-word work unfashionably refusing to submit to the voguish over-rational worldly secularisation finding expression in atheism, deism and an attitude of indifference to the authority of the scriptures and moral theology, an insouciant attitude encapsulated and approved of in 1733 in the famous couplet of Alexander Pope, Defoe's contemporary:

For modes of faith, let graceless zealots fight
He can't be wrong
Whose life is in the right.[15]

Religious Courtship is a fierce rejection of such a relaxed view; its didactic message is unequivocally spelled out in what reads today far more as a Shavian play than a novel or tract. It portrays within the sedate ambience of an upper middle-class family home a kindly widower seeking to find suitable and good husbands for his three grown-up unmarried daughters. The daughters, well endowed with virtue, looks and dowries, are in a position to choose among their suitors. Through continuous dialogue between the sisters and their aunts, Defoe's script enables us to assay the varying temperaments of these high-minded, well brought up ladies, ever mindful of the pledge they had given to their dying mother to marry no man unless he was genuinely religious and, of course, Protestant. The good widower is exasperated by his daughters' scrupulousness; but they are adamant. Wealth, rank, goodness, all such qualities in a suitor were of no account unless he were religious; and not nominally so but deeply committed. The rigour of the tests and surveillance to be applied to evaluate his commitment varies between the sisters but all are in agreement that no true love can abide in a home unless husband and wife can pray together, and, ideally, have children and servants who, properly instructed, would join them in daily worship.

The criteria insisted upon by Defoe's three daughters are to be differentiated from those operating in the taboos maintained by the devout Muslim and the strictly Orthodox Jew against miscegenation with a Gentile; race, bloodline, circumcision and such like are no barriers to a loving and happy marriage if the partners are as one in unswerving allegiance to the Protestant faith. If that prevails, the marriage is blessed; if the husband defaults in that allegiance, his continuing virtues—kindness, consideration and generosity—are of no avail; the marriage is doomed.

Defoe illustrates the inevitable nemesis of such a mixed marriage by allowing one of the sisters, with insufficient investigation and with her father's full approval, to marry a most eligible Italian; the dénouement comes with a horrifying discovery that the Italian, although otherwise a model husband, is a closet Roman Catholic who keeps in a locked room in the matrimonial home a secret shrine at which he makes his private obeisances. Tainted by the presence of Catholic icons in the home, the wife is fated thereafter to live in anguish and sin, a perdition shared by her father, who blames himself for having brought about such a terrible misadventure.

Many more stories of disasters resulting from similar misalliances are unremittingly spelt out; but before we condemn the whole work as an ugly display of bigotry, we should note that there are singular features of this tale and its telling that act as caveats to such a sweeping simplistic judgement. It can be easily overlooked that this story is in fact a paean of praise to the wisdom of wooing and a denigration of the shallowness of men. All the main protagonists are women, and it is their vigorous assertions and spiritual beliefs which, in the outcomes portrayed by Defoe, are vindicated; the indifference of men to a communion of religious observances by husband and wife is not to be regarded as a mere peccadillo; it is fatal to marriage.

In no work of Defoe's does his psychic bi-sexuality reveal itself more than here, where we see him wholly identifying with the daughters; it is women's happiness that is under threat if the religious anchorage is cut free. Historians such as Lawrence Stone, who have depicted the erosion of religious observance and daily family prayers led by the father as a liberating influence and an attack upon oppressive patriarchy, would find no confirmation of such theorising in Defoe's women, for they see that liberation as a trap, far more likely to disadvantage women than to give them greater freedom and equality. In *Religious Courtship*, the eldest daughter, in ringing tones, instructs her youngest sister to be wary of accepting that the risks entailed in marriage are unaffected by the fashionable decline in religious observances:

> I am firm in my opinion; . . . It is true, there is a hazard in every part of the change of life; we risk our peace, our affection, our liberty, our fortunes; but we ought never to risk our religion. . . . Because religion itself is less in fashion than it used to be . . . also marriages are now wholly taken up with mirth and gay things; but in those days matrimony seems to have been understood, as it really is in itself, a solemn and serious thing; not to be ventured on rashly, considered slightly, or performed with levity and looseness; 'tis a transaction of the greatest weight, attended with circumstances of the greatest importance, and consequences of the utmost concern to our welfare or misery; the happiness of life, the prosperity of families, and indeed the interest of the soul, is exceedingly dependent on the good or bad conduct of both parties in this affair; and to run headlong upon it, is rightly compared to a horse rushing into the battle, and argues a miserable thoughtlessness of what is before us.[16]

Defoe's views, as expressed through his fictional daughters, cannot be regarded as those of a reactionary bigot. At the time he wrote *Religious Courtship*, his sons having moved out of the family home, he was living in a wholly feminine household with his wife and three daughters. Their pervasive presence and his own feminine sensibilities made him acutely aware of the positive contribution that women's conservatism, their natural disposition to conserve and care expressed in religious commitment, could make to bringing a blessed harmony into a home; but he knew too how Britain had, in his lifetime, been torn apart by religious dissension and that to bring into partnership two people of different faiths was a grave risk, that the religious dissension which had occasioned the destabilisation of the state could be imported into the domestic scene, and similar turbulent consequences could result. Those biographers of Defoe who treat *Religious Courtship* as a work of naked religious prejudice, or as a lapse of taste, fail to understand the full significance of this remarkable sermon.

Indeed, the extraordinary timing of this well crafted sermon tells us how important it was to Defoe himself that it be delivered without any delay. He was anxious to pre-empt any charge that the racy novels he was publishing were titillations, condonations of the promiscuous behaviour of the characters peopling his tales. *Religious Courtship* was published a month after *Moll Flanders* and, a little more than eighteen months later, *Roxana* was to appear. Twentieth-century feminists can perhaps claim the daughters of *Religious Courtship* as well as *Moll Flanders*, but their feminism, if such it was, manifested itself in entirely different forms; the upright reprimanding daughters asserted their moral authority over their wimpish suitors; Moll and Roxana, living breathtakingly independent lives, violated every moral tenet and religious principle maintained by the daughters. Rapt prayer and worship gave the daughters their stability and happiness; Moll found her raptures elsewhere, in adultery, wealth, incest and bigamy. Defoe was playing with fire when he allowed Moll to tell her tale, and he knew it.

Everything points to the two works, *Religious Courtship* and *Moll Flanders*, having been conceived simultaneously; not even Defoe at his most prolific could have completed *Religious Courtship*, so challenging and lengthy a work, in a few weeks. He was probably writing both at the same time. The Preacher could only dare to permit his lustful feminine imagination to soar, to revel in his anti-heroines, to enjoy vicariously their anti-social frolicking and manipulations, by putting in place a total disavowal of their irresponsible lasciviousness; *Religious Courtship* was that magnificent disavowal. Those critics who see it as insufferable, intolerant humbug, as a precursor to suffocating Victorian values, are wrong. Without *Religious Courtship* the concupiscence and wickedness enveloping *Moll Flanders* and *Roxana*—over which they, and posterity, unashamedly salivate—would never have been available.

★　★　★　★　★　★　★　★　★　★

In 2004 a long-suppressed piece,[17] written by Freud in 1932, surfaced; the recipient, a brilliant and astonishing American ambassador to whom, at the time, it was addressed for publication, took fright. He understood the full implications of its contents and feared the reactions which could follow if it were published, for Freud, in wandering outside his original brief of providing a diagnosis of the effete policies of President Woodrow Wilson in terms of the feminine negative Oedipal arrest, identified too the consequence of the same condition in Christ. The diplomat, William Bullitt, then contemplating leaving the diplomatic service to enter national politics, appreciated that to be associated with Freud in affirming an interpretation of the central tenets of Christian belief that many would regard as outrageous would be electorally disastrous—so Freud's short but extraordinarily significant little piece was hidden away. Today we find, on reading the newly found fragment, that it illuminates still further for us the psychic dynamics operating in the passionate Dissenter convictions and fierce anti-Catholicism continuously expressed by Defoe and, in particular, preached in *Religious Courtship*.

The fragment, originally intended as part of an introduction to a joint work by Freud and Bullitt, a psychological study of Woodrow Wilson, does not appear in the expurgated, and perhaps garbled, version of that book, not published until 1967; it was evidently still regarded as being too disconcerting to be tolerated. In this hitherto unpublished introduction to the book, we find once again that Freud insists that the most important of the Oedipal problems besetting the child is his relationship with his father; unequivocally he returns to his emphases on the determining influence of the negative Oedipus complex, and that, not his problematic relationship with his mother, is of greater significance; the child has to deal "with the more important of the two Oedipal problems—the relationship with the father". When Freud then proceeds on that premise to scrutinise the psyche of the committed Christian, we find he is presenting a clinical picture of a man who displays an abundance of the traits we have in this essay repetitively attributed to Defoe. Freud explosively tells us:

> A man whose passivity towards his father could not find a direct outlet will often have recourse to a double identification. He will identify with his father and also seek out a younger man whom he identifies with himself and on whom he bestows the same love that he wished for from his father but that remained unsatisfied because of his passivity toward the father. In this way he may become an active homosexual. In many cases a man whose passive attitude toward the father has not found direct expression will find that expression by identifying with Jesus Christ. This identification is a regular occurrence, so to speak, in the psyche of a Christian; according to the testimony of psychoanalysis it can be demonstrated to exist in completely normal people. That should not surprise us, for this identification accomplishes the feat of miraculously reconciling two extremely powerful and absolutely contradictory wishes by fulfilling both at the same time. These two wishes are to be completely passive and subservient toward the father, to be completely feminine, and on the other hand to be completely masculine, powerful and authoritative like the father. Christ was able to fulfil both these wishes: by humbly submitting to the will of God the Father, he was able to become God himself; in other words, by surrendering to total femininity he was able to attain the ultimate goal of masculinity. Thus, it is understandable that identification with Christ is so frequently used to deal with the more important of the two Oedipal problems—the relationship with the father.

> . . . Christ is, after all, the perfect reconciliation between masculinity and femininity. Belief in his divinity includes the belief that one can realize the most daring dreams of activity by means of the utmost passivity; in submitting unreservedly to the father, one triumphs over him and becomes God oneself. This mechanism of reconciling opposing impulses of masculinity in the constitutionally bisexual human being by identifying with Christ is something so satisfying that it assures the Christian religion a long existence. People will not readily be inclined to give up something that rescues them from the most

difficult conflict they have to struggle with. They will continue to
identify with Christ for a long time to come.

As we have seen, the "most difficult conflict" in the lifespan of man
which Freud is identifying, the infantile negative Oedipus complex,
was only tenuously and imperfectly resolved by Defoe. He needed
far more than most to find in Christ "the perfect reconciliation
between masculinity and femininity"; his intactness depended upon
the "mechanism of reconciling opposing impulses of masculinity
in the constitutionally bisexual human being". Any interference
with the smooth operation of that mechanism was seen not as mere
tampering but as a lethal intervention; there had to be for Defoe
certainty that the mechanism could never be unlocked. The complaints made against Defoe's *Religious Courtship*, deploring its lack
of ecumenical tolerance, its passionate insistence on the exclusive
verity of a particular religious conviction, arose because Defoe could
not permit himself any doctrinal weakness that might undermine
the containment his brand of Protestantism afforded; in identifying
with God the Father, and God the Son, he stilled the turbulence that
would otherwise have arisen if the legacy of the homosexual components within the Oedipal situation sought more direct expression.
He dare not yield in any way to his youthful temptations to be a
disbeliever; when he inveighed against atheists, his invective reveals
the dogmatism that is always the hallmark of over-compensated
doubt. To treat Defoe's religious and political ideas, as for all ideo-
logies, as the offspring of pure reason would be to assign them a
parentage as mythological as that of Pallas Athene. The tenacity and
persistence shown by the great Protestant Dissenter as he waged his
religious and political wars in his pamphlets, and in *Religious Courtship*, tells us more of the underlying passions, not the rationale, that
informed and sustained them.

And those passions especially lit up his denunciations of Popery.
We have drawn attention to the horror and consternation Defoe
evoked in *Religious Courtship* when telling of the daughter who was
"undone" by innocently marrying a closet Catholic; the wife and her
family were led to the discovery of the husband's secret by becoming aware of his addiction to the paintings he kept in a locked room;
they were paintings of the Virgin Mary and Christ. Nothing could
inflame Defoe more than any hint of Mariolatry; the worship of

Mary was, for Defoe, the ultimate heresy. His brand of Protestantism was a carefully designed construct assuring his unconscious need to be at one with his father; he, usurping the mother's role, became the exclusive lover of the father; the mother had to be subordinate. To bring back as an icon Mary the Mother into the centrality of the Christian myth, to diminish the significance of God the Father, was for Defoe an affront which threatened the nice balance for which he yearned, what Freud called in his fragment the "perfect reconciliation between masculinity and femininity".

To suggest that the lifelong political battles of Defoe to achieve and defend a Protestant constitutional settlement for Britain, and his consequent uncompromising diatribes against any Jacobite infiltration, are mere epiphenomena reflecting the struggle of his Oedipal conflicts would be absurdly reductive; but the passion with which he fought those battles certainly has its source in those earliest turbulences. In Britain today, when presented with desiccated lacklustre political manifestoes by leaders who only simulate passion, we perhaps look back with nostalgia to a Defoe who, curious as its source may have been, was possessed with an authentic fervour; endowed with such rare élan, the provocative testaments in *Religious Courtship* continue to engage us.

Notes

1. Defoe, D., *Serious Reflections: A Vision of the Angelic World*.
2. Bastien, L., *Defoe's Early Life*, Macmillan, 1981.
3. Defoe, D., *Meditations*, p. 5, quoted in Novak, M. E., *Daniel Defoe: Master of Fictions*, Oxford University Press, 2001.
4. Laplanche, J. and Pontalis, J. B., *The Language of Psychoanalysis*, Hogarth Press, 1973.
5. Fenichel, O., *The Psychoanalytical Theory of Neurosis*, Routledge & Kegan Paul, 1946.
6. See Chapter 3.
7. See Chapter 8, p. 102.
8. Stone, L., *The Family, Sex and Marriage in England 1500–1801*, Penguin Books, 1979.
9. Khan, M., *The Privacy of the Self*, International Psychoanalytical Library, Hogarth Press, 1974.

10. Defoe, D., *Religious Courtship*, 1722.
11. Woolf, V., *The Common Reader, Volume 1*, Vintage, 2003.
12. Novak, *Daniel Defoe: Master of Fictions*.
13. Defoe, D., *A Scots Poem*.
14. West, R., *The Life and Strange Surprising Adventures of Daniel Defoe*, Harpers, 1997.
15. Pope, A., *An Essay on Man*, 1733.
16. Defoe, D., *Religious Courtship*.
17. Roazen, P., Oedipus at Versailles, *Times Literary Supplement*, 22 April 2005.

CHAPTER FOURTEEN

The feminist

When, in 1727, George II came to the throne, in "affaires of the heart", as the pretty beautifying phrase goes, he followed the example of his father, who, on quitting Hanover for London, had brought with him two aged mistresses and soon acquired more. He continued the Hanoverian tradition, betraying his beautiful wife, Queen Caroline, with a succession of mistresses. Defoe, loathing such casualness, in a work published in the same year as the enthronement of George II, nostalgically mourned the loss of the rectitude of the late Queen Mary and Queen Anne. His implied criticism of the Hanoverian kings, written against the prevailing current, was contained in his greatest non-fiction work, *Conjugal Lewdness or Matrimonial Whoredom*, a fierce denunciation of the coarsening of values which accompanied an increasingly permissive society.

Social historians, however, following Lawrence Stone, eager to pursue their own thesis, have, sometimes by distorted extrapolations, sought to reduce this massive treatise to use it merely as an illustration of the ongoing reassessment of the power relations between the sexes; and, noting its pleas for equality and sharing within marriage, declare it to be a manifesto on behalf of companionate marriage.

Contrariwise, sensing such a reading could place Defoe as an advo-
cate of an anaemic passionless status being accorded to marriage,
some of Defoe's biographers have defiantly insisted that the work is
"a hymn to the joys of sex".[1] Such interpretations fall short. A full
appreciation of the work would not treat it as a paean to either
companionate marriage or sex; but in this work we can, if we dare,
join Defoe in an epiphany, in a festival where the Holy Ordinance
of marriage—as Defoe describes it—is celebrated, and where
worship is directed with all the fervour of a devout Christian to the
most beguiling and redeeming of all the pagan gods, to Eros, the
God of Love.

Conjugal Lewdness is certainly no "ascetic" guide, as Lawrence
Stone would suggest,[2] to the tepid pleasures of companionate marriage; nor, though it is fearless in exploring sexuality, is it a dated sex
manual. It is a catechism instructing us how, in marriage—and only
in the exclusiveness of marriage—it is possible to enjoy the greatest
delight obtainable on this earth, truly to love and be loved. It is not a
piece of romantic juvenilia. Defoe explicitly presents the work as
that of an old man; indeed, four years later, he was dead. It is, and is
intended to be, a most serious work, a distillation of the wisdom of
age. It was written after Crusoe, Moll Flanders and his darkest novel,
Roxana. It is drained of all the titillation that may be found in those
novels and deliberately excludes any near-pornographic asides.
From the outset he warns the reader, and indeed himself, that they
were not being lured by the eye-catching title of his treatise into
reading a work that would provide a moralistic cover to their pruri-
ence; there was to be no shoddy window-dressing to market this
product.

Lewdness was to be stigmatised as such, not treated as elegant
frivolity; adultery was not to be lightly dismissed as gallantry.
Defoe was not writing as a prim prude; he was declaring his war
upon the encroaching and pervasive permissive society's wish to
prettify and legitimise the encouragement they gave to those whose
pollutants would snuff out the sacred flame, who would gut Love.
And since he knew the resentment his strictures would provoke,
he was determined to pre-empt those who, by compelling him to
use circumlocutions, would stifle or dilute his Philippic. In no way
would he accommodate those who under a pretence of good taste
or delicacy would have him avoid a scrutiny of their deviances and

sexual indiscipline; and no area of human behaviour which impinged on the sacred state of matrimony would be excluded. He warned, in demotic mood, that he would be clear and blunt, never submitting to either external censorship or self-censorship; and that warning was, as the work unfolded, proved indeed to be no idle threat.

All the skills Defoe had developed as a journalist, all the insights into personal motivation explored in his novels *Crusoe, Moll Flanders* and *Roxana*, were now put into the service of this assault on those whose lifestyles denigrated true love and their apologists. His was the riposte of the passionate Puritan refusing to tolerate the ugly discourtesies that his society, like ours today, was heaping upon the sensuous love available to the committed joined in matrimony. He could not, to strengthen his case, draw upon the intimations and language of the classics, a deficiency which the literati of his day never failed to mock; as a Dissenter he was barred from Oxford and Cambridge and their classical education. But he had another resource upon which, never more than in this work, he bountifully and creatively drew; never more than here was there a more cunning exegesis of the Hebrew Bible used to validate an argument. Reading Defoe today brings home to us that, with the demise of the teaching of the classics and, now, with the Bible being a closed book to many, our technological society, while affecting to have perfected the art of communication, has been struck dumb; and beyond the acquisitive reach of Hellenic and Hebrew articulation, our public discourse is, for the most part, conducted in grunts.

But here, in *Conjugal Lewdness*, Defoe delivers his reprimands clearly, unequivocally, marshalling his case with a forensic skill every trained lawyer would envy. In the 120,000-word work, chapter after chapter, never prolix and only repetitious to ensure emphasis, cumulatively, using as aids his own sardonic wit and the borrowed concrete imagery of Old Testament chroniclers, he constructs his indictment against all who would besmirch the supreme virtue of sensibility between partners in matrimony. And although his excursus takes him into the marriage-bed, still he does not desist: he scorns euphemism, the device of the pusillanimous to avoid giving offence; no disguises are permitted in this work; here he does not, as was his usual wont, permit himself anonymity or the use of the pseudonym. He unashamedly declares his authorship. It is Defoe's most truthful production; and, lacking concealment, its authenticity makes us startlingly aware of the hermaphroditic qualities so deeply striated in the work; the signature appended to the treatise is that of the man but the voice we hear is that of a woman.

In the preamble to the main work, when we are succinctly informed what is being argued, we immediately hear the feminine voice; with a "young lady" acting as the medium, we are told that the nature and causes of the maladies afflicting matrimony can be diagnosed and that, under a strict regime, prophylactics are available to remedy the condition:[3]

> I am Arguing to remove the Occasion of those Abuses which make the Matrimony ruinous, and a Disaster both to the Man and to the Maid.

> This would secure the Affection of the Parties before they marry; they would be united before they were joined, they would be married even before they were wedded, the Love would be possessed before the Persons, and they would have exchanged Hearts before they exchanged the Words of, I, S, Take thee N; in short, Matrimony without Love is the Cart before the Horse, and Love without Matrimony is the Horse without any Cart at all.

> Marrying is not such a frightful Thing that we should be terrified at the thoughts of it, yet it is far from being such a trifling Thing either that we should run Headlong or Blindfold into it, without so much as looking before us. 'Twas a prudent Saying of a young Lady who wanted neither Wit nor Fortune to recommend her, that marrying on the woman's side was a Horse rushing into the Battle, who depending upon the Hand that rules him has no Weapon of his own either offensive or defensive; whereas, on the Man's side, like the Soldier, he has both Armour to preserve himself, and Weapons to make him be fear'd by his Adversary.

And as he begins, so throughout the work, cataloguing the "Abuses" which ruin matrimony and slay "Love", the disadvantages endured by women are unsparingly recited. He brings to their predicaments an understanding far beyond the capacity of most men. We have insistently proposed that many of Defoe's guilt-ridden dilemmas were determined in infancy by his early failure to relinquish the unconscious desire to be his father's lover; but in this work, that feminine identification is put into the service of a rare empathy with all womankind.

When we remark on Defoe's psychic bi-sexuality, we are drawing attention to a quality far removed from that to be found in the novels of bi-sexuals such as Benjamin Disraeli and Oscar Wilde. For them, acting out their homosexual yearnings in their private lives was insufficient; they must needs people their novels with clones whose homoerotic escapades, covertly told, excited them and, no doubt, their readers. Disraeli in his early novels, all autobiographical, lacked the discretion he imposed upon himself as he climbed the greasy pole of politics; we continuously, in those early works, find lingering references to Greek and Roman male friendships. In his novels *Vivian Grey, The Young Duke, Alroy, Contarini Fleming, Henrietta Temple* and *Venetia*, the male heroes often look like girls, often are dandies, sometimes getting tangled with handsome young men, and are frequently put into homoerotic situations, spending hours in Turkish baths or dressing in female costumes. In *Venetia* Disraeli makes open references to Byron's Thyrza's verses, love poems addressed to a boy, and his Byronic hero remarks on two figures of the classical world whose same-sex experiences were well known: "I think of the ancients ... Alcibiades and Alexander the Great are my favourites. They were young, beautiful, and conquerors; a great combination."[4] Disraeli, ever the chancer, gambled on those familiar with classical literature understanding what he was conveying, while those who might be shocked would never find him out.[5] Nor did they. But Wilde, lacking Disraeli's discretion and political skills, was entrapped. He suffered the same fate as his alter ego Dorian Gray and, to posterity's grievous loss, destroyed himself.

But the love whose name could not be spoken by those supreme egotists, Disraeli and Wilde, was not the love which Defoe preached. Their love was self-love, a love limited by physical boundaries, emotionally circumscribed, restricted by gender. Their narcissism ensured their fictional characters were mere replications, never permitted to escape their creators' embraces. But Defoe's love violated all such gender boundaries; impossibly ambitious, he nobly sought to reach out to the platonic ideal, to reclaim the hermaphrodism which Aristophanes, in Plato's *Symposium*, taught once belonged to us all:

First of all, you must learn the constitution of man and the modifications which it has undergone, for originally it was different from what it is now. In the first place there were three sexes, not, as with us, two, male and female; the third partook of the nature of both the others and has vanished, though its name survives. The hermaphrodite was a distinct sex in form as well as in name, with the characteristics of both male and female, but now the name alone remains, and that solely as a term of abuse. . . . Each of us then is the mere broken tally of a man, the result of a bisection which has reduced us to a condition like that of a flatfish, and each of us is perpetually in search of a corresponding tally.[6]

Defoe may have lacked familiarity with the classics but certainly not with the Pentateuch. The biblical passages he quotes underwriting his argument reveal how deeply affected he was by the chroniclers of the Books of Moses; he had wholly absorbed, from the telling of the God of the Hebrews, the notion of a hermaphrodite organism which had explicitly male and female characteristics; for woman as well as man, Genesis insists, was created in the image of the God, who evidently contained both elements; and being so created, Eve springs from Adam's rib. This concept of a primal divine hermaphrodism, found of course in the creation account of so many cultures, arises from the wish to believe that the Ultimate Being is a unity in which all present pairs of opposites, including the sexes, are contained. Ancient myths abound of a time when the eternal male, Father Sky, and the eternal female, Mother Earth, were locked in unending embrace; there was neither duality nor multiplicity, only one hermaphrodite creation. It was only later, when the cosmic egg was broken, that creation took place. The sexes were separated and have ever since longed to be re-united, each in the other. The tirade that Defoe mounts in *Conjugal Lewdness* is against all those "abuses" which harden and perpetuate gender divisions; those divisions must be courageously acknowledged, not denied, but as long as those "abuses" continue, no appointment can be made for the fulfilment of that yearning for reunion; with the disabilities in place, no coupling can bring the bliss giving us intimations of the paradisical unity that once upon a time was the possession of humankind.

Expectantly, having been thus alerted by Defoe that he will categorise the abuses that devastate matrimony, we await their identification; and then the male reader is soon discomfited and, indeed, shocked to discover that Defoe holds that of all the "abuses", none is more deserving of punishment than the one which offends a woman's periodicity.

Menstruation is a subject that men avoid in private conversation and is almost unmentionable in public discourse. Although politicians are quick to claim credit for every benefit brought to the public, Gordon Brown, as Chancellor, could not bring himself in a recent Budget Statement even to mention that millions would gain from the VAT exemption he was granting to sanitary towels. But Defoe was possessed of no such diffidence; the woman in him ensured that no squeamishness inhibited his engagement with the subject. Only in very recent times has the male prejudice against acknowledging on television the fact of menstruation been overcome; that has come about because what was once regarded as bad taste, as unmentionable, has been overcome by greed for advertising revenue. Now products are presented in a manner intended to deny the very reality of the existence of menstruation; with such products one can ski, dance and climb mountains; menstruation is trivialised. But Defoe, with his feminine sensibility, understood the elemental significance of periodicity; to deny that significance and, worse, untimely invade a woman's space was an "Abhorrent Crime".

In *Conjugal Lewdness*, both Nature and God are invoked by Defoe to justify his condemnation. He reminds

> those that are guilty, that the more modern Brutes of the Forest, who obey the Laws of Sex, and follow the Dictates of meer Nature, do not act thus; The Wild Ass, which the Scripture represents as the most vitiated ungoverned of all the Forest, yet the text says, in her Months you shall find her; she has her Seasons, and so have all the rest of the beastly Creatures, and they all observe them strictly and suitably to the reasons of Nature.

And then Defoe calls on scripture to reinforce the warnings that Nature gives to those who would defy her commands:

> How can any Persons who are really guilty of this conjugal Uncleanness, reproach an Author for the Sin of naming what they are not ashamed of doing? I look upon the Crime with Abhorrence, and I could refer you to the Scripture, where it is branded with a Title that

deserves it; as I say, I look on the Crime with Abhorrence, for I add, that I look on the persons with something beyond it, and can only add this of them, that as they were not to be touch'd under the Law, so they are not to be named under the Gospel. God would not take them for Jews 'til they were wash'd, and I shall never take them for Christians 'til they reform; let them read their Reproof at large in Leviticus XI.

Defoe is citing a Levitican command that coitus must be forgone during a woman's menstruation and for seven days thereafter; more, in what to the obtuse may seem a bewildering *non sequitur*, after those seven days have passed, on the eighth day the woman, separately, leaving the man to do likewise, "shall take unto her two turtles, or two young pigeons, and bring them unto the priest, to the door of the Tabernacle of the congregation. And the priest shall offer the one for the sin offering and the other for a burnt offering; and the priest shall make an atonement for her before the Lord."

Defoe's denunciation of those breaching the injunction cannot be regarded as a mere aesthetic revulsion; although in his condemnation reverberations echo of the ancient tribes' protective taboo against the horrors of contaminated blood, that too, in itself, does not adequately explain the fierceness of his diatribe. There was, for Defoe the Bible scholar, no ambiguity about the heinousness of the sin for which God in Leviticus required this monthly atonement. And those, Defoe insists, who blasphemously fly against the face of the Lord are outlaws beyond the Law, untouched by the grace of the Gospel. For the sin which the offenders were committing was original sin, the sin that encompassed all subsequent sins and of which woman, by her periods and by the pain and labour of childbirth, was given a perpetual reminder; in her menstruation she was suffering, as it has often been popularly named, "the curse", which followed when, in the Garden of Eden, she disobeyed. Transcending the male misogyny of blaming woman as the temptress for our human plight, the feminine in Defoe reached out to her; for him she was not Eve the Seducer but the true "Dolorosa", the woman of sorrows, and his indignation that she, in her most vulnerable and piteous of times, should be mocked by "Brutal" insensitive male intervention was boundless. For Defoe menstrual discharges were the tears of a distressed woman; on such occasions she should be comforted and her inner space respected.

Latterday self-proclaimed feminists, having achieved relative emancipation reluctantly granted by man, too often tacitly accept, and recommend to the female sex, the self-made male image as the model to be equalled; they would smudge the biological differentiation between man and woman; Defoe, on the contrary, by so dramatically drawing attention to women's periodicity, understood and emphasised a woman's distinctiveness; his was a feminism free from the penis envy that afflicts so many contemporary militant feminists with their querulous demands for state subsidies for child-caring to relieve them of motherhood and free them to compete equally with men in the market place.

Defoe's feminist demand was far grander. His was a demand for a recognition that it is a woman's inner space which is the rock bottom of the biological differentiation between man and woman. The human foetus must be carried inside the womb for a given number of weeks, the infant must be suckled or at any rate raised within a maternal world; years of specialised woman-hours are to be devoted to the child. No wonder that the little girl, the bearer of ova and maternal powers, tends to survive her birth more surely and is a tougher creature, able as she grows up to be more resistant to not a few man-killing diseases and to enjoy a longer life expectancy. The survival of the species depends upon her physical strength and upon her capacity to fulfil the biological imperative, as an adult to react more vividly, more personally and with greater compassion to the different needs of others—her reactions stemming from her responses to her child. When Defoe advertised menstruation it was because he wanted to declare, not conceal, women's distinctiveness, to acknowledge the creativity and tragedy pre-determined by her especial biology. The feminists of the twenty-first century who continue to deny their biology are no fellow-travellers of Defoe. They are engaged in a disastrous course, in an act of self-immolation; they impoverish their own personal relationships and deprive all of us of the social inventions and institutions which we desperately need to guard and cultivate that which nurses and nourishes, cares for and tolerates, includes and preserves us.

Repeatedly, during my legislative efforts, I was made aware of the importance of this "inner space" in the feminine cycle. Before entering the Commons, as a solicitor with a substantial divorce practice, I had already been made acutely conscious of the profound despair and hurt a woman can suffer on the breakdown of a longstanding marriage, pain that so often, in the case of the husband, was a wonder, arousing both his empathic horror and a refusal to understand it. During the long campaign before my Divorce Act of 1969 reached the Statute Book, the anguish that engulfed me from negative and positive responses coming from women throughout Britain brought me an understanding that the woman's inner space was not only the very centre of fulfilment but also the centre of despair, for to be left empty was to be drained of the blood of her body, the warmth of her heart, the stuff of life. Erik Erikson, the early psychoanalyst whose divinations are more those of the artist than the clinician, has not exaggerated in writing that such hurt can be re-experienced in each menstruation: "It is crying to heaven in the mourning of the child; and it becomes a permanent scar in the menopause."[7] It is an impertinence on the part of men to interpret this suffering by suggesting that women want, above all, what a man has: an exterior equipment and ease of access to woman's inner space; and it is foolishness on the part of militant feminists who, by their shrill demands for so-called equality, provide corroboration of simplistic penis-envy theorising. The "void" that can arise within the inner space of a woman has a tragic profundity that cannot be explained away by male chauvinistic presentations, or by the denials of the gender-feminists of the 1980s and 1990s. Beyond their naive and superficial renderings of women's perplexities, in Defoe's daring meditation on menstruation, so accusatory of male arrogance, so unprecedented in English literature, we are abruptly halted and, to our discomfort, commanded to gaze upon his hermeneutic findings of womankind's anguish. His denunciation of male indifference to the dolour, ordained and intractable, is a chilling reproof to every man. Unpalatable as the facts may be to some militant feminists, it was not a woman who was Britain's first feminist: it was the man Daniel Defoe; it was he who understood, far better than they do themselves, what lies behind their frantic protestations.

Defoe insisted that Nature would bring dire punishment upon those who, by coitus, breached the boundaries set by Leviticus: they, and the children thus illicitly conceived, would be physically disfigured, literally "branded" by "Marks of Infamy"; for Defoe, psyche and soma were one indivisible; the sinners would pay a terrible price for ravaging the sacred groves of a woman's space. His anticipations of psychosomatic diagnoses of sickness are sometimes extravagant, often erroneous, but they cannot be dismissed as intemperate ravings. Indeed, belatedly, after psychoanalysts retreated for so long from the sexuality and the body-ego concepts that Freud related to the very foundations of the psyche,[8] we now find women analysts engaging in seminars which try to interpret the language of the menarchial;[9] it does not, of course, speak to them of the stigmata that Defoe imagined upon the miscreants who had disobeyed Nature's law, but it does identify the soul sickness which can find bodily expressions—as in severe menstrual pain or in pre-menstrual behavioural instability. These analysts cannot help their clients without relating the somatic concomitants of the illness they present to the conflicts buried in their unconscious. Defoe's attribution of a physically expressed disease to an unnatural desire, although archaic in its formulation, is not to be scorned as primitive superstition; in his own inimitable way he was telling us that biology is destiny, that the intractable vicissitudes that woman, the child-producer, experiences must be respected and that those who would ignore the monthly reminder of her role and her worth should be outlawed.

When, however, women claim Defoe as an early feminist, they rarely cite *Conjugal Lewdness* as proof. Still seared by the extravagances of the gender-feminists of the past century, such women suspect as patronising any focus on the irrevocable disadvantages of women; they, understandably, prefer to concentrate on the man-made handicaps. They therefore choose to call in aid of their claim Defoe's earlier optimistic and romantic little essay *The Education of Women*, which is devoid of the tragic overtones of the ecclesiastical preacher to be found in *Conjugal Lewdness*. There, the youthful idealistic ameliorist tells us not of the intractable biological differences between the sexes but of how all differences can be surmounted:

> The great distinguishing difference, which is seen in the world between men and women, is in their education; . . . The soul is placed in the body like a rough diamond; and must be polished, or the lustre of it will never appear. And 'tis manifest, that as the rational soul distinguishes us from brutes; so education carries on the distinction, and makes some less brutish than others. This is too evident to need any demonstration. But why then should women be denied the

benefit of instruction? If knowledge and understanding had been useless additions to the sex, God Almighty would never have given them capacities; for he made nothing needless. . . . And, without partiality, a woman of sense and manners is the finest and most delicate part of God's Creation, the glory of Her Maker, and the great instance of His singular regard to man, His darling creature: to whom He gave the best gift either God could bestow or man receive. And 'tis the sordidest piece of folly and ingratitude in the world, to withhold from the sex the due lustre which the advantages of education gives to the natural beauty of their minds.

A woman well bred and well taught, furnished with the additional accomplishments of knowledge and behaviour, is a creature without comparison. Her society is the emblem of sublimer enjoyments, her person is angelic, and her conversation heavenly. She is all softness and sweetness, peace, love, wit, and delight. She is every way suitable to the sublimest wish, and the man that has such a one to his portion, has nothing to do but to rejoice in her, and be thankful.[10]

Defoe, in this essentially naive essay with its embarrassing idealisation and over-valuation of woman's virtues, was looking forward to a millennium of domestic bliss that would result from improved female education. It is a work certainly not lacking in self-interest: the goal was to have wives whose education would benefit husbands. Defoe makes that unequivocally clear: "Not that I am for exalting the female government in the least; but in short, I would have men take women for companions and educate to be fit for it." Although the pungency of his argument could not be excelled, originality of content cannot be claimed. Defoe was adopting views presented by some distinguished women writers during the decades preceding his contribution.[11] In 1675 Mrs Woolley, who had herself been a mistress of a school, a governess and the wife of a Free School usher, thus displayed her feelings in a pamphlet:

Vain man is apt to think we are merely intended for the world's propagation, and to keep its human inhabitants sweet and clean, but, by their leaves, had we the same literature, he would find our brains as fruitful as our bodies . . . most in this depraved age think a woman learned enough if she can distinguish a husband's bed from another's.

And in 1706 Mary Astell had put forward the argument that men were destroying the possibility of marital companionship by depriving girls of a good education: "How can a man respect his wife when he has a contemptible opinion of her and her sex . . . so that folly and a woman are equivalent terms with him?" And indeed John Locke, albeit ambivalently, long before Defoe, had advocated a limited education for women—not for themselves, but rather to improve their capacity to educate their children in their earliest years. To recall Defoe's precursors when commenting on that essay is not intended to detract from the little work, for it is a splendid and cunning polemic subverting misogyny; but one suspects the exaggeration of its seminal significance and its ready acceptance, in particular by women academics, as a weighty contribution to the long battle against male prejudice come about because it offers a deceptively simplistic solution to a complex conundrum and, as a bonus, offers flattery, for it tells of "angelic" ladies conducting "heavenly conversations" offering men "sweetness" and "delight". Defoe himself in the wistful conclusion of his essay acknowledges the dream-like quality of his aspirations: the realisation of his ideal future—of well educated women ministering to the needs of men—is postponed indefinitely: "those Happy Days (if ever they shall be) . . . when men will be wise enough . . . to mend the defect of education in the female sex".

But a decade later when Defoe returns, in *Conjugal Lewdness*, to a scrutiny of the marriage relationship, one finds in that sombre work, so free of persiflage, no day-dreaming; the obstacles and impediments that must be overcome to achieve true and creative harmony within a marriage are unsparingly set out; the goal is achievable but there are no short cuts; jejune romantic posturings will not magically conjure up a lasting bliss. Reversing the social and educational disadvantages of women is not enough. Man has to acknowledge the separateness of women, to address woman as woman, to have and cultivate the sensibility to respect and respond to her essential differentiation, to her rhythm, to her especial sexuality. Defoe's manifesto is far more than a call to end the obvious man-made discriminations against womankind, far more than a plea for women's emancipation and far more than a demand that man should graciously, by an act of manumission, liberate womenfolk. When we follow Defoe in his explorations of the "Abuses" which he is indicting we are indeed being led by Britain's first feminist, the heterosexual male who, because of his extraordinary identification with the feminine side of his nature, could articulate his hermeneutical findings and tell us not only of women's creativity but of her accompanying anguishes, of her labour pains, emblematic of her fated condition, woman the dolorosa.

Like all true prophets, he was telling a society what it had no wish to hear. He was preaching that man was diminished when he approaches his woman totally lacking the exquisite delicacy her inescapable travails demand; he was defiantly preaching a doctrine of sensibility to one of the most coarse societies that has ever prevailed in Britain. The fact is that the presentation of the age of the Georges as a world of elegance is profoundly misleading; the physical remains of the period, the terraced houses by Wood, the palaces by Kent and Adams, the prints by Baskerville, the china by Wedgwood, the delicate furniture, the paintings depicting diaphanously clothed ladies toying with fragile teacups and attended by young men immaculate in silk and satin, all create an illusion of a world of calm urbanity and restrained good breeding. That world may have been inhabited by the small wealthy class; but, as the historian Sir John Plumb well taught us, the overwhelming majority of London's denizens lived in a savage city replete with "violence and aggression, with coarse language and gruff manners, with dirt, disease and lust".[12] When Defoe wrote *Conjugal Lewdness* London was a stinking mud-bespattered metropolis pulsating with slums where thieves flourished, tuberculosis was rampant and infants died like flies. He was living among what Plumb described as "a callous people" whose popular sights were the lunatics in Bedlam, the whipping of half-naked women at the Bridewell, the stoning to death of pilloried men and women and the public hangings at Tyburn where a girl and a boy might be seen dangling between a highwayman and a murderer. The most obvious feature of English life in the eighteenth century was its love of aggression: "Rarely has the world known a more aggressive society, or one in which passions were more openly or violently expressed." No nation rioted more easily or more savagely; angry mobs, burning and looting, were as prevalent as disease and as frequent in the countryside as in the great towns.

With this as the ugly backcloth, it is all the more astonishing that

Defoe was capable of distancing himself from the surrounding vicious social turbulence and of uncompromisingly affirming, in *Conjugal Lewdness*, that the supreme virtue was constraint and that only by its exercise within the "holy ordinance" of marriage could man and woman find sexual fulfilment and the happiness of true love. A man who all his life had been so heavily engaged in the political battles of his era, now disengaged; in this mature work he sheds illusions that all humanity's dilemmas were capable of political resolution; only in unsullied personal relations between man and wife can the tragedy of life be eased. All our public clamour and our conceits, our bittersweet successes, our fulfilled and unfulfilled ambitions, can be relegated if we truly love. It is a romantic conclusion presented in starkly brutal terms; the "abuses" which sabotage true love must be identified, acknowledged and eliminated or mitigated; the saboteurs are to be condemned and outlawed.

★   ★   ★   ★   ★   ★   ★   ★   ★   ★

Defoe's severity and judgemental hectoring may not commend him to today's professional gentle mediating marriage guidance counsellors; but they should hesitate before disqualifying him from being awarded the accolade of Britain's first marriage guidance counsellor. His unsparing investigation of marriage disharmony levers to the surface the buried animosity, the unspoken humiliations, that can subvert a conjugal relationship. Because he wrote as a woman he insisted that the married woman must enjoy respect, admiration and the right to enjoy her sexuality; she was not to be treated as either angel or whore. So, understanding her needs, Defoe, having left in his meditations on women's periodicity his male readers discomfited, and perhaps squirming, proceeds to discuss next their greatest fear, impotence, and he focuses upon the particular consequence to the wife of that condition, of the deprivation she suffers: "She is strong, in perfect vigour, the Spirits high, the Blood hot, and perhaps boiling; Nature forward, and craving Desire unsatisfied." When writing of a man's impotence and of a woman "not able to receive the embraces of her lord without the utmost extremity of pain and disorder", Defoe knew he was wandering into dangerous territory, an excursion upon which his already discomfited and castigated male readers would resist accompanying him; impotence and female frigidity make for frightening, not attractive, viewing. But he would not desist; he would not diminish or exaggerate the

significance and importance of sexuality within a marriage but was
determined too, however elisively, to insist that the total absence of
sex in marriage was a threat to its stability, that the issue could not
be ignored or sidetracked, that it must be faced and, if possible,
remedied; but if it was intractable, then partners with understanding
and mutual sympathy could come to terms with the condition and
still live in love and harmony.

Acutely aware that his credentials as a diagnostician and healer
able to proffer prophylactics to remedy or mitigate the banes of impotence and vaginisimus could be challenged, he pretends that "Such
infirmities, Physicians, Acoucheurs or Surgeons, and Anatomists
understand, and can describe them; 'tis none of my Business, much
less my Design." But this disclaimer is but a placatory ruse to
reassure apprehensive readers that they will not, as with his meditation on menstruation, be assailed, that he will spare them and himself the embarrassment of a merciless probe into the humiliating
condition; and then, having thus disarmed them, gently, he in fact
insouciantly leads them into a sympathetic review of both the psychological and physical precipitates that bring about a devastated
sexless marriage. But when couples come together:

> their Constitutions may, as too often their Tempers may and do, dif-
> fer from one another, with respect to these Things, to the greatest
> Extreme; one is weak, faint and the Spirits low, Nature unable to
> answer what is expected; another perhaps is reduced by Child-
> bearing, too sick and too long together, by Accident in often hard
> and difficult Travail, Injuries received by unskilful Hands, or many
> other Incidents and Circumstances not to be named; by these, I say
> the Person is reduced, debillitated, and render'd unfit to give the
> Satisfaction which has formerly been found; On the other hand, the
> Man is reduced by a tedious, lingering decay, which Physicians call
> a Consumption; or by other acute Distempers, which he can, as is
> said before, account for without scandal; and to which Men are fre-
> quently subject, and as much disabled by them, as Women are in the
> cases mentioned just now; such as Stone, Gout, Palsies, Epilepsies,
> Rheumaticks, Dropsies, and such like.

Defoe, as was his wont, by intuition here conflates psyche and soma,
or, to use his own vocabulary, soul and body, in order to present his
description of the woes of the impotent and the frigid; he tells of a

woman, after bearing two children, becoming cold and being "actually destroyed, I might have said murthered" through having to submit to "conjugal Violences", and of a man who "sits under the Weight of his own Deficiencies; he is ashamed to decline the Duty of the Marriage-bed, disdains to be thought unable to satisfy". Defoe, now sixty-seven, himself suffering from gout and gallstones, well knew the organic origins of some sexual handicaps, but, anticipating in an extraordinary fashion present-day clinicians' findings, he clearly understood that the causation of most sexual inhibitions displayed in impotence and frigidity was not physical; the sickness lay in the soul, and, at first, we find the usually decisive, indeed the over-decisive, Defoe hesitating to engage in the required demanding soul-searching.

Today's clinicians with patients suffering from impotence or frigidity, when considering the aetiology of the sexual inadequacies of their patients, do not exclude their physical ailments or the widespread use, as prophylactics, of psychotropic drugs which may induce a marked decline in their sexual drive; and they acknowledge that sometimes anatomical factors, such as malformations or cancer of the penis or the susceptibility of the clitoris to displacement during intercourse, are the source of the troubles; but they have long since learned that these cases are infrequent in comparison with those arising from psychological disorders, and that surgery or pharmacology is rarely an answer to their patients' problems.[13] With men a common type of impotency results from an unconscious identification of the wife with the mother or sister, leading to the assertion of the incest taboo, and the consequences which appear are the inhibiting castration anxieties, leaving him too fearful to perform; and with some neurotic women one frequent cause of frigidity is that the woman is using it both as a weapon against her husband and as a punishment for her guilty self; she inflicts upon herself dyspareunia—painful intercourse—in which the vaginal sphincter muscles close tightly and obstruct, or partially obstruct, the entry of the penis. Many and various are the psychic conflicts that find physical expression in a man's impotence and a woman's frigidity.

Defoe's recommendation that the understanding and treatment of impotence and frigidity should be left to "Acouchers and Anatomists", his " 'tis none of my Business", was an evasion; two hundred years before Freud's divinations of the unconscious forces masking these conditions, Defoe well understood that the answers could not be given by those who at most claimed a professional capacity to deal with physical ailments. But he hesitated; a probe could open his own wounds; intuitively he would have known that castration anxieties are the inhibitors resulting in impotence. Defoe's manhood was always under threat from his especial feminine identification, and a full scrutiny of the phenomena of impotence would awaken his anxieties. Yet he could not forbear to leave the subject so unsatisfactorily suspended. Somehow, without threat to himself, he wanted to awaken his readers to the possibilities that impotence and frigidity, with all their attendant woes, could be overcome or mitigated. So, distancing himself from the pain and discomfort that the further needed investigation could bring to him personally, he used his wondrous imagination to create a Never-Never land where the hapless married partners would, under state aegis, be brought together and, in a private court presided over by experienced persuaders, could thus unburden themselves; Defoe, centuries before psychotherapists or marriage guidance counsellors, in informal or formal settings, proffered opportunities for healing catharses, was canvassing the need for such facilities.

Deadpan, without a hint of irony, Defoe in this hitherto brutally frank and realistic dissertation suddenly, with no suggestion that what he was about to tell was anything but fact, launches into an aside telling of the benign family courts of the "Turks". The credulous reader is invited to believe in the existence and efficacy of these courts equipped to deal wisely with the sexual problems of man and wife. In pursuit of this fiction, Defoe tells us how seriously the Turks take the weighty problem:

> The Turks think this very Case, whether of the Man's Side or the Woman's, to be so weighty, as that it deserves the interposition of Authority; the Grand Vizier in Person, where he can be applied to, and in more extraordinary cases, hears the causes himself; in other cases the graver Kadelefchers, and Judges determine it; where both the Man and Wife are fully examined and Judgement given as the circumstances require. I am assured also, that Judgement is given in those cases, not in a ludicrous manner with game and sport, and a Court, or rather Crowd, standing round to laugh and make a jest either of one Side or other; but with a solemn Gravity, suitable at

least to the dignity of the Judge who passes the Sentence, and to the reverence which both Sides pay to the Laws themselves.

And, lest it be thought inappropriate to propose to a Christian people the use of a Muslim juridical technique to resolve marital sexual problems, Defoe attempts to reassure any doubting readers by claiming the ancient lineage and universality of this therapeutic method:

> Nor is the Method wholly Turkish, and to be objected against as a piece of Mahometan Original; but 'tis founded upon the antient usage of all the Eastern Countries, in whose customs it is to be found, though with some variation, even as far back as the Phenician and Carthaginian Empires, and as the Egyptian and Persian Governments and Monarchies.

For Defoe to claim that history and geography provided clear corroboration of the value of the method was, of course, outrageous *chutzpah*; but he was never loath, in a good cause, to imaginatively provide the fictions to support his case. He was too vulnerable himself to attempt to explicate unequivocally the aetiology of impotence and frigidity; but, at one remove, he conjured up the forum in which partners, by privately talking together with an intermediary, could discharge the emotions attaching to a previously repressed experience which was the inhibitory precipitate of their unfortunate condition, a forum where, to use today's psychoanalytical language, they could abreact.

Defoe, however, was far too much of a realist to believe that there was any imminent possibility of such marriage counselling becoming available, but his sympathy for the wife unable to "receive" her husband was too great to leave her without some comfort, and so he invented a romantic tale which could bring some solace:

> There was a certain reigning Prince not long ago alive in the World; I do not say there are many such left, who after having had five Sons, and most of them Men of Fame as well as high Birth, and still living, had this particular Circumstance attending his Marriage-bed; his Princess was reduced to such Weakness, by frequent Child-bearing, that she was not able to receive the Embraces of her lord without the

utmost Extremity of Pain and disorder; and went so far that she was at last obliged to discover it to him, but did it with so much Modesty and Goodness, that she offered him to consent to his taking any other Lady which he might approve of to supply her place.

She insisted upon the reasonableness of it, in that she believed her consenting to it, and from such evident adversity, might make it lawful; nay, she pressed the Prince to it very earnestly, offering herself to find out an agreeable person for it, and to bring her to him.

The generous Prince received her first Declaration, intimating her own weakness and infirmity, with a concern of Pity and Affection as became a tender Husband, which he always had been to her, and assured her he would not offend her, or offer anything to injure or disorder her. He smiled at her Proposal but told her, No; since providence had thought fit to deny him the satisfaction he used to have in the embraces of his own wife, he hoped he was too much of a Christian as not to break God's Laws to gratify natural desires; and that he had so much the Government of himself also as to not let his appetite get the mastery of his reason; and with this noble Resolution declined the offer his wife made him of another Lady, and kept himself single, as it may be called, to the last.

It is a "pretty, happy-ever-after" fairy-story extolling the virtues of nobility and self-sacrifice, and no doubt its imagining brought some comfort to the ageing Defoe mourning the loss of his own virility. But, more, the tale was a fitting conclusion to the section within Defoe's tome which so courageously and stoically wrestled with the problem of sexual disorders that can wreak such havoc within a marital relationship. The miseries of impotence and frigidity announce the capitulation of life and zest to depression and fears. In any promiscuous society, like ours and Defoe's, overvaluing sexual prowess, obsessed with tumescences and orgasms but frightened of true love and commitment, impotence and frigidity become terrifying impairments. Today we see widespread efforts made to ward off the impairment by desperate pill-popping of Viagra or so-called "chemical treatments" at the proliferating, profit-making "clinics"; the websites and the columns of agony aunts reveal how considerable are present-day anxieties that penile erections and orgasms are not always available; in women's magazines

these are the subjects of endless articles, often graphically illustrated; but nevertheless in private discourse it is spoken of fur-
tively, in whispers; it is not a subject dwelt upon at the dinner
tables of the so-called emancipated chattering classes. In *Conjugal
Lewdness* Defoe shows no such diffidence; he outspokenly confronts
the condition, remarkably anticipates the aid that psychotherapists
today can sometimes provide and bestows an exquisite compassion
upon those suffering from the ailment. Only the curmudgeonly can
withhold admiration from this man who, against the current, in a
coarse vulgar and Philistine era, so boldly and sensitively asserted
the humanistic values and insights that could and should belong to
a civilised society.

His fervour and confidence in asserting those humanist values
came primarily from a profound and particular religious conviction; and this becomes increasingly transparent as he moves us
away from his consideration of the dilemmas of the sexless marriage and invites us to condemn contraception and abortion. It
was Defoe's belief that nowhere had a magnanimous God more
revealed His generosity than in His readiness to share His creativity with humankind; it was that belief that had led Defoe to dwell
upon the tragedy of sexual disability which bars the sufferers from
enjoying the divine gift; and that belief was why Defoe regarded
those who, by contraception and abortion, dared to reject creativity
as abhorrent blasphemers. And because women, not men, were the
supreme creators—men being mere incidental fertilisers—practices
frustrating women, denying their capacity to bring forth a child,
were violations, "abuses", that fell far more harshly upon women.
Those married women who colluded in such avoidance strategies
were self-destructive, were betraying themselves and their sex:

> What! Give herself away for nothing! Mortgage the Mirth, the Free-
> dom, the Levity and all the Pleasures of her Virgin-state, the Honour
> and Authority of being her own, and at her own dispose, and all
> this to be a Barren Doe, a wife without children; a Dishonour to her
> Husband, and a Reproach to herself! Can any Woman in her Wits do
> thus? ... In a word, she would have the Use of the Man, but she
> would not act the Part of the woman; she would have him to be the
> Husband, but she would not be a Wife and, if you bear the blunt Stile
> that some People put it into, she would only keep a Stallion.

Such sentiments were out of kilter with the mood of the increasingly promiscuous society of Defoe's day; devotees of the new permissiveness could not have relished his diatribes against those who, by lacking a sense of wonder at the creative potential of the sperm and ovum, would endeavour in coition to sever sex from birth; for Defoe that left sex impoverished, joyless, a poor thing. The delights of sex were enhanced by its association with holy creation; without that link, sex became trivialised—and for Defoe there was no sin more heinous than loveless, trivial sex. And to ensure his readers would fully grasp how great was the sin, Defoe regales us with gruesome tales of the punishments, physical and psychological, brought upon themselves by men, and especially women, who sought by potions and other means to thwart conception or to precipitate miscarriages.

Defoe was too passionate a life-lover, too aware, as we have seen in our readings of *The Plague* and of *The Storm*, of the threat that the masochistic attractions of death posed to him personally and to society, to condone the casualness of life deniers; unequivocally he stigmatised those who, by contraception or abortion, extinguished life as "murderers". He was impatient with those who rested their case for and against the right to abort on more equivocal issues, on notions of when the foetus acquired a soul; nor was he a Papist absolutist. The paramount consideration was to protect and conserve a woman's creativity; if that preservation endangered the woman, and in no other circumstances, should a birth be terminated. No man less in touch with his femininity than was Defoe would have dared to have been so condemnatory of the woman who despised herself and "shamed" her sex by giving up her most precious and unique asset, creativity, for frivolous copulation. It was with a woman's voice that Defoe, as one woman to another, erupted, denouncing such a woman as a whore and laying down the strict conditions which alone could acquit her of the charge:

> Had the Lady been with Child, and had a dangerous Travail, had she been frequently with child, but always subject to Abortions, or constant and dangerous Miscarriages; had she conceived any hurt in the delivery of her former Children, which threatened Dangers if she came again; or had several other Circumstances attended her, less proper to mention than those; had she been abused by Midwives, or weakened by Distempers or Disasters, this would alter the Case.

But the Circumstance I insist upon is, when the woman marries, takes a man to bed to her, with all the Circumstances that are to be understood, without obliging us to express them; lives with him, and lies with him every Night, and yet professes to desire she may have no children; these are the Circumstances I insist upon, the Aggravations of which admits no abatement, and for which I do not know one modest Word of Excuse can be said; this is what I call Conjugal Lewdness, nor can I see anything else in it; 'twas the plain end of her marrying; 'tis in vain to call it by other Names, and cover it with other Excuses; 'tis nothing but Whoring under the shelter or cover of the Law, we may paint it out and dress it up as we will.

The intemperance of Defoe's polemic may estrange some but my own involvement in the parliamentary proceedings concerning contraception and abortion preceding the legislative changes of the 1960s makes me aware and, perhaps, more understanding of the emotional turbulences inevitably accompanying open debates on these issues; they can, and perhaps should, prompt impassioned and conflicting extravagances by opinionated protagonists, for they bring out of the shadows into the public arena dangerous and profound concerns which timid politicians and governments, to the detriment of their electorates, prefer to ignore or suppress.

When, in 1967, after a long struggle, I succeeded in placing on the Statute Book my Family Planning Act, an Act which for the first time gave to local authorities the right to set up or support family planning clinics where contraceptive advice could be given to all and for which some, or nil, payment need be charged, I was yet again ruefully reminded how in politics you can choose your enemies but not your allies. Although I am proud that my seminal Act was to lead, after I and others pressurised the Government, to the establishment in 1974, within the National Health Service, of a full family planning service with contraceptive advice freely given to all, nevertheless I recall with distaste the arguments of many of those who supported my campaigning.[14] I recoiled from the essential morbidity of their enthusiasm for my cause. I spoke of planning parenthood and personal choice; they spoke of birth control, with the emphasis on control. They described unplanned children as "mistakes", with no appreciation of the unconscious need and demand of a woman for a child that often will mock at all contraceptives. They labelled the woman using no regular contraceptive technique as being "at risk", as if pregnancy was a disease. I wanted to aid parents to have planned, well spaced and happier families; they unconsciously begrudged the establishment of a family at all. They, of course, were zealous population planners, always apocalyptic in their prophesies of the consequences of over-population. All these "allies" were, in short, like deniers of the same ilk who so enraged Defoe. It is therefore no paradox that I should have some sympathies with his fierce denunciations.

And even more so do resonances resound for me as I read Defoe's condemnation of abortion and abortionists, of women the creators becoming the destroyers. When in 1967 the Abortion Bill was before Parliament, all my persistent attempts to modify its provisions, so that while addressing genuine concerns, life should never be treated in a cavalier fashion, were unsuccessful. The militant feminists of the day were determined to have a Bill that, in effect, gave them abortion on demand, and under a banner proclaiming their right to choose they savaged me for presumptuously questioning their motivation and succeeded in reaching their objectives. When, in 1973, I recorded the background to these events I commented in terms that I now find were only marginally less severe than the responses of Defoe:

> For my part I could never regard an abortion Bill, narrowly or widely drawn, as a triumph. Every failure we make to plan so that every life within its puny transient span can live out its full potentiality is a defeat, just as the hanging of a murderer, every imprisonment of a rapist or traitor is a defeat for the community; these are the signs that the community does not know how to gauge loyalty, and an admittance by the nation of its failure to know how to deal with its failures. An abortion can result from a defeat because of a failure of medical science as yet unable to rescue a malformed unborn child from its fate; it can be precipitated by the selfishness of a society too indifferent to save women and children from intolerable housing conditions; it can come from a vengeful society now sophisticating its hostility to the illicit love of the unmarried by proffering abortion rather than providing the financial and social support desperately needed. Worst of all, it is a defeat for women. It is illusory to claim abortion on demand is an extension of women's freedom; on the contrary, it is an enslavement. It enslaves her to the selfishness of the narcissistic lover

fearful of taking the step towards parenting and maturation, even as it enslaves too her husband who treats her as a convenience to be periodically flushed out. Abortion on demand is a triumph not for women but for the men who fear to love, to give themselves to love, the thwarted men who, evoking their initial expelling, of rejection as babes, release their hatred upon all womankind, working off their own scores against mothers by slaying motherhood. Legislation can sing with love and concern; but it can also be replete with envy and revenge. The politics of the abortionist lobby are the politics of hate.[15]

Such a perspective differs little from that maintained by Defoe in *Conjugal Lewdness*. He refused to concede that a woman had a fundamental right to abort herself; she had a fundamental right of choice of a different order, the right to love, and as the work unfolds in chapter after chapter he vehemently assails those who, in his society, by denying her that right, maimed her, preventing her fulfilment. She alone, he insisted, has the right to choose whom she can marry, free of parental or any other pressures; it was her right to refuse to enter into a marriage governed by material or status considerations and no woman, when yearning for another, should be coerced into matrimony. Repeatedly he imports into his argument the governing principles which he often stated in the columns of his *Review*: "The great duty between man and wife is love, and the only obedience is obligingness on both sides; Love knows no superior or inferior, no imperious Command on one hand, no reluctant Subjection on the other." Without love, Defoe maintained, neither virtue nor fidelity, nor "Conscience of the Conjugal Duty", nor religion, nor "goodness in submission" on the part of the wife could create a good marriage.

As Defoe scholars have pointed out,[16] his view of the role of women was far removed from those of writers of his period like Richard Steele, who often claimed in his *Spectator* to be a "friend" to woman and "Guardian to the Fair". Steele's claim to be the champion of women was doubtless influenced by his wish to increase the circulation of *The Spectator*; the number of potential women readers was growing. But Steele never conceded equality to women. He deplored any ambition in women on the grounds that it was undesirable for themselves as well as for men: "for their own Happiness and Comfort, as well as that of those for whom they were

born", they ought to consider themselves "no other than an additional Part of the Species" made to adorn their fathers, husbands,
brothers or children. Steele's ideal wife has:

> no other concern but to please the Man I love; he is the End of
> every Care I have; if I dress 'tis for him, if I read a Poem or Play
> 'tis to qualify myself for a Conversation agreeable to his Taste; he
> is almost the End of my Devotions, half my Prayers are for his
> Happiness.[17]

Such ideal women were soon to be depicted in Henry Fielding's
novels. In his *Amelia*, the heroine is idealised only by her divestment
of the normal rights and claims of a human being; she is an angel,
ready constantly to give up everything to an errant husband. These
patronising attitudes to women displayed by Steele and Fielding
are not to be found in Defoe; he treated women as equals; he could
not do otherwise; his singular temperament made him as much a
woman as a man. Coleridge's comment that "the truth is a great
mind must be androgynous" is certainly apposite to Defoe; and
when Virginia Woolf, aware of Coleridge's comment, wrote in *A
Room of One's Own* that "in each of us two powers preside, one male
one female", she was in error in Defoe's case in adding that in the
man's mind the man predominates, and in the woman the woman's.
Defoe's psychic hermaphrodism ensured that neither the man's voice
nor the woman's predominated.

Proffering women stylised sentiments and refined emotions was
regarded by Defoe's literary contemporaries as sufficient compensation to balance the prevailing glaring inequalities between the sexes;
but Defoe knew that the imbalances, if they were to be redressed
to produce relationships in which love flourished, needed more
than the corrective of flowery words and extravagant praise. It
is true that on occasion, with tongue in cheek, as in his *Historical
Collections* and his feuilleton *Education of Women*, he played the flirt
and in fashionable manner over-praised women; but there are no
such insipid sentimentalities to be found in *Religious Education* or
Conjugal Lewdness when we find him seriously engaged in discuss-
ing the relationship between husband and wife. Defoe's own preoccupation with money, upon which we have frequently remarked,
and his own feminine sense of practicability, distance him from

the vapourings of his literary contemporaries. Not for him the notion that marriage requires a woman to be economically dependent upon the man. The economic exploitation of wives was an issue which the sentimentalist particularly wanted to smother in finer feelings;[18] but Defoe incited women to gain economic independence. He counselled that a woman should not marry without assurance that her husband had an estate and would use it to provide for her: "You must have his Estate appear, your Part be settled, and the Land bound to you . . . you will have it under Hand and Seal, so that he shall not be able to go back." In the next century Charles Dickens was to sneer at what he claimed was Defoe's "insensibility" to romance, but it has been well said that it was Dickens, not Defoe, who was hostile and exploitative towards woman.[19] Defoe saw marriage as a mutual relationship in which both parties expected concrete gains—because he saw women in the same terms as he saw men.

Perhaps that is why Defoe, who could become so impassioned over faults that today we may regard as mere peccadilloes, nevertheless appears to have a much more relaxed attitude to the importance of chastity[20] and did not even condemn out of hand the wife who committed the paramount sin of adultery. He declared that it was a man's business to "preserve the Affection of his Wife entire", for "if she is once brought . . . to have an aversion to him . . . she must . . . be more Christian than he ought to expect of her, if she does not single out some other Object of her Affections". This tolerance puts us on enquiry. Did Defoe come with clean hands? On at least two occasions, once in respect of a fishwife (an oyster-seller), and another in respect of a woman at whose home he was sheltering from debtors, his enemies accused him of adultery, charges which he heatedly denied. But was he never an errant husband? And did his transgressions reveal themselves in an over-determined insistence upon the values and exclusiveness of what he described as the "holy ordinance of marriage"? Was *Conjugal Lewdness*, at least in part, a reparative confessional?

Defoe himself has given us the answer. It is to be found within the interstices of the poem he set out on the title page of *Conjugal Lewdness*. The relevance of his poem to the content of the work may not immediately be apparent, but before the work ends the attentive reader will have understood its full significance:

Loose Thought, at first, like subterranean Fires
Burn inward, smothering, with unchast Desire;
But getting Vent, to Rage and Fury turn,
Burst in Volcano's, and like Aetna burn;
The Heat increases as the Flames aspire,
And turns the solid Hills to liquid Fire.
So sensual Flames, when raging in the Soul,
First vitiate all the Parts, then fire the Whole;
Burn up the Bright, the Beauteous, the Sublime,
And turn our lawful Pleasures into Crime.

Defoe had clearly been seared by his lapses. He had experienced
"the subterranean Fires". His condemnation of the promiscuous
society was a projection of the condemnation he imposed upon himself. At all costs, "the Bright, the Beauteous, the Sublime" was to be
protected, insulated from scorching lust. If his passions had been
less torrid, his sermonising would have been tepid; but he knew, as
his poem corroborates, the full power and strength of human sexuality; and he, as the extraordinary container of both man's desires and
woman's passions, affirms that that driving power, that force, must
be harnessed, never squandered. Only then, with all obstacles, all
"abuses", removed, within the boundary walls of marriage, could
the "Sublime" be attained. Defoe was aligning himself with the force
described by Aristophanes in Plato's *Symposium*: "the force which
calls back the hearts of our original nature; it tries to make one of
two and heal the wound of human nature . . . Eros is the name for
our pursuit of wholeness, for our desire to be complete."[21] It is, of
course, an impossible desire, a vain pursuit even for someone like a
Daniel Defoe, advantaged by a hermaphrodite disposition. But it is
a grand chase. In recent years some women psychoanalysts have
joined in this pursuit of the hermaphrodite ideal. They have, in
particular, drawn on the work of the great French anthropologist
Georges Bataille, who made a fundamental distinction between
the "animal" and "normal" sexuality and what he regarded as
"true" human sexuality blessed with an eroticism, possessed of a
profound desire and a deep longing to return to continuity.[22] This,
Bataille proposes, is the profound desire in us discontinuous beings
which sends us on the quest to re-establish the lost continuity
from which we have been severed, and so escape from our lonely

separateness and fill the gap. The Israeli psychoanalyst Ruth Stein has sympathetically interpreted Bataille:

> Though it is impossible to cross the borders and totally emerge with the other, the very conceiving of such a possibility enables one to look with the other human beings into the abyss that lies between them, and to feel together the dizziness accruing from a joint looking. This to Bataille is essentially what arouses sexual excitement, what creates sexual ripples and shudders that transform plain "animal sexuality" into eroticism, with its heightened mental and spiritual power.[23]

Conjugal Lewdness is a testament to Defoe's belief in such transcendental possibilities. His was a conviction that the bi-sexuality which was ever being played out in his interior life could be exteriorised and bear an analogous fusion; a "sublime beauteous" coming together could be enacted. Believing human beings could, by a scrupulous maturing of love in marriage, in sex release their potential to fuse with each other and the universe, he deplored those who in his society, as in ours, wasted their especial endowment in grubby and silly recreational sex. We today would be wise to heed the reproaches of this passionate Puritan.

Notes

1. West, R., *The Life and Strange Surprising Adventures of Daniel Defoe*, Harpers, 1997.
2. Stone, L., *The Family, Sex and Marriage in England, 1500–1800*, Penguin Books, 1979.
3. Defoe, D., *Conjugal Lewdness or Matrimonial Whoredom*, 1727.
4. Disraeli, B., *Venetia*, 1837.
5. Kuhs, W., *Times Literary Supplement*, 26 November 2004.
6. Plato, *Symposium*, c.371 BC.
7. Erikson, E., Inner and outer space: reflections on womanhood, *Dadelus*, 93 (1964), 582–606.
8. See Chapter 3, pp. 16–17.
9. Panel discussion, What has happened to the body in psycho-analysis?, International Psycho-analytical Association, March 2004.
10. Defoe, D., *The Education of Women*, 1719.

11. Stone, *The Family, Sex and Marriage in England 1500–1801*, Penguin Books, 1979.
12. Plumb, J. H., *The First Four Georges*, Fontana Collins, 1983.
13. Abse, D. W., *Sexual Disorder and Marriage: Marriage Counselling in Medical Practice*, University of North Carolina Press, 1964.
14. Abse, L., *Fellatio, Masochism and Politics*, Robson Books, 2000, pp. 173–5.
15. Abse, L., *Private Member*, Macdonalds, 1973, p. 217.
16. Rogers, K., *Women in the Eighteenth Century*, A. M. Hakkert, 1976.
17. Steele, R., *The Spectator*, nos 254 and 342.
18. Rogers, *Women in the Eighteenth Century*.
19. Ibid.
20. Ibid.
21. Plato, *Symposium*.
22. Bataille, G., *Eroticism: Death and Sexuality*, San Francisco Lights Books, 1996.
23. Stein, R., The poignant, the excessive and the enigmatic in sexuality, *International Journal of Psychoanalysis*, 7 (April 1998).

CHAPTER FIFTEEN

Crusoe's island

T imorous literary critics and hesitant social historians continue to fear engagement with Defoe's challenging, and sometimes chilling, work *Conjugal Lewdness*; it lies neglected. But the island story of Robinson Crusoe has become overloaded with comment and interpretation. Ever since its first publication in 1719, it has commanded attention. During Defoe's lifetime there were six reprintings and almost at once the novel was pirated, plagiarised, abridged and imitated in English, and translated into German, French and Dutch. It has been calculated that by the end of the following century there existed, including adaptations, translations and English editions, some seven hundred versions of the Crusoe story. The responses and resonances Crusoe has occasioned continue, never more than in the twentieth century and, as now, into the twenty-first. In a recent masterful essay, Doreen Roberts tells us: "The Crusoe story has the almost autonomous life, the resonance and versatility of a myth, and Crusoe, whether admired or deplored, is a culture-hero, 'the English Ulysses', as James Joyce called him."[1] We have had Crusoe presented to us as light entertainment in play, film, panto, and even "Crusoe on ice"; and we have had, within the avalanche of literature on the true meaning of *Crusoe*, darker intimations; Crusoe the racist, Crusoe the imperialist, Crusoe the anti-feminist, Crusoe the devil, even Crusoe as God.[2] None of us, as children or as adults, seem able to resist the lure of the island tale; sometimes it excites, sometimes thrills or repels us, but always prompting admiration of the creativity, resilience and stamina that we are witnessing. When Defoe, the stubby, scruffy, warty boatman, offers us a trip to this desolate island, despite his appearance and the arid destination, none of us seem capable of refusing his invitation. Desert islands are irresistible.

It has ever been so; in every region of the world the belief may be found that there does exist somewhere, usually in a western sea, a magical island. In Europe it goes under various names: Meropis, the Continent of Kronos, Ogygia, Atlantis, the Garden of the Hesperides and The Fortunate Isle. On mediaeval maps we find the actual position of the isle; it can be seen in Hereford Cathedral's "Mappa Mundi" of the thirteenth century, as in the twelfth-century map of the world in Corpus Christi College, Cambridge. The location is always in the west, a compass point which from the Odyssey[3] onwards has always been associated with the idea of death; indeed, in not a few languages a usual expression for dying is "to go west".

Despite its name, "The Fortunate Isle" in folk beliefs, as in the individual unconscious, is the abode of the dead;[4] the Isle is a uterine conception of death, a womb symbol; in dying one simply returns from whence one came. The lure of an island visit, which we all experience, is not only in all the paradisical delights that we fantasise will await us, but also in the hidden pleasurable masochistic desires which on the island will find consummation in death. The mediaeval caricatures of the concept of the Fortunate Isle, which we find in Cockaigne and Schlarassenland where roast ducks parade in the streets and wine flows in the rivers, tells us only of the one side of the island, the side where the sun always shines and nature is bountiful; but there is a darker, sunless, menacing side where dead souls wander. In our imagination, according to our temperament and, indeed, according to our mood, we make our choice of the landing-stage upon which we shall disembark, that marked "Eden" or that inscribed "Tsunami". Predictably, Defoe, as we have repeatedly observed, ever only precariously holding his masochism in check, made his choice and placed Crusoe on a bleak, inhospitable, barren isle.

In our daytime reveries, in our dreams, nostalgically we look back to an imagined intra-uterine life where we enjoyed instant gratifications; there, in an amniotic sac the foetus floated peacefully, with the placenta feeding it, providing it with oxygen and cleaning its blood of carbon dioxide and waste. To that ideal, in fantasy we return; but the return revives less agreeable sensations, the constrictions imposed in the newly cramped womb as it lengthens and gains weight, which presage the distress it suffers as involuntarily it is painfully expelled. A voyage to our womb-island may involve a very rough crossing; perhaps that is why even a little innocent trip to an island is accompanied by an especial frisson not present when one makes a mainland journey. Upon Crusoe Defoe imposed more than a frisson of fear; a mighty storm had to be braved before, shipwrecked, he scrambled on to his forlorn isle. Yet, whatever the hazards, few can turn a deaf ear to the siren calls inviting us to the magic isle; and often, by circuitous routes and improbable transport, we yield.

I cannot deny that there must have been a strong undercurrent to the tug which took me to the Shetland Islands to campaign against devolution to Scotland and Wales; to plead with Taiwan ministers in the island's capital Taipei for copyright protection on behalf of British publishers; and to address large gatherings on the island of Mauritius under the chairmanship of the former prime minister, the famed "Ram" who, confusing me with my brother Dannie, always introduced me as a "poet-politician". I would not plead mere chance that I have found myself on the platform at packed meetings at the Mansion House in Ireland's capital, urging the creation of a divorce law in Eire; or that for some years I became, in effect, the MP for the Seychelles, after a visit in the days before the islands had an airport and independence, as I insisted on putting its problems before the Commons; and I doubt whether it was just coincidence that in the midst of the early Tamil troubles in Sri Lanka, I found myself in heavy discussions with the then President Jayawardene in Colombo. The rational explanations I would afford for my presence on all these and other islands would rightly be suspect; Prospero's magic, sometimes black, reigns over all of us and the incantations coming from islands can dangerously bemuse us.

We covet our imagined wondrous isles; we will not release them from our dreams, and though they may be chimerical, we will not

easily yield to reality and see them as they are. On the Northern
Ireland issue, as on the Falklands, the politicians of all parties
fiercely attack interlopers who dare to scoff at their hallucinations.
No interventions I made during my thirty years in the Commons
brought upon me more fierce vituperation than when, in vain, I
sought to free our debates from the mythology in which they were
entangled. Ernest Jones, in his brilliant 1922 essay *The Island of
Ireland*, as relevant today as when it was written, has illuminated
for us how pernicious was the mythopoeia which bedevilled all
attempts to bring about a peaceful settlement in Northern Ireland. In
1974 I was howled down in a parliament vowing that no response
except extermination was to be the answer to the IRA, when
I insisted that talks were inevitable and desirable; and when, in defiance of the Government's Trappist stance, I went to Ulster and clan-
destinely in a no-go area met the assembled leadership of the IRA,
I found in the imagery enveloping their presentations chastening
corroboration of Ernest Jones's assertion that there was no other
culture more impregnated than the Irish with the various beliefs and
legends of an island paradise. The number of Erse names for it are
legion: Thierna na Oge (the Country of Youth), Tir-Innanbeo (the
Land of the Living), Tir Tairgare (the Land of Promise), Tirn-aill
(the Other Land), Mad Mell (the Agreeable Plain).

And even as the Magic Isles have so many names, so has the land
where the Catholic cult of the virgin mother reigns. The feminine
names abound: Caitlin Ni Houlihan, Morrin Ni Cullinan, Roisin
Dub (Little Black Rose), Shan van Vocht (Old Woman), Sau Bheau
Bhoctc (Dark Rosaleen), and the names of three Queens of Tuatha Di
Dannan, Eire, Bauba and Fodhla; all these names evoke ideas of
woman, mother, nurse and virgin. The two themes are connected;
surrealistically the Magic Islands and Ireland are superimposed
upon each other, glorified idealisations of an Irishman's birthplace.
With the English still refusing to abandon their right to call their
kingdom the British Isles, violence continues in Northern Ireland.
Britannia—with her Union Jack embossed heavily upon her shield
by the Ulster Unionists—has no place in the hierarchy of Irish
mythological figures. The myths collide in the heavens and on the
ground; men possessed by their fables relentlessly still slay each
other.

So too Thatcher's fantasies of the congruence between the island race of Britain and the kelpers of the Falklands, and her vision of the Malvinas as the Arcadian Isles, a glorified idealisation of every Englishman's birthplace, took us into an avoidable war. When, with only a few of us demurring, to applause Thatcher brought her speech to an end in the fateful Commons debate declaring war on the Argentine, she put forward an absurd proposition which cannot bear serious scrutiny: "The people of the Falklands, like the people of the United Kingdom, are an island race." No matter that an "island race" is a phantasmagoria, when dismayed I listened to her ringing declaration, I knew myth had overflown reality. Britain was on her way to regain Atlantis.

★ ★ ★ ★ ★ ★ ★ ★ ★ ★

As in all myths, unresolved ambiguities prevail in the magic island legend; logic is absent, definitive conclusions are eschewed, contradictions are unacknowledged and, in the archipelago of isles our unconscious constructs, we can find both paradisical atolls where all wishes are granted and others that are the cemeteries of dead souls. Although a tsunami may punish us for our hubris, still, never more than today, and responding to the travel agents' glossy brochures, by the thousands we make our hedonistic choice and escape to an island paradise in the sun where no shadows fall and no sinister intimations mar a brief sojourn. In this hiatus between burdensome weeks of disenjoyed work and days of insistent mortgage repayments, we act out our fantasies; and our hope is that, at least for a while, refreshed, indeed re-born, we return inoculated against the sickness prevailing in our faithless, narcissistic, competitive capitalist world. The magic island fantasy has always had a therapeutic function; and today the island, equipped with spas and providing life-enhancing massages, is sought to bring relief from the malady endemic to our dysfunctional society. On our chosen island we can dream of a world remote from apocalyptic threats of nuclear bombs, terrorists and ecological disasters.

So too did Defoe seek to use the telling of his island tale as therapy; but, even as the austere island of *Crusoe* is far removed from the packaged languorous Hawaii holiday island visited by work-depleted modern man, so must the ailment suffered by Defoe be differentiated from contemporary man's sickness. Defoe's sickness was psychosomatic; it was not occasioned by lack of communality or the sort of external societal pressures that press down upon today's alienated man, leaving him unable to tolerate the continued strain of his individuation; he goes off to his chosen island to obtain relief from the stresses contemporary capitalism has imposed upon him. But Defoe's dis-ease was lodged in his psyche; it was no infection he had picked up from a decomposing world; it sprang from an illness he had contracted in his mother's clumsy arms in his earliest days on earth. And the name we give to this excruciating malady is loneliness.

The gifted Defoe scholar G. A. Starr has perceptively identified the symptoms of the illness when writing of "Crusoe's elaborate self-enclosure", of "the task that preoccupies most of Defoe's characters ... each seeking a 'safe harbour' ... from the painful sense of his own isolation which is more or less explicitly regarded as punishment for his own or his parents' misdeeds".[5] That aloneness pervades Defoe's works. No man could have been more engaged in the politics and controversies of his period; he lived for most of his life amidst the tumult of public affairs and yet he walked alone. He was ever the loner, never fully committed to any faction or party. John Donne tells us that "no man is an island"; but that is a half-truth, an inspirational and moral declaration reminding us of our obligations to community; it is a denial of the full reality. When the bells toll, it is the survivors who hear them, not the dead man carried in the hearse to his grave. We may live together but we die alone; and it is that premonition of the inevitable which had possessed Defoe from his beginning to his end.

Never more than in that epic of loneliness, *Robinson Crusoe*, do we see Defoe using his works as therapy, as self-medication; none of his works more validates the hypothesis that an unempathic mother had left him singularly bereft of the comfort that soothing, reassuring nursing can provide; a solicitous mother can create the illusion of the intra-uterine state,[6] bestowing the warm darkness and the quiet; without it the babe's expulsion from the womb leaves him terrifyingly separate, alone; brusque weaning can leave the babe, bereft of his sustainer, fearful of abandonment; and a strict controlling mother peremptorily demanding he evacuates his bowels can leave the babe empty, desolated by his separation from his golden eggs, not a triumphant creator. The capacity to be alone, to enjoy and not to interpret solitude as threatening, originates, as the paediatrician and psychoanalyst Donald Winnicott has so eloquently explicated,[7] with the infant's experience of being alone in the presence of his mother. If the child's immediate needs for physical contact, food and warmth have been satisfied and there was no further need for the mother to be concerned with providing anything, nor any need for the child to be looking immediately to the mother for anything, then, at such moments, there is a blissful stillness. This relatedness between mother and child is the basis of a capacity to be alone. The paradox, Winnicott indicated, of the capacity to be alone is based on the experience of being alone in the presence of someone and without a sufficiency of this experience the capacity to be alone cannot be developed. A remote mother cannot bestow this capacity upon her child; for such a babe, solitude is not bliss; it is a menacing experience. And all his life he is fated to carry that painful sense of isolation which Starr finds in Defoe's characters.

Some of Defoe's pain was indeed to be unloaded on to his fictional characters, enabling him, with a lightened load, refusing to despair, to carry on stoically. The pains, however, were chronic, too grievous to be easily disposed of by him. The temptation would surely have been great to dose himself with analgesics even as does twenty-first-century man when he attempts to gain temporary relief from societally induced anomie in the holiday fantasy of a bountiful, aphrodisiacal island in the sun; but Defoe scorned such placebos. His psychic wound was deep and open; if the bleeding was to be staunched and a fatal suppuration was to be avoided, a radical rethink was required and a radical remedy found.

Some theologians making anthropological forays into biblical narratives have taught us that the original chroniclers displayed a different mode of thought, far different from our own mental process;[8] it was such a mental procedure, radically different to our usual analytic thinking, that Defoe used when, in a bid to cure his loneliness, he created the story of Robinson Crusoe. This mode of thought has been named "analogical thinking"; many cultures construct their world through such analogical thinking, which is more primitive than but not necessarily inferior to although so different from ours: "In analogical thinking, reality is seen as a complex system of correspondences in which given components may throw light on their counterparts or actually symbolise them."[9] We see such a correspondence being marvellously portrayed in the isolation and aloneness of Crusoe and the well nigh insufferable loneliness endured by Defoe.

Such a mode of thought was in an idiom with which Defoe was familiar; the man who as a child had been required to write out the whole of the Pentateuch[10] was well attuned, by osmosis if not consciously, to the manifold correspondences that abound between the literal texts of the Bible and that of an imagined cosmos. These correspondences, ever recurring in Talmudic commentaries of the rabbis, seem to have re-emerged in the interpretations of some latterday theological scholars.[11] The correspondences in Defoe's case were not, however, to be found in the stars, not in God's heaven, but on his fantasised island.

Analogical thinking may indeed yield truths still unproven. We recall Blake's proverb from hell: "What is now proved was once only imagined." The imagined correspondences may be too easily dismissed as superstitious magic by the more prosaic; sometimes they give answers to problems unheard by the over-rational. The Hebrew chroniclers sometimes found their correspondences in their Tabernacle, and sometimes modern theologians find them in the cosmos and, much less subtly, the tabloid astrologers find them in the stars.

Such a mode of thought easily accommodates, indeed welcomes, what the prudent would treat as extravagances. Defoe's fantasised island, where correspondences with his own desolate psychic conditions proliferated, was an ideal venue on which such an extravagance could be enacted; it was to be the island where therapy was to be made available for those stricken with the malady of loneliness. The treatment was the antithesis of that provided by today's easily accessible holiday island; instead of total relaxation, aromatherapy, thalassotherapy, yoga-like meditation and a diversity of massages, with every delicious food and every physical need serviced, Crusoe's isolated island offered a terrifyingly strict regime, a punitive sentence of solitary confinement where survival depended upon desperately arduous work; loneliness was to be trumped by utter loneliness, disease conquered by even more virulent infections. Only those who submitted for years to such a pitiless regime would leave the island purged of their sickness.

Robinson Crusoe is the work of Defoe the physician; here he is writing out a detailed prescription of the bitter potions to be taken as a cure for loneliness. But Defoe is no orthodox medical practitioner; he subscribes to the heretical medical tradition of homeopathy, a system of therapeutics based upon the "law of similars", *similia similibus curantur.* From the time of Hippocrates down to sixteenth-century Paracelsus until its formal exposition at the end of the eighteenth century by Samuel Hahnemann, in one form or another, homeopathy has been practised; in the medical profession in the twentieth century, it came under the stigma of being a dissenting sect but perhaps today, given the royal patronage bestowed on alternative medicine, it may be regarded by some with a little less scepticism. Among homoeopathists the longstanding debate has been how small or large should be the dosage of effective material given to the sick; on this question, Defoe certainly had no doubts. To treat his own loneliness, he inflicted upon his alter ego huge doses of aloneness. Even those condemned to life imprisonment, suffering solitary confinement, must have gaolers; but there were no custodians on Crusoe's island. For years he was left to fend for himself, utterly alone.

After twenty-five years of such treatment, Defoe displayed doubts. He feared that Crusoe on the sexless island could not continue to tolerate the regime imposed upon him; relief from the tensions was needed; onanism was not adequate; the dosage had to be reduced if the therapy was to succeed. To temper the isolation, Defoe produced Friday.

In introducing Friday, Defoe was following a pattern which Starr has, with insight, noted. Defoe's characters have a remarkable aptitude for acquiring surrogate parents and children:

> This pattern extends to such conduct manuals as The Family Instructor and Religious Courtship as well as the better-known first-person narratives; in all these books attachments between the sexes tend to be weaker than familial or quasi-familiar ones involving the dominance of one party—parent, child, master, mentor, governess, or God —and the submission of the other. Love is mentioned, but guilt and anxiety are the prevailing emotions, and give a sombre undertone.[12]

The filial relationship which, as mentor, Crusoe developed with Friday indeed has sombre and transgressive undertones. No imaginative novelist gives all of his self to one of his characters; the autobiographical emerges in some form in all the protagonists peopling his narrative, and although more explicit, the Defoe and Crusoe equation is not exclusive; it in no way eliminates the Defoe–Friday equivalence. A novel gives an author the freedom, denied to him in real life, to play many parts, and to play them simultaneously. On his uninhabited island, Defoe, banishing all, with no interfering woman or mothering figure coming between them, placed two men who could, as master and servant, as father and son, give themselves to each other. With Defoe in full authorial control, he could enjoy both the dominance of a father and the passivity of a son; it is a powerful homoerotic fantasy. He was, in disguise, once again conjuring up the primal Oedipal fantasy, never relinquished, of being lover to his father; earlier yearnings had been acted out in the services he had rendered to William of Orange and First Lord of the Treasury, Robert Harley, but the meaner politics of the Hanoverian era could throw up no grand figure upon whom he could lavish his affections; thus denied, to posterity's advantage, in fantasy, insulated from some of the guilts in the real world that are brought to intensive relationships between father and son, Defoe created a story where he played both roles, Crusoe the solicitous father and Friday the obedient loving son. And to ensure that he, like his readers, could savour to the full the eroticism pervading the emotionally charged situation, and would not mistake the nature of the relationship, Defoe excised the pigment from Friday's skin; he was not to be permitted the affectation of innocence; only the colour-blind readers—and they over the centuries have proved to be millions—could still believe in Friday the innocent; Friday was to be no white boy, pure as snow; he was to be deliciously tawny, almost black as sin, container of dark savage passions.

Lasciviously, lingering over the physical details, Defoe describes his sex-bomb:

> He was a comely, handsome fellow, perfectly well-made, with straight long limbs, not too large, tall, and well-shaped and, as I reckon, about twenty-six years of age. He had a very good countenance, not a fierce and surly aspect, but seemed to have something manly in his face; and yet he had all the sweetness and softness of an European in his countenance too, especially when he smiled. His hair was long and black, not curled like wool; his forehead very high and large; and a great vivacity and sparkling sharpness in his eyes. The colour of his skin was not quite black, but very tawny; and was not of an ugly, yellow, nauseous tawny as the Brazilians and Virginians, and other natives of America are, but of a bright kind of dun olive colour, that

had in it something very agreeable though not very easy to describe. His face was round and plump, his nose small, not flat like the Negro's; a very good mouth, thin lips, and his fine teeth well set, and white as ivory.

And not content with this erotic idealisation of Friday's physique, Defoe, in the manner of all lovers over-valuing their belovèd, projected upon his noble savage every saintly quality:

> never man had a more faithful, loving, sincere servant than Friday was to me; without passions, sullenness, or designs, perfectly obliged and engaged; his very affections were tied to me, like those of a child to a father; and I daresay he would have sacrificed his life for the saving mine, upon any occasion whatsoever.

That such a perfect being should have had withheld from him the "great lamp of instruction, the Spirit of God" threw Crusoe into a "melancholy". Defoe has Crusoe on the brink of blasphemy, questioning the justice of a dispensation that gives us the holy instruction while hiding the "life-saving knowledge from so many millions of souls, who if I might judge by this poor savage, would make a much better use of it than we did". We observe Defoe becoming fearful of permitting Crusoe to pursue further his dangerous questionings:

> I sometimes was led too far to invade the sovereignty of Providence, and as it were arraign the justice of so arbitrary a disposition of things, that should hide their plight from some, and reveal it to others, and yet expect a like duty from both. But I shut it up, and checked my thoughts with this conclusion: first, that we did not know by what light of law he should be condemned; but that as God was necessarily, and, by the nature of His being, infinitely holy and just, so it could not be that of these creatures were all sentenced to absence from Himself, it was on account of sinning against that light, which, as the Scriptures says, was a law to themselves.

And, to close the argument without disclosing what was the sin against the light that had brought such terrible retribution, Crusoe turned from that scriptural quote from Romans to another biblical quote, this time from Isaiah, telling us to accept God's will without challenge: "And as we are all the clay in the hand of the potter, no vessel could say to Him, 'Why hast thou formed me thus?' "

But Defoe, the biblical scholar who had as a boy translated Genesis into shorthand, well knew the nature of the sin that Ham, the ancestor of his savage, had committed, bringing about a curse upon all his descendants. Defoe, the incessant Bible-quoter, had the courage to query the justice of the curse, but not to direct Crusoe to the passage in Genesis which told how it arose. They are the ten short verses which would have appalling consequences; they were to provide a God-given sanction to the slave trade even as they were to provide the Boers of the Dutch Reform Church with a theological justification for the sons of Ham paying the price of oppressive apartheid laws. The curse contained in the verses is unequivocal but the real offence occasioning the curse is hidden in sinister silence:

> And the sons of Noah, that went forth of the ark, were Shem, and Ham, and Japheth; and Ham is the father of Canaan. These are the three sons of Noah; and of them was the whole earth over-spread. And Noah began to be an husbandman, and he planted a vineyard; And he drank of the wine, and was drunken; and he was uncovered within his tent. And Ham, the father of Canaan, saw the nakedness of his father, and told his two brothers without. And Shem and Japheth took a garment, and laid it upon both their shoulders, and went backward, and covered the nakedness of their father; and their faces were backward, and they saw not their father's nakedness. And Noah awoke from his wine, and knew what his younger son had done unto him. And he said, Cursed be Canaan; a servant of servants shall he be unto his brethren. And he said Blessed be the Lord God of Shem; and Canaan shall be his servant. God shall enlarge Japheth, and he shall dwell in the tents of Shem; and Canaan shall be his servant.[13]

There are huge and significant gaps in the chronicler's tale; either the original story has been heavily censored or, even from the beginning, the events in Noah's tent were too awful to be told. We do not look for our legends to follow strict rules of causality but that an inadvertent glimpse by a son of his father's nakedness should have such dire consequences for one-third of the human race is indeed a singularly unconvincing recounting. The myth, as told, conceals more than it reveals. One of the most lively of modern-day rabbis, recognising the lacunae in the story, has suggested that Ham laughed at the drunken Noah's nakedness, and that this was the cause of Noah's anger.[14] Such an anodyne explanation, that a son's innocent tease of a father should have caused such a disproportionate response, is not persuasive. There are far more likely and far more explosive interpretations to be found in the interstices of the abrupt verses. In the tent a sexual encounter had taken place, one surely more than a concupiscent gaze. When any sacred taboo is broken, a curse must fall upon the miscreant; that is the iron rule to be found in all the Greek and Hebrew myths; and when so terrible a curse is in place, one bringing, as Defoe laments, the injustice that fell upon Friday, descendant of Ham, then we know a taboo has been violated. It is the full horror of such a transgression that envelops the biblical fable. The chronicler seeks to acquit the father of guilt, pleading his drunken stupor as extenuation; but a scapegoat has to be found; for so heinous an offence as this was, the punishment must be forever, a permanent deterrent to those like Defoe who may otherwise yield to the temptation of acting out the primal fantasy of becoming the exclusive lover of the father. In the fable, to guard themselves from the temptation to which Ham had yielded, Shem and Japheth walked backwards, shielding their eye from the naked form; for their renunciation, they were rewarded, even as Ham was punished for his default.

When Defoe calls Crusoe to meditate on the injustice of Friday's condition, he dare not direct him to this Noah fable; to be found there were too many dangerous resonances with his own condition; homosexual incest was a threat to be distanced, not courted. And as Defoe explains, Crusoe had decided to "shut-up" and "check" his thoughts. And so fleeing from the discomforts of such troubling thinking, Defoe gave Crusoe a respite and let him enjoy three years of erotic fantasising before deciding that the therapeutic gains of enforced banishment had reached their limits; and he brought the two men back to the mainland.

For Defoe the homecoming was the triumphant vindication of his homeopathic treatment. Crusoe, without any outside agencies, dependent upon no one but himself, alone, had faced the loneliness, and conquered the disabling malady. And Defoe shared the remission he had granted to his creation; for the next decade, in the years when *Moll Flanders* and *Roxana* were to be written, the physic he had given Crusoe was also to keep Defoe free from the deadly infection.

Thus unencumbered, with renewed energy, at the age of sixty, the genius of Defoe suddenly burst into a winter blossom unexampled in the whole field of literature.

Notes

1. Roberts, D., Introduction to *Robinson Crusoe*, Wordsworth Classics, 2000.
2. Gardam, J., *The Independent*, 17 December 2004.
3. Homer, *The Odyssey*, XX, 356.
4. Jones, E., *The Island of Ireland*, Stonehill Publishing Company, 1974.
5. Starr, G. A., Introduction to *Moll Flanders*, Oxford University Press, 1998.
6. See Chapter 5, p. 222.
7. See Chapter 9, p. 130.
8. Douglas, M., *Jacob's Tears: the Priestly Work of Reconciliation*, Oxford University Press, 2004.
9. Alter, R., *London Review of Books*, 3 March 2005.
10. See Chapter 3, p. 27.
11. Douglas, *Jacob's Tears*.
12. Starr, Introduction to *Moll Flanders*.
13. Genesis, 9: 18–27.
14. Brichto, Rabbi Dr S., *Genesis*, Sinclair-Stevenson, 2000.

CHAPTER SIXTEEN

Moll Flanders

W hen Defoe, so late in life, turned to novel-writing and, through his conduct manuals, to an exploration of the human heart, the times were indeed decisively changing. It was perhaps in response to those changes that we find Defoe relinquishing his intense engagement in the politics of the day and releasing all his extraordinary energy into imaginative works and didactic insightful psychologising treatises.

Politics had become mean. The grand themes which had taken young Defoe on to the battlefield at Sedgemoor and later, upholding his Dissenting convictions, had sent him to prison, were played out; the historian Sir John Plumb has instructed us that "there was no real clash of conflicting political systems . . . The aim of politics was not directed to liberties—they had been won in 1688—nor to social justice, but to the pursuit of office."[1] It was a type of politics with which today in Britain we are lamentably familiar; and just as today, when conviction politics are pejoratively stigmatised as ideological and political activists are disenchanted, so too would Defoe have found the miserable politicking of George I's court demeaning. He was too big a fish to swim in such shallow waters.

Contemptuous of the shabby provincial German world of the

231

Hanoverians, Defoe turned his back on its drab political squalor and, in his novels, created his own world; from that vantage point the vanities of the world he had left behind are unsparingly recounted, exposed and ironically mocked; with pity and understanding the hapless inhabitants, weighed down with their self-deceptions, are depicted staggering on their way to Calvary.

In these fictions, such is Defoe's art, a facsimile is produced indistinguishable from the real world. He was in fact engaged in a task of adaptation to a disagreeable world that psychoanalysts, following Ferenczi, have described as being in an auto-plastic mode.[2] There are two ways of adjusting to reality: by means of adjusting reality to make it fit one's needs, or by means of changing oneself to fit in with reality; these reactions have been named as alloplastic and autoplastic; the former is witnessed as man, through technology, conquers the environment, the latter when man is engaged in courageous introspection, an exercise that tends to bring painful insights that have to be faced through the calibration by introspective work into personal resource. Defoe in his major novels embarked on just such an introspective exploration but ingeniously he protected himself from much of the pain of self-discovery by allowing it to be borne by the protagonists who peopled his works. In their self-questionings, their doubts, their meditations, their constant monitoring of motivation, he was practising what in our post-Freudian days we could perhaps dub self-analysis. All authentic novel-writing, like biography, is partly autobiographical; in this voyage into his interior life, Defoe cunningly contrived to gain the relief that, by way of catharsis, was granted to him as he told of the transgressions of his creations, of their sins, those that he would have liked to commit but dared not; and all this could be enjoyed by him, and indeed his readers, without suffering any attendant guilts.

But Defoe, ever the risk-taker, was playing a dangerous game, and nowhere can this be observed more acutely than in *Moll Flanders*. As a female raconteur he abandons all gender boundaries and, in this hermaphrodite guise, conjoins with Moll, with some little moralising asides, to make the stolen fruit even sweeter: every taboo is breached, every sin—incest, adultery, bigamy, thieving, infanticide and lesbianism—is to be thrillingly experienced.

Defoe was now playing with fire; such exotic, inflammatory fantasies could become dangerously out of control; preventative action had to be taken; the incendiarist who has put his torch to a pyre of illicit desires was, as the flames spread, now in danger of being consumed. Aware of the encroaching danger, even as Moll lawlessly romped, simultaneously, Defoe erected his first defence against the lure of her temptations; as we have seen,[3] the austere work of *Religious Courtship* was in place shielding him from becoming a victim of his own passionate imagination, and also from any charge that he was inciting, and condoning, the anti-social frolicking and manipulations of his anti-heroine.

But even the repudiations of *Religious Courtship* did not suffice to quell the riotous fantasies now assailing the man; the delights gained in identifying with Moll's escapades could not yet be relinquished. In little more than a year, Defoe was back inviting us to join him in his ambivalent rejoicing in the vices of Roxana. But he was determined to conquer his addiction; *Roxana* was to be his final novel. Mobilising all his resources to extirpate the insidious cancer destroying his moral fibre, he was, ere long, using his pen like a scalpel; in *Conjugal Lewdness* he first identifies every ugly symptom of the disease, ruthlessly cuts out its site and, even more, prescribes the balm—true monogamous love—to heal the wound. In contrast to the infidelities and disorders in *Moll Flanders*, he posits the rewards to be found in love and marriage:

> upon the solid Foundations of real marriage, personal Virtue, similitude of Tempers, mutual Delights; that see good Sense, good humour, Wit, and agreeable Temper in one another, and know it when they see it, and how to judge of it. . . . It would call for a Volume, not a Page, to describe the happiness of this Couple. Possession does not lessen, but heightens their Enjoyments; the Flame does not exhaust it self by burning but encreases by its continuance; 'tis young in its remotest Age; Time makes no Abatement; they are never surfeited, never satiated.[4]

Nowhere has Defoe affirmed more eloquently his faith that men and women, if they cleave together, can lose their separateness and become as one. Observance of the rules laid down in *Conjugal Lewdness* is the essential prerequisite to the attainment of the hermaphrodite ideal; only thus can Adam regain his rib. Defoe's declaration is a total repudiation of the misconduct, tantalising and seductive though it may be, of his creation Moll Flanders, of the vanity that narcissistically, by manipulatively gaining wealth and status, they can attain serenity. That is a condition reserved for those men and women ready to renounce themselves for each other; in such a merger, and not in Moll's desperate strivings, can happiness be gained. Any reading of the two novels that fails to acknowledge the over-riding disavowals to which they are subject is incomplete.

Yet to define the transgressive novels or *Conjugal Lewdness* merely in terms of each other, to regard the works as antithetical, could be simplistic and misleading; they share the same teleology. In the novels and in *Conjugal Lewdness* Defoe's purpose is to be found in his pursuit of the hermaphrodite ideal; he was never prepared to concede that his male gender necessitated the forfeiture of his singular feminine endowment; he would never accept that mono-sexual man is condemned for life to be but one half of the sexual tandem. In *Conjugal Lewdness* he declares that it is within the holy ordinance of marriage that the fusion of the sexes can be achieved. Like the perfect ephebe, Hermaphrodite, the child of Hermes and Aphrodite and gifted with the attributes of both these gods, man and woman too could live as gods. Defoe, doubtless enjoying the confidence that came from his long and successful marriage to his Mary, was, in *Conjugal Lewdness*, romantically asserting that man's *urphantasies* could be lived out in real life. It is the illusion in which the poets encourage us to believe:

My true-love hath my heart, and I have his,
By just exchange one to the other given;
I hold his dear, and mine he cannot miss,
There never was a better bargain driven:
My true-love hath my heart, and I have his.

His heart in me keeps him and me in one,
My heart in him his thoughts and senses guides:
He loves my heart, for once it was his own,
I cherish his because in me it bides:
My true-love hath my heart, and I have his.[5]

More prosaically, one of the leading French psychoanalysts has reminded us: "The fantasy of being both male and female, of possessing the white and black magic of both sexes, of being father and mother, or of being self-engendered—who in his child's heart might not long for this?"[6] That longing is made explicit in *Conjugal Lewdness*, unlike in the novels, for there is made the optimistic claim that the hermaphroditic goal can be reached by way of consummation within the idealised perfect marriage. That same longing operates in *Moll Flanders*, but there the route to the goal is far less accessible, far more circuitous, far more hazardous; the directions to be followed to reach the yearned-for destination are enfolded, not immediately discoverable, within the hidden agenda of both novels; their directions lead to the signpost pointing the way with an inscribed injunction anticipating one of William Blake's *Proverbs of Hell*: "The road of excess leads to the palace of wisdom." It is on such a fearsome road, initially accompanied by Defoe, that Moll travels; always her daring is sustained by the illusion that at the end she will find the hermaphroditic gifts that are the privilege of gods and earthworms.

To ensure she was on the right road, the excesses had to be far more than petty defiances. Defoe himself sets the pace, challenges the given differentiation and as the raconteur becomes a woman; his metamorphosis is total, not that of a mere female impersonator. He is acting as did the early Gnostics who acclaimed the Gospel of Thomas wherein Christ taught:

> When you make two human beings into one, and when you make the inside as the outside, and the outside as the inside and the top as the bottom! And if you make the male and female into one so that the male is no longer male and the female no longer female, then you will enter into the Kingdom.[7]

This indeed was heretical doctrine in total contradiction to the Old Testament's insistence upon the maintenance of boundaries. The prophet Jeremiah's fierce condemnation of those who cross the ordained barriers was insolently defied by Defoe, who, compounding his own sin of wiping out gender boundaries, incited his creations to commit adultery, incest and murder. He was deaf to God's warning that there are lines that must never be crossed:

> Fear ye not me? saith the Lord; will ye not tremble at My presence, which have placed the sand for the bound of the sea by a perpetual decree, that it cannot pass it; and though the waves thereof toss

themselves, yet can they not prevail; though they roar, yet can they not pass over it?[8]

Jeremiah's beautiful metaphor speaks to us of a boundary that can be regarded as the prototype of all boundaries and barriers, and consequently all differences. Mankind, always fretting at the restrictions, is ever endeavouring to go beyond the narrow limits of his condition; nostalgically he recalls the dark chaos that preceded God's creation of the earth when it was without form, before He divided the light from the darkness, before He placed a firmament in the midst of the waters and let it divide both the waters from the waters, and the waters which were under the firmament from those which were above.[9] Always there have been those who believed God, by insisting on boundaries, botched the job and that a new start must be made. This belief is linked, sometimes quite openly, with perversions as in the case of Dionysian rites involving inter-sexual disguises. Mircea Eliade has written of these rites:

> Their aim is regression to primordial confusion . . . and their goal is the symbolic restoration of "chaos", the state of unity without differentiation that preceded the Creation. This return to confusion manifests itself in a supreme act of regeneration and an enormous increase in power.[10]

An attempt is being made to reverse the way leading from indistinctness to separation and demarcation. As the remarkable French psychoanalyst Janine Chasseguet-Smirgel has pointed out, here we are very close to the worshippers of Satan and religions of the Devil:

> A black mass is a parody of the sacrifice of Christ. In it the cross is placed upside down or facing the wall; the mass is said backwards and the Tetragrammaton is pronounced the wrong way round and is accompanied by sexual orgies. In every case there is a reversal of values leading to a return to primal chaos.[11]

It is the pain of separateness, of aloneness, that we have repeatedly suggested is the condition Defoe finds well nigh intolerable. One of the creative stratagems he devises to bring relief has given us that epic of isolation *Robinson Crusoe*,[12] but in *Moll Flanders* and *Roxana* too he seeks a way to escape from the anguish of individuation. It is that anguish which the practitioners of Dionysian rites, Satan worshippers and the early Gnostics all sought to relieve. They were all possessed with an alchemical conception of the world, a belief that they could find, usually in group sex where anonymity not individuality prevailed, a magic formula for the undoing of all transmutations of elements of the undifferentiated primordial material from which they were created; there was to be no separation; all would be mixed in this new anal shit-world[13] which would supplant the rule-bound Kingdom of God. From this perspective we do not see Defoe-Moll, or indeed Defoe-Roxana, merely as cross-dressing players in a self-indulgent pantomime; they are in fact profoundly subversive. When Defoe wrote these novels as a female raconteur he was certainly not engaged in a mere literary device.

Nor, when he assumed his hermaphroditic persona was he engaged in the masquerade, the superficial tease of today's groomed and perfumed "metropolitan" men, the women-envious soccer celebrities who wear women's clothes and accoutrements, and claim they are in touch with their feminine side; but their enhanced facials and moisturisers are but skin-deep; Defoe's fractured self could not be healed by a beautician.

In *Conjugal Lewdness* we have found Defoe aspiring to exteriorise and thus assuage his inner psychic bi-sexuality by a "sublime beauteous" coming together where sanctified sex melts all divisions and, obeying the holy ordinance of marriage, a fusion would result where male and female were as one with themselves and the universe. But, in blasphemous contrast, in *Moll Flanders*, in an attempt to achieve the same end, he took the sacrilegious course; like the Dionysian and Satan worshippers he made a bid to be released from the bondage of one-dimensional gender; in the sex orgies of those zealots, there were no inhibitions, no commandments, no prohibited orifices; their frantic ecstasies conjured up a homogeneous marshland devoid of demarcation lines and frontiers where the pervert was king and redeemer; it was the land of anti-Jehovah and anti-Christ, the kingdom of the Devil. Only by a hair's breadth did Defoe distance himself from that domain. But, imitatively, he smashed all boundaries and, like a hermaphroditic god, created Moll, and later Roxana, and, as observer and participant, then wallowed in their deviances.

Defoe was, in those novels, creatively restructuring his most perverse and earliest fantasies. Always there is an enigmatic relationship

THE BI-SEXUALITY OF DANIEL DEFOE

between perversion and creativity. The human infant's sexual drive
is not channelled into any one single direction; it is polymorphous
perverse, regarding all erotic roles as interchangeable,[14] and none in
adulthood, Freud has asserted, leave behind all traces of that primal
lability: "No healthy person therefore can fail to make some addition
to what might be called perverse to the normal sexual aim";[15] but
some are cursed and for them even the most elaborate preliminary
foreplay cannot encourage them to move on to find their full satisfaction in genital sex; they are fixated. These are the wretched per-
verts to be found in every society. But before ever condemning
them, we should reflect that all men hide within themselves a polymorphous child—even as they also contain a polymorphous nexus
of creative resources.[16] The pervert is a laggard, left behind while
most of us, more or less, abandon our boundless polymorphous
world, move on, settle for genitality, only able to carry as baggage
the memories and dreams of the perversions practised once upon a
time without prohibition. The vicissitudes we have noted of Defoe's
pre-genital infancy ensured that he was heavily loaded with such
luggage.[17] When he unpacked, he gave the contents to posterity; the
marvellously transmuted recollections of his infantile perversions
became the enchanted fables of *Moll Flanders* and *Roxana*.

★   ★   ★   ★   ★   ★   ★   ★   ★   ★

Emancipated from the burden of maleness, yet able to remain confident as a father of at least eight children of his heterosexuality,
Defoe, in the form of Moll, abandoned all conventionally bound
rules and from almost the first pages of his novel delighted in the
perversions coyly enacted or fantasised by his wayward feminine
self. He began with troilism, revelling in becoming a woman who
could simultaneously enjoy two men—but not any two men. These
were brothers and the spice of the occasion was its barely concealed
attempt to subvert all consanguinity laws, those categorising
degrees of relationships within which sex and marriage are permitted or prohibited. These are matters which can arouse strong passions; indeed, in the history of family law, no Bill was more fiercely
contested over so many years as that seeking to permit a man to
marry his deceased wife's sister; all such rules in place have one
over-riding object, to build a fence around the ecclesiastical laws
which criminalise incest.

Defoe was fully conscious of what he was about when he told of virginal Moll first becoming the secret mistress of one brother and then marrying the other. In his depiction of this threesome he went almost as far as he dared. The lover first placed the drunken husband-to-be in the honeymoon bed with Moll, and lustful Moll then tells us:

> I never was in Bed with my Husband, but I wished myself in the Arms of his Brother ... in short, I committed Adultery and Incest with him every Day in my Desires, which without doubt was as effectually Criminal in the Nature of the Guilt, as if I had actually done it.

This curtain-raiser to the tale of Moll's transgressions yet again illustrates how deeply striated in Defoe's psyche was the polymorphous perverse instinctual life of his early pre-genital infancy. He was ever seeking a socially sanctioned outlet where the perversions, sometimes encoded, could be savoured; and Moll, for this purpose, was the perfect foil. Moll, on behalf of Defoe, could confess, as she does, to incestuous longings; and on to her, Defoe could displace his own unconscious desire, the never-relinquished yearning of his negative Oedipal phase, of being a woman able to receive as lover his own father; and to ensure that his incestuous love should be exclusive, not even Moll, his own creation, is permitted to have a father; he, in the novel, is banned; significantly, he is never mentioned; Defoe permits no competitor even in his imagination; only he, not Moll, must luxuriate in the forbidden embraces of a father. At one remove, however, by ingenious circumlocution, Moll throughout the novel is permitted to break restraining consanguinity rules; incest and hints of incest hover over the novel, their ambiguities concealing the author's illicit and most profound desire, to be possessed by his own begetter.

That repressed wish emerges compulsively, overtly, insufficiently disguised, as Defoe creates the circumstances enabling Moll, with her first husband dead, to marry her brother. It is too dangerous to Defoe, morphised as Moll, to permit an explosion of the ultimate taboo of an incestuous relationship between father and son, so he cunningly displaces his own desire and, with Moll's father removed from the dark tale, provides her, as substitute, with a sibling, innocent as Moll, with whom in Virginia she, as a wife, enjoys the prohibited pleasures of incest. Not until she is blessed with children and had years of delightful transgression does Defoe, fearing his own condonation of this outrageous cohabitation, draw back from giving it a happy ending; reluctantly he ends the ideal which he was relishing, reveals the horror of the relationship to the participants and sends the stricken Moll alone back to England.

Defoe walked too near the edge for his own comfort in that adventure of Moll; one false step and his own secret could have been advertised. On the next occasion, when he sends the widow on her predatory way and invites us to participate in his perverted thrills, he is more circumspect. A precondition of any relationship he conjured up was that there was a third person looming in the shadows, usually a disabled or mentally sick wife; only thus could the recounting of an adulterous affair have for Defoe the necessary resonance recapitulating the primal fantasy where, with his mother present but excluded, he had imagined his own father-and-son love affair. The man who, while Moll was husband-hunting in the spa at Bath, engaged her attention was, apart from his "Great Estate", most suitably qualified in Defoe's tale to be her lover; for he had a wife "distempered in her Head" who was "under the Conduct of her own Relations".

I doubt if it is possible to understand the bizarre relationship Defoe then invents for Moll and her Bath lover without appreciating the full significance of Defoe placing in the background this ominous mad wife. Far away from this woman of whom, apart from her mental sickness, we are told nothing, Defoe puts her husband with Moll into bed lying every night naked side by side, permitting them at most an embrace, but never, over a period of two years, any sexual expression whatsoever. The vow, spontaneous and unsolicited, of the Bath Gentleman when he first wooed Moll was scrupulously observed. "If", he had told her, "he was naked in bed with her, he would as sacredly preserve her virtue as he would defend it if she was assaulted by a ravisher"; meanwhile, he insisted, he would wait for some opportunity to give him an undoubted "Testimony" of it. Because he loved her, he bewilderingly explained to Moll, he could not injure her. Although Defoe scholars from academia have, more than any other of his works, attempted deconstructions of *Moll Flanders*, none appear to have dwelt upon this weird ambivalent tryst, one that Defoe, to make certain its importance was not belittled as a passing episode, subsequently gave eight years of Moll's life, during which she, eventually, gave birth to three children.

Yet if one asks the right questions, answers can be found explaining what drove Defoe to convert an unremarkable and entirely forgivable adulterous association into a horror story. The basic story is simple: a wealthy man, burdened by his chronically sick wife, in melancholic mood, seeks recreation in the "gallantry" centre of Bath and there meets an attractive widow on the prowl whom he eventually sets up, suitably ensconced, as his faithful mistress. But why is the telling of such a commonplace transparent event so bedevilled with perverse asides and penitential lamentations? Why, before allowing the affair to be consummated, does Defoe inflict upon this sophisticated and sexually experienced couple, much attracted to each other, the torment of sharing, in the nude, a sexless bed?

The delays cannot be satisfactorily explained away as mere titillation, a tease to hold the reader in suspense, an amusing tale of an endurance test, a depiction of a foreplay diversion to allow the reader, with mounting excitement, to enjoy a little postponement of the inevitable culmination; there may be faint echoes of such a subtext in the recounting, but it would indeed require a singular pornographically minded reader not to weary of a thrill that, to be climaxed, has to be sustained for two years. Nor can the imposed delay be given a rationale by attributing erectile dysfunction or impotence to the Bath Gentleman. Defoe causes Moll expressly to repudiate such an interpretation by affirming that his self-discipline was more "amazing" for "he was a strong vigorous brisk Person"; and Defoe, too, has Moll making it unequivocally clear that "he did not act thus on the principle of Religion at all".

But Defoe realises that some explanation is called for to account for such kinky behaviour. Lamely he tries to cheat us into believing it was a symptom of the Madonna–Whore syndrome, that such was the affection of the Gentleman for his angel that he could not defile her. Given the circumstances of their meeting in notoriously promiscuous Bath, the Gentleman may have regarded the widow a whore but surely could never credibly be thought to have held her to have virginal qualities; and since the barrier ultimately—after they had had a few too many drinks together and sexual intercourse took place and continued—so easily collapsed, the motivation behind the Gentleman's scruples, as suggested by Defoe, is indeed highly suspect. It becomes even more so when we witness the extraordinarily disproportionate display of guilt by the protagonists when at last, after years of lying nude together, they cross the boundary and, "with shame and horror of soul", coitus ensued. And although three children are soon born within the relationship, still its "horror" hovers; it does not vanish; an illness suffered by the Gentleman causes him to reflect on his "criminal correspondence", to look upon his adultery "with a just and religious Abhorrence", and with such "an Abhorrence of the Sin" came a "detestation of the fellow Sinner; you can expect no other". Crushed with guilt, "strooked with a dire remorse", to escape his dilemma, we are asked by Defoe to be so credulous as to believe that this hardened adulterer, suddenly repentant, with no reproach from his sinning mistress, abruptly ends the affair.

Defoe has never asserted a more improbable episode in his tale-telling; it is unconvincing, the motivation and behaviour of his characters so askew because it is palpably false, a clumsy concealment. When Moll slept with one brother and married the other, the incest motif was barely concealed; when she inadvertently married her own brother, it was explicit; but here too, although Defoe clumsily attempts to camouflage its presence, it is again the underlying theme. The intimacy of these two case-hardened serial adulterers is, in itself, a mere peccadillo; such an event can hardly be regarded as earth-shaking; the shock, horror and penitentials occasioned do not arise from an adultery; they arise from the violation in Defoe's mind of an awesome and threatening taboo. Adultery is but the veil covering criminal incest. Behind the figure of the unnamed Gentleman looms the father, and Defoe is encapsulated within Moll. The exquisite temptation both so desperately seek to avoid, ambivalently, so precariously distanced as they lie in the nude side by side, is homosexual incest; it is the ghastliness of the ultimate consummation that precipitates the unbounded remorse, the lamentations and, finally, the intolerable guilty pressures compelling the end of the heinous coupling. The manifest content of such a tale as told by Defoe, and, indeed, as in all our dreams, can be comparatively innocuous but the unacceptable latent content must remain hidden, unacknowledged; if acted out, the terrible punishment it attracts is the curse of original sin that fell upon the disobedient Adam and Eve when expelled from Eden.

In the Bath Gentleman episode Defoe stumbles; his presentation of Moll's liaison is too inconsistent. But, more usually, with considerable literary skill, he entices us to engage in the exciting adventures of his heroine and, thus distracted, only subliminally are we aware that as an accompaniment to the story a musical composition is being played, one containing an insistent perverse leitmotif. In *Moll Flanders* Defoe is singularly reminding us that perversion and creativity have a common primitive origin in the pre-genital phase of our development;[18] the irredeemable pervert deflects his instinctual drive to a fetish, while the creative writer sublimates that self-same drive and, thus desexualised, a work of art can emerge.[19] Defoe, however, refuses to be confined to the choice of either desexualised sublimation or the claims of perversion. When he is in full authorial control, we often see his capacity to harness, not abandon, his perverse incest fantasy and, thus reined in, to place it at the service of his creativity.

His guile ensures the complicity of his readers. In the hermaphroditic production of *Moll Flanders*, staged at Defoe's theatre, he and his actors are never gender-bound, never confined to playing one role; all can, and do, play many parts, untrammelled by the bondage of a fixed sexual identity. Here the audience can revel in the cross-generational interchanges as in the cross-dressing; they are spared the acute discomfort that would be occasioned by awareness of the dynamic generated by the dialogue and action. The underlying theme, the source of the élan, informing the production, is ever-present but disguised; without any impropriety, without any embarrassment, without guilt, the audience shares with Defoe the exquisite pleasures of the incest fantasies which he so obligingly dextrously cloaks in the elaborate and colourful costumes adorning his commissioned players. It is unsurprising that such splendid theatre, so discreetly presenting our most transgressive perversion, has gained applause from the time of its first showing in 1722.

With Moll now depicted on film and television the acclamations continue, and critics in the English departments of universities on both sides of the Atlantic continue to engage in disputations addressed to assessments of the literary merits of the work; but the incest theme which evokes resonances today even as it did in the eighteenth century and which is the lure that has attracted, innocent of its presence, a vast readership, is rarely commented upon. Defoe's ruse to allow it to be heard but not seen has been remarkably successful. That would indeed have brought much pleasure to our inimitable master of deceptions.

★ ★ ★ ★ ★ ★ ★ ★ ★ ★ ★

In *Moll Flanders* there is another significant and insistent theme but, unlike the incest motif, it is one brazenly and clamorously proclaimed; the downfall of Moll, her descent into criminality, her incarceration in Newgate Gaol and subsequent deportation are all made to be the consequence of her inordinate and compulsive greed. Defoe does not permit her to conceal her motivation. All he allows her is an eloquent plea claiming that despite her resistances, she was possessed by the Devil:

> the busy Devils that so industriously drew me in, had too fast hold of me to let me go back; but as Property brought me into the Mire, so Avarice kept me in 'til there was no going back . . . Avarice stepped in and said "Go on, go on" . . . thus I that was once in the Devil's Clutches, was held fast there as with a Charm, and had no power to go without the circle, 'til I was engulph'd in Labyrinth of Trouble too great to get out at all.

It is a feature of feminist literary critics that despite Moll's firm affirmation that she and the devil are responsible for her misdeeds, they nevertheless insist she is not culpable; her avarice, they claim, was not an irrational response to the prevailing societal conditions which left single women, unmarried mothers and widows without inheritance exposed to terrifying insecurities. The days had passed when women of all classes had held important places in the life of the community; licensing, and apprenticeships not open to women, meant there were no opportunities to gain a decent wage in a respectable profession; such employment as was available to women was menial, over-stretched, ill-paid and irregular; the death by starvation of abandoned women was not infrequent.[20] At one stage or another of her marital career, they would suggest, Moll exemplified all those varieties of abandoned women. In a spirited feminist essay, the American academic Miriam Lerenbaum has powerfully presented Moll's defence:

> If she anxiously tallies her assets at the close of each of her marriages,

it is not because she is paranoid or obsessively greedy, or a symbol of the capitalist spirit, but because she has a clear and accurate picture of her possible fate.[21]

Such an apologia would be persuasive if we were unaware of the coprophiliac compulsions that Defoe projected upon so many of his fictional characters. Defoe, as we have seen in our exploration of his other works, notably *The King of Pirates*, could never resist the vicarious pleasures he gained by depicting adventurers revelling in ill-gotten accumulations of shit equivalents, of gold and jewellery. Always the sympathetic feminist, Defoe certainly does not minimise the serious disadvantages facing Moll as a penniless young woman and as an impoverished widow; indeed, indulging his persistent penchant to ablate the parents of his fictional personages, he adds to Moll's handicaps by making her a foundling. But although these encumbrances were real and severe, she never proffers them as sufficient excuse or explanation to justify her descent into criminality. When she declares her avariciousness we must take her at her word; even when she has acquired by theft and fraud sufficient to have financial security, still she cannot desist. Defoe places no restraints upon her incontinent law-breaking; indeed, that all commandments must be broken is a prerequisite to the success of Defoe's scheme, that of creating a novel where the blessing of a perfect relationship where man and woman are one, where the hermaphrodite ideal is attained, and the breaking of them ultimately falls to his heroine.

First, however, she must sin, sin grievously; only then can she be redeemed. Defoe steers her towards the sacrilegious course that, as we have remarked, has been prefigured by so many frenzied zealots like the Dionysians, the early Gnostics and the followers of Satan.

To achieve his purpose he exploits his and Moll's anality. It would be repetitious to direct attention to the aetiology which, we have claimed, explains his compulsive prurient interest in wealth, in its creation and loss as illustrated in his economic works, and in its illicit accumulation as recorded in his tales of adventure. In *Moll Flanders*, however, the accent is not upon an attempt to regain through the acquisition of money the coprophiliac pleasures prohibited by a martinet mother; here, rather, we witness an attempt to reclaim other lost infantile delights—those pleasures accompanying the act of defecation.

A need to control and manipulate in adult life is one of the traits associated with those who have suffered peremptory and unsympathetic toilet-training; denied as an infant the pleasures of manipulative sphincter control, the adult may, as a manipulative personality, seek compensations in subtle dominances over others. These determining early frustrations of Defoe, projected upon Moll, are assuaged as she constantly creates, in her relations with her lovers and husbands, situations in which they believe they are taking initiatives when in fact she has cunningly contrived to bring them about. Apart from one display of innocence which occasioned her first seduction, she is, although pretending otherwise, totally in control in all her liaisons. As Starr has remarked: "The men she has to do with tend to be timid and solicitous towards her, and the roles of initiative and passivity assigned to male and female in the account of her first seduction are virtually reversed in most later episodes."[22] It is she, not any of the unsuspecting men, who is the predator.

With such masterly command, Defoe sends Moll on her way to begin as a petty thief and then to become a formidable criminal meriting imprisonment and the threat of the gallows. Defoe is determined that her wickedness must be untempered; only then can she qualify for repentance and subsequent redemption. To ensure she obtains the necessary qualification, Defoe depicts her making a total commitment to lawlessness; her final marriage is to a hunted outlaw, a highwayman. The two, by their rapaciousness and avarice, fully pass the test to be sufficiently evil to be the beneficiaries of redemptive repentance; that Defoe grants them, and thus pardoned, exemption gained, Moll and her pliant husband are sent to the colonies where, assisted by the now prosperous son of her previous incestuous marriage, in perfect union, they are to live happily ever after.

The novel is indeed a piquant comedy where Defoe, his fantasies unleashed, to our shared pleasure, has granted his characters, himself and us absolution; all his, and our, secret wishes for transgression have, in the end, been permitted and enjoyed without attracting deserved punishment; by acting out in this tale his repressed unconscious fantasies, Defoe gained a temporary amnesty from his guilt-ridden conscience. But with the happy ending, with Moll having a loving son and a loyal dependent infantilised husband, he gained even more; he was applying a relieving balm to one of his deepest wounds, that inflicted upon him as a little boy when, by her premature death, his mother had "deserted" him, leaving him to an unfeeling stepmother who, by sending him to boarding school, expelled him from the family home.

Those feelings of abandonment Defoe shared with the foundling, Moll. Starr has drawn attention to Moll's passion, which

> emerges most clearly in the heroine's recurring attachment to older women each of whom she "learnt to call Mother"—"the good motherly Nurse" in Colchester, the "midwife-governess at the Sign of the Cradle", and the mother-in-law who turns out to be her real mother; . . . But one "mother" leaves her in the lurch by dying, another countenances incest, a third proposes abortion and later leads her "as it were by the Hand" into a labyrinth of crime; none proved quite equal to Moll's filial longings.[23]

To ensure, however, that the novel concludes as comedy not tragedy, Defoe overcomes her frustration in failing to find an ideal mother by elevating her to that role. She becomes the good mother to the son she once abandoned even as she becomes the mothering wife to the immature erstwhile highwayman; and since Defoe never denies himself the opportunity to identify fully with Moll, the reversal of roles by Moll brings comfort to Defoe. By fantasising himself as the good mother he lacked, he overcomes some of the traumatic consequences, still in place, of his own feelings of abandonment as a child. Yet again, as we have seen in our explorations of the Plague and Crusoe,[24] Defoe is using his story-telling as therapy; and since in *Moll Flanders* his elliptical recitals of his self-medication invariably bring us thrills, amusement and so much naughtiness, we surely should not begrudge the author his hypochondriacal self-indulgence. Rather, in our enjoyment, like many generations of readers before us, we should admit to our complicity.

Notes

1. Plumb, J. H., *The First Four Georges*, Fontana Collins, 1983.
2. Waelder, R., *Progress and Revolution*, International Universities Press, 1967.

3. See Chapter 13, pp. 181–182.

4. Defoe, D., *Conjugal Lewdness or Matrimonial Whoredom*, 1727.

5. Sidney, Sir P., *A Ditty*.

6. McDougal, J., *Plea for a Measure of Abnormality*, Free Association Books, 1990.

7. The Gospel of Thomas.

8. Jeremiah, 5: 22.

9. Genesis, 1: 1–7.

10. Eliade, M., *Mephistophélès et l'Androgyne*, Gallimard, 1962.

11. Chasseguet-Smirgel, J., *Creativity and Perversion*, Free Association Books, 1985.

12. See Chapter 14.

13. Chasseguet-Smirgel, *Creativity and Perversion*.

14. Rycroft, C., *A Critical Dictionary of Psychoanalysis*, Nelson, 1968.

15. Freud, S., *Three Essays on Sexuality*, SE, vol.VII.

16. McDougal, *Plea for a Measure of Abnormality*.

17. See Chapter 3.

18. Freud, S., *Three Essays on Sexuality*.

19. McDougal, *Plea for a Measure of Abnormality*.

20. George, D., *London Life in the Eighteenth Century*, Penguin, 1966.

21. Lerenbaum, M., Moll Flanders, in *The Authority of Experience*, University of Massachusetts Press, 1988.

22. Starr, G. A., Introduction to *Moll Flanders*, Oxford University Press, 1998.

23. Ibid.

24. See Chapters 6 and 15.

CHAPTER SEVENTEEN

Roxana

Reflecting his temperament, Defoe was never given to present his stories in calm, modulated tones; his protagonists, like their author, were subject to violent changes of mood; sometimes triumphalism prevailed, sometimes utter despair; the comedy of *Moll Flanders* was, two years later, succeeded by the tragedy of *Roxana*. Gone were the manic denials of Moll, gone were the optimistic assumptions that perdition does not necessarily follow upon sin, that guilts could be erased by repentance, that happiness, in the end, was still available even to the most errant.

Such sanguinity is no part of Defoe's sombre last novel. Its painful conclusion, that the immoral can never escape retribution, was repeatedly incised in subsequent pirated editions. Happy endings in at least three different forms were provided by enterprising booksellers who knew their readers could not tolerate the anguish of recognition in the affirmation that no matter what the stratagems devised, men and women cannot evade the fate decreed by their tragic destiny; there are choices but they are limited and if, for immediate advantage, they opt self-indulgently then their ultimate degradation will be excruciatingly mortifying.

The story of Roxana is that of a beautiful woman who made just such a fatal choice; she scorns the comforts and virtues of middle-class respectability to become a courtesan to the wealthy and the titled. Although in the telling of her adventures and misadventures distinctive themes from *Moll Flanders* come into play, there are nevertheless many congruences, not least in her addiction to the accumulation of wealth. Indeed, she leads her life in pursuit of wealth. Even as that of a penitent autobiographer, supposedly chastened by "calamities", her narration is excited by the thought of the loot that she remembers:

> So we opened the Box; there was in it indeed, what I did not expect ... Goldsmiths' Bills, and Stock in the English East India Company ... Rents of the Town-house in Paris, amounting in the whole to the 5,800 Crowns per Annum ... the Sum of 30,000 Rix-dollars in the Bank of Amsterdam.

Her story is full of the magical sums of the different currencies that she collects—denominations that she casts up all over again as she recalls her history.[1]

Defoe in *Roxana* has, however, more perverse and sophisticated delights than, by depiction of avarice, a vicarious dabble in coprophilia; in the first few pages of his recital of Roxana's adventures, he hastens to introduce us to the joys of lesbianism, troilism and caudalism.[2] Although these indulgences are always accompanied by forebodings, the sins are made even more exciting by the very threat of punishment; the risks add to the thrills. To accommodate his fantasies, Defoe initially places Roxana in a well furnished house where she has been abandoned and left penniless by her handsome fool of a husband; there we are first tentatively introduced to the lesbian theme when in the commodious home we find Defoe putting Roxana's pretty maid, Amy, in bed with her mistress, which, it is revealed, is a sleeping arrangement most agreeable to both women. We are spared the details of any physical intimacy but we are excited by the protestations of love that pour out from Amy: "Dear Madam," says Amy, "if I will starve for your sake, I will be a Whore or anything for your sake; why, I would die for you, if I were put to it."

The titillation continues as Amy vows that in order to rid Roxana of her economic distress she herself is ready to lie with Roxana's landlord, who, in an exchange of favours, is prepared to give the required financial assistance; if Roxana's virtue inhibits her from acceding to the landlord's importunings, then Amy will, on Roxana's behalf, give herself to him. Thus Defoe sets the scene for the creation of a *ménage à trois*; he is anticipating one of the cherished conventions of pornographic lesbian representations that was to be established by one of his contemporaries, John Cleland:[3] that female homosexuality is at best a sort of warm-up to heterosexual sex—a necessary but ultimately temporary phase during the apprenticeship of the female libertine.[4]

Defoe does not hold himself, or us, in suspense for long; excitedly he unfolds his tale. Roxana yields to the landlord and becomes his well paid mistress; disappointed that she has not conceived, and, with the biblical story of the barren Rachel putting her handmaid to bed with Jacob invoked as a possible holy sanction, Defoe provides us with a bodice-ripping episode of troilism. Roxana recites the tale in lascivious detail:

> At Night, when we came to go to-Bed, Amy came into the Chamber to undress me, and her Master slipd into Bed first; then I began, and told him all that Amy had said about my not being with-Child, and of her being with-Child twice in that time; Ay, Mrs Amy, says he, I believe so too, Come hither and we'll try; but Amy did not go; Go, you Fool, says I, can't you, I freely give you both Leave; but Amy would not go; Nay, you Whore, says I, you said, if I would put you to-Bed you would with all your Heart; and with that, I started out, pull'd off her Stockings and Shooes, and all her Cloaths, Piece by Piece, and let her to the Bed, to him; Here, says I, try what you can do with your maid Amy; she pull'd back a little, would not let me pull off her Cloaths at first, but it was hot Weather and she had not many Cloaths on, and particularly, no Stays on; and at last, when she see I was in earnest, she let me do what I wou'd; so I fairly stripped her, and then threw open the Bed, and thrust her in. I need say no more. . . . Amy, I daresay, began now to repent, and would fain have got out of Bed again; but he said to her, Nay, Amy, you see your Mistress put you to-Bed, 'tis all her doing, you must blame her; so he held her fast, and the Wench being Naked in the Bed with him, was too late to look back, so she lay still and let him do what he wou'd.

Defoe's detailed recounting of this incident, contrasting as it does with his usual habit in his novels of leaving us outside the bedroom door of his inamorata, underlines its significance. It is not to be interpreted merely as a vignette invented by a populist journalist to feed the pornographic appetites of his readers. The shameless gaze of Roxana at the coupling of her husband and maid provides Defoe, ever the Peeping-Tom,[5] with an oneiric recollection of the primal scene; the voyeurism is a violation of the privacy and sanctity of the parents' sexual intercourse, a defiant taunt levelled at parents who would dare to exclude the son from their conjugal bliss.

The assault on Amy, when Defoe, through Roxana, strips her, is a sadistic attack on the mother who, by a reversal of authority, must now be mocked and, under the command of the son, ordered to submit to rape. In this episode Defoe's imagination has indeed run riot, releasing all his repressed feelings of vengeance against the women, his mother and stepmother, who had denied him the exclusive love of his father and then failed to provide him with the compensation of their love. The conflict afflicting all of us in the earliest stages of our infantile development between the wish to observe our parents' sexual relationship and the wish to deny away its reality is here depicted, and a vicious resolution of the dilemma is presented; it is an ugly recital, but when the unconscious, unmediated, emerges, expect no mercy; the id is no gentleman.

And after their outrageous frolic, despite the remorse that immediately afflicted the sinners, Defoe has found too many delights in the troilistic situation to allow it to be treated as an isolated lapse. He ensures that Roxana continues to incite an acquiescent Amy to engage in the threesome, and spurs the hesitant landlord to accept, albeit ambivalently, the role of the husband with two wives, the one the Wife of Affection, the other the Wife of Aversion, against whom, while practising his abhorrent Vice, he has murderous thoughts.

By conjuring up this tale of troilism early in the novel, Defoe was creating a template determining the shape and content of the whole work. Troilism afforded him a multitude of opportunities for fantasising which were unavailable, or limited, in a dyadic setting; the tentative troilism episode to be found in Moll Flanders,[6] when he had two brothers bedding down with Moll, lacked the element of simultaneity that is present as Roxana, Amy and the landlord grapple with each other. Later in the novel, Defoe, ever thrilled by the frisson accompanying troilism, tells of Roxana and Amy enjoying themselves in a shared bed when the Lord, Roxana's current lover, unexpectedly came upon them. Pleading that only fear of lightning had caused the two women thus to cling to each other, Roxana, to satisfy the suspicious Lord that their bedfellow was only an innocent female and not a male, condones a sexual assault in her presence by the Lord upon Amy and this dispels all the Lord's doubts about the gender of Roxana's bedmate. Defoe allows the bizarre incident to be described as a "Jest". In telling it, Defoe is once again indulging in a long-time appetite. Even as a young man, as his poetry reveals, he was an ardent admirer of the libertine political stances of John Wilmot, Earl of Rochester; it would not be over-speculative to suggest that Wilmot's delicious erotic poems, including "The Disabled Debauchee",[7] so often laced with themes of troilism, were excitations that lingered on to find their place in Defoe's near-pornographic depictions in *Roxana*.

The gifts and blessings of the authentic and exclusive monogamous relationship—the ideal which Defoe so insistently espoused in his *Religious Courtship* and *Conjugal Lewdness* as attainable—require renunciations; the developmental task of the infant to lay the foundations upon which mature adult heterosexual relations can be securely built requires painful relinquishments; the father must be given up as a lover and the mother as an object of desire. Troilism, in fantasy or practice, tells of the regressive wish to deny the inevitability of such renunciations, of the yearning for the impossible, for the imagined time when the babe was the holy ghost in blasphemous unity with father and mother, a member of a trinity who was one. When three are in one bed they are enacting a scene of an event that never took place but which was once fantasised, and the evocation of that fantasy, bringing with it a temporary freedom from painful choices or renunciations, is the illusory reward gained by the participants. The temptation for Defoe to reclaim such a respite was enormous; the recitals of imagined conflict-free troilism acted as emollients easing the wounds, never healed, suffered in his early Oedipal struggles.

More, a respite so obtained brought Defoe other and significant gains; by discarding the dyad in favour of other computations, of threesomes or foursomes, he could join Roxana in a release without overtly acknowledging its aberrant nature, the Sapphic subtleties which bound her so closely to Amy. Cunningly he inserted episodes in the tale which enabled the two women, separated only by a ceiling, to enjoy each other, each using her man merely as an instrument to facilitate the consummation of their homoerotic desires. When Roxana becomes the mistress of a prince, Amy sleeps with the prince's gentleman servant. Yet

> to cut it short amounted to no more than this, that like Mistress, like maid; as they had many leisure Hours together below, while they waited respectively, when his lord and I were together above; I say, they could hardly avoid the usual question one to another, namely, Why must not they do the same thing below, that we did above?

G. A. Starr, the Defoe scholar, has remarked that in all Defoe's first person works, attachments between the sexes are depicted as weaker than those of the quasi-familial nature;[8] and in none of these are the homosexual components loaded upon them more overtly than in the intimate relationship between Roxana and Amy. Only nominally is that relationship one of mistress and maid; the mistress is in every crisis dependent upon the maid. When Roxana is immobilised by anxiety and indecision it is Amy, increasingly becoming a protective mother figure, who takes the decisions and acts upon them; their ages and roles are reversed. Defoe gives Amy a place within the pantheon dedicated to maternal figures whom we have seen in *Moll Flanders*, overlooking, sheltering or provoking that anti-heroine.[9] Amy is yet another seductive mother inciting her charge to temptations.

Indeed, beneath all the relationships between Defoe's anti-heroines and their mother-surrogates a pathological undercurrent flows. The liaisons depicted are essentially conspiratorial; intimacies and shared secrets abound; tender maternal concerns exist but are subordinate to Sapphic imperatives, often passionate and sometimes destructive. Imported into these relationships are all Defoe's own forbidden filial yearnings; his bi-sexuality, imaginatively deployed and displaced, enables him to become the daughter, and the same homosexual passivity he wished to offer to his father could therefore now be put into play between Moll, Roxana and their mother-surrogates. His creative capacity to shift on to his characters his own unresolved problems, and so lighten his own load, is extraordinary; and no less wondrous, informed by his feminine identification, is his hermeneutic understanding of the homoerotic bonds between mother and daughter, between surrogate mother Amy and Roxana.

The central place of a mother in a woman's life means that she is born, and continues to live, with a legacy of a homoerotic bond, and that female heterosexuality will always be accompanied by a strong homosexual undercurrent.[10] Nowadays, some of Europe's women psychoanalysts are led to conclude, from the clinical material they have assembled, that the penis envy identified by Freud as existing among women arises because women feel handicapped in the means available to them to express their homosexuality.[11] Such women analysts therefore regard the continuous female bi-sexuality of all women not so much as a consequence of a nostalgia for an inadequate clitoris which, to attain femininity, the woman has to give up, but, rather, as an ongoing homosexual longing for her early love, her mother. Most men, unlike Defoe, find women's homosexuality threatening and resent the intimacy of a mother and her girl-child. Indeed, we find that the Jewish God was a jealous God, for the myth tells us that men, not women, were created in "His" image; women were a mere by-product of a man's rib. The Greek depreciation of woman's creative role was no less; Athene was born from the head of Zeus.

In reality, in contrast to the myths, women can, in their daughters, recreate themselves, but the very closeness that can arise between mother and daughter brings its own hazards. It can, at its most benign, bring about the transmission of good mothering and move the daughter towards the joyful acceptance of her femininity and, in turn, her ultimate role. Other and less than good enough mothering can cause hiccups in the girl's development; then she remains still frustrated, still wanting the active possession of her early love, her mother. Unlike male homosexuality, little has been written about female homosexuality, and the importance of the ongoing homosexual relationship between girl and mother which shadows all the adult heterosexuality of a woman is extraordinarily unremarked. But Defoe, advantaged by the insights afforded by his feminine sensibility, in the tragic figure of restless, unfulfilled, status-seeking Roxana, has bequeathed to posterity a true *dolorosa*, a woman who in her sexual ambiguity, promiscuities and protestations is a paradigm containing so many of the discontents not only of the women of his day but also of those unblessed and without moorings living in this confused twenty-first century.

* * * * * * * * * *

Roxana in her fifties is depicted by Defoe contemplating the sick dynamic driving her to her own destruction; her avarice had contributed to her moral downfall, but she acknowledges that greed has not been the dominating motivation. She was now financially secure, worth £50,000, with "£2,500 per year coming in upon good land securities", yet she continues on her shameless pursuit for acclamation; vanity was the spur, her narcissism, never mortified, never assuaged. She knew "avarice could have no pretence" to justify her continued misconduct; only her vanity remains a viable motive.[12] She remarks: "Necessity first debauched me, and poverty made me a whore at the beginning, so excess of avarice for getting money and excess of vanity continued me in the crime."

Roxana was the emblematic name Defoe bestows upon his antiheroine and later it was to become the title of his novel; Roxana's real name was Susan but Roxana was the name that unequivocally advertises her limitless narcissism, for she had earned it in an extraordinary display of exhibitionism that, in the story, captivates the whole of London society. As courtesan to an aristocrat, she hosts at her home a lavish masquerade attended by the dukes and lords and, no less, in disguise, by the king himself. There, bejewelled and dressed in an exotic Turkish costume, she performs an unforgettable erotic dance which so excites the assembly that, unable to contain themselves, the aroused men in her audience burst into applause, repeatedly proclaiming "Roxana! Roxana!"

In Defoe's day "Roxana" had become the generic name for an oriental queen, suggesting ambition, wickedness and exoticism. In her regal display on that ostentatious occasion, Roxana earns her title but seals her own fate. She had over-reached herself. She was to pay a heavy price for her self-indulgence; the event and the Turkish dress she wore were to haunt her to the end of her days. All her later attempts to bury her shameful past, to conceal her life as a whore, were to be thwarted as the story of the Turkish dance repetitiously re-emerged; in the end, to silence the tell-tale daughter threatening the status and security she had gained as a respected countess, she was complicit in her murder. In the tale of the killing by a mother of her child, Defoe presents a terrifying exposure of the destructiveness that can possess a narcissistic woman.

His depiction of the terrible process at work in Roxana, of her alternating disturbed states of mind as, in manic or depressive moods, she struggled with her narcissism, has been described by Defoe scholars as the finest piece he ever wrote.[13] Freud, although never failing to stress the tentative nature of his explorations of femininity, nevertheless unequivocally, time and again, noted the importance of narcissism in female sexuality. In his short, dense, seminal paper entitled *On Narcissism*, he describes a particular type of narcissistic woman as being basically a representative of all women; such a woman, albeit perhaps caricatured, was Roxana. Freud made his clinical judgements by drawing on the morbid manifestations of narcissism of his women patients; Defoe, by anticipating Freud's findings by two centuries, ever more revealed his genius in his delineation of the characteristics of his narcissistic anti-heroine; the traits and dilemmas that Freud catalogued as belonging to such women are all to be found in the character Defoe so marvellously created.

Freud insisted that the narcissistic woman wants "to be loved". To be loved means, primarily, to be chosen and loved for "herself". She wants to be specially valued in a narcissistic way. Adopting Freud's view, the French psychoanalyst Béla Grunberger has pertinently commented:

> We must try to understand this peculiarity of womanhood which confronts us in this characteristic way. We must try to understand why women seek narcissistic gratification above all else, even to the detriment of their own sexual needs, and why they offer themselves sexually in order to be loved; whereas men tend to seek sexual satisfaction primarily, giving their partners narcissistic gratification only in order to obtain their own sexual satisfaction.[14]

When a woman like Roxana affirms, as she explicitly does, her refusal to accept the subjugation of the laws covering the conventional matrimonial state, and demands the right to the same sexual freedom, she risks the danger of being unable to invent a love-life other than narcissistically. Her bodily self will become increasingly important, extending from her body to her clothes, to her jewellery and accessories, to her home, to all the material premises of her love-life; but her actual love-life will be impoverished. Freud's narcissistic woman[15] who put all her libido in what he calls "her narcissistic cathexis"[16] can no longer cathect her sexual instincts and so becomes frigid; Roxana has only tepid sexual relations with her men; her passion is reserved for her duplicates, Amy and other significant women in her life; they are mirror-images, penis-less figures with whom, in lesbian embrace, she hugs herself.

Freud has noted that men are frequently attracted to such women; they are reminded of their own narcissistic tendencies and see in these women a successful narcissistic integrity which they themselves have not been able to achieve. A beautiful woman, such as Roxana, can lure them, for she achieves a rare seductive narcissistic autonomy; by cathecting herself narcissistically, she becomes charming and desirable, a *femme fatale*.

For many women love, as a narcissistic form of sexuality, can be enriching; being admired, liked, loved, having a certain radiance or possessing a certain influence, are all narcissistically enhancing factors; but this benign consequence was not one open to Roxana. Her narcissism was chronic; she failed to achieve a balance between her narcissism and her instinctual needs; in the strangulation of affect which leaves her conspicuously lacking in maternal feeling, we witness her incapacity even to extend her bodily self to her own children. Her desertion and distancing of her many legitimate and illegitimate children, and her insouciance when she loses a babe or has a miscarriage, jar; even allowing for the social mores of her day, which accorded little respect for children's needs and rights, her self-regard at the expense of her offspring is repellent and Defoe, the moralist, ensures retribution is exacted as he sends his countess anti-heroine to her doom.

D. H. Lawrence once wrote "One sheds one's sickness in books— repeats and presents one's emotions to be master of them"; and doubtless it would be possible to relate many of Defoe's personal anguishes to the oft-times aberrant and selfish behaviour of Roxana, and indeed other characters whom he places in his last novel. But such a deconstruction could become an iconoclastic injustice, for the novel is far more than an attempt by Defoe at self-therapy; it is a study unsurpassed in English literature or contemporary psychoanalysis of the narcissism of womankind. In *Roxana* Defoe achieved the creative detachment that Coleridge described as "aloofness"; in such contemplation Defoe has given us a work of art. We would risk the deserved charge of spoliation and appear prurient if we enthusiastically attempted to dismember such a work; we may find it more rewarding to leave the work intact, note its acknowledgement that it suffers an omission and discover the significance of a censorship which Defoe has imposed upon Roxana, barring her from telling us anything of three years and a month in her life as a whore.

★ ★ ★ ★ ★ ★ ★ ★ ★ ★

In his scrutiny of male impotence, we have seen Defoe insisting upon and affirming the legitimacy of a woman's demand for sexual satisfaction;[17] he was indeed quite prepared to countenance the adultery of a woman suffering from an inadequate husband who failed to serve her. But today's vulgar error, that in sex women can find their fulfilment and that achieving an orgasm to match man's ejaculation should be the holy grail and sought by all women, was no part of Defoe's catechism. He was too much of a woman himself to believe the act of copulation could answer a woman's most profound needs. In his depiction of Roxana, Defoe relegates sex and instead brings into prominence the other needs of all womankind, each specific and exaggerated in Roxana's case, but nevertheless felt by all women. Defoe's empathy ensures that we understand that lust was never the irresistible imperative spurring Roxana on in her promiscuous adventures.

Roxana wishes, above all, to be what today we dub a "celebrity", but a celebrity of a particular kind, one whose vanity would not be content with the admiration of a mere brewer, jeweller or merchant, whatever might be their appearance or age, however "obliging" or "gentlemanly"; no matter how sexually besotted with her, whatever money they showered upon her, still her narcissism was unassuaged by their attentions. Her secret desire, revealed in her Turkish dance, was expressed in a fantasy of being not lowly, plebeian Susan, not even, as she was to become, a countess, but becoming a queen, admired by all her subjects. Defoe indulges himself, and ourselves, by permitting Roxana to be mistress to a lord and to a prince, but then he takes fright; his imagination is taking him into awesomely dangerous quarters; he wishes but fears to allow us sight of a king entering her boudoir; for three years and a month, however, the bedroom door is closed. All that Defoe, as narrator, with considerable trepidation has to tell us is contained in a short paragraph:

> There is a Scene which came in here, which I must cover from humane Eyes or Ears; for three years and about a month, here Roxana

liv'd retir'd, having been oblig'd to make an Excursion, in a Manner, and with a Person, which Duty, and a private Vow, obliges her not to reveal, at least, not yet.

"At least, not yet" ambivalently expresses an intention that one day the kiss-and-tell revelatory story will be told; in fact the novel ends without such a recital. Defoe did not dare to fulfil the intention, for it would have revealed the unavowed[18] motivation behind the concealment of Roxana's thirty-seven month amorous adventure which was the apogee of her career as a courtesan. Unconvincingly Defoe professes that it would be lese majesty to say more. If that indeed was the case, why, one asks, has the narrator tantalisingly even mentioned the episode; and why, when we have been told so openly and in such detail of Roxana's affaires with so many other men, has such a mood of *terribilata* enveloped this particular liaison, one so awesome that it must be shielded "from humane Eyes or Ears"?

In suppressing Roxana's liaison with a king, Defoe is engaged in one of his familiar stratagems. We should not be deceived. As ever, he is attempting, by the fantasising of apposite events and characters, to circumvent and subvert the prohibitions against his passive homosexual incestuous longings. Precariously, unobserved, he seeks to fulfil these secret desires as Roxana, with whom Defoe identifies, captures the king's lascivious attentions and triumphantly, so chosen, submits to the royal embrace and enjoys the illicit love-making of the king—the father of his people.

So paper-thin is the camouflage Defoe uses in this synoptic, one-paragraph recording of this most significant event in Roxana's life that one suspects he is inviting the thrill of being discovered; of all the many games of hide and seek that we find in his works, this spiel is the most naive. Looming behind the depicted king is the authoritarian ruler of Defoe's first household, his father, while Roxana is the feminised version of Daniel himself. The extraordinary reticence Defoe imposes on the narrator stems not from "Duty" or etiquette or from a commendable refusal to exploit the capture of the king by a kiss-and-tell story; it is part of Defoe's half-hearted cover-up of an imagined agony and ecstasy which he is sharing with Roxana in a criminal, incestuous act. In real life, we have seen Defoe using another king, William of Orange, to regain a reminiscence of his earliest intimacies with his own father;[19] here we see him again using a royal figure as a fantasised father surrogate; but he is frightened of recording the doubts of such an outrageous defiance of the ultimate taboo. He was fearful his imagination was getting out of control;[20] to save himself, he gagged the narrator.

Eschewing psychologising, but noting how Roxana and Defoe's other characters are always engaging in a fevered pursuit of wealth, has led many economists, political theorists, sociologists and literary critics to fasten on to Defoe's fictional creations and to declare them to be classical examples in literature of *Homo economicus*. Exceptionally, others, recoiling from such a coarse interpretation, have said that his characters, for all their pursuit of money, are unique in their *nouveau riche* point of view and that they owe this to their creator:

> they do not worship wealth for its own sake but are fascinated by it because of the style of life that they know it can buy in the fluid society of the late seventeenth and early eighteenth centuries—hence their key interest in such details as fine clothes, gorgeous equipages, liveried servants, handsome houses. Defoe's characters, in short, do not pursue wealth so much as pursue gentility, which they know wealth can buy them.[21]

Yet even such tempered, perceptive assessments suggesting that Roxana's pursuit of a king can be explained by her dominant desire to rise above her class are inadequate. Defoe's usual unabashed and often prolix recitals of the antics of his status-seeking marionettes become hushed when Roxana goes to the king; there is no celebration of her triumphant fulfilment of her aspiration to move in the highest possible circles. Defoe does not want any further scrutiny of the liaison lest it be revealed as a masquerade, a charade intended to direct attention away from its true intent, that of the telling of a tale—not of the consummation of a relationship between a king and his mistress, but that of a love whose name cannot be told between a father and a son.

Such transgressive fantasising merited severe punishment; to exculpate himself, Defoe inflicted upon Roxana the wrath of God. With the most heinous crime unmentionable, he focuses upon her other great crime, her complicity in the murder of her daughter, to justify the punishment she must suffer. She must fall "into a dread Course of Calamities". She is brought low again; the "Blast of Heaven" unremittingly pursues her and Defoe, fearful of being found guilty by association, distances himself from her, abandons her to terrible fate and abruptly ends the novel. His damaging imaginings had brought him to the edge of the abyss; but he had learned his lesson. Never again would he write a novel.

Notes

1. Mullan, J., Introduction to *Roxana*, Oxford Classic Paperbacks, 1998.
2. Term used for a man or woman looking at their partner having sexual intercourse with one or more adult partners (www.aegsa.com/glossary).
3. Cleland, J., *Memoirs of a Woman of Pleasure*, Oxford University Press, 1985.
4. Castles, T., *The Literature of Lesbianism*, Columbia University Press, 2003.
5. See Chapter 8, p. 93.
6. See Chapter 16, p. 238.
7. Adlard, J., *John Wilmot*, Carcanet Press, 1974.
8. Starr, G. A., Introduction to *Moll Flanders*, Oxford University Press, 1998.
9. See Chapter 16.
10. Abse, L, *Fellatio, Masochism, Politics and Love*, Robson Books, 2000, pp. 28–33.
11. Haleberstaet-Freud, H., Electra versus Oedipus, *International Journal of Psychoanalysis*, 7 (1998), 41.
12. Shinagel, M., *Daniel Defoe and Middle-class Gentility*, Harvard University Press, 1968.
13. Blewett, D., Introduction to *Roxana*, Penguin Books, 1987.
14. Grunberger, B., *Outline for the Study of Narcissism in Female Sexuality*, Karnac Books, 1992.
15. Freud, S., *On Narcissism: An Introduction*, SE, Volume 14.
16. A term invented by Freud's translators of *Besetzung* ("interest"), the word Freud used to describe the quantity of energy attaching to a mental structure.
17. See Chapter 14, p. 201.
18. Freud, S., *Forgetting of Intention in Psychopathology of Everyday Life*, SE, Volume 6.
19. See Chapter 9, p. 108.
20. Shinagel, *Daniel Defoe and Middle-class Gentility*.
21. Ibid.

CHAPTER EIGHTEEN

Apocalypse: *The Political History of the Devil*

T he Devil and Defoe were more than old acquaintances and, in
1726, having quit his novel-writing, Defoe paid his respects
to him by writing his biography; it is a work that has proved
to be of singular and discomfiting relevance to contemporary political dilemmas. *The Political History of the Devil* was one of the last
major works of Defoe to be published in his lifetime; there he presented, not for the first time, a fearless defence of his "friend",
acknowledging his defects but exonerating him from so many of the
accusations that throughout history had been falsely heaped upon
the hapless fallen angel.

Six years earlier Defoe had already come to the Devil's aid in
his *Vision of the Angelik World*,[1] where, adumbrating *The Political
History of the Devil*, he gave this ironic reflection upon the capabil-
ity of humanity to conduct evil deeds without the interference of
the Devil:

> I must do the Devil the justice, as to own, that he is the most slan-
> der'd, most abus'd Creature alive; Thousands of Crimes relayed to
> his Charge that he is not guilty of; Thousands of our own Infirmities
> we load him with which he has no Hand in; and Thousands of our

Sins, which, bad as he is, he knows nothing of; calling him our
Tempter, and pretending we did so and so, as the Devil would have it,
when on the contrary the Devil had no say in it, and we were only led
away of our own Lust and enticed.[2]

When *The Political History of the Devil* was published that admonition
to those who strove to project their crimes upon the Devil was
again vigorously repeated in the verse he placed on the frontispiece
of the book:

Bad as he is, the Devil may be Abus'd,
Be falsly charg'd, and causelessly accus'd,
When Man, unwilling to be blam'd alone,
Shift off those crimes on Him which are their Own.

This little verse, as in his earlier intimations in *Vision of the Angelik
World*, was giving notice that he was involved in a disengagement
exercise; he wished to release man, over-eager to escape personal
responsibility, from an anthropomorphic delusion; the Devil with
all his wiles was in themselves; absolution could not be gained
by exteriorising their evil and attributing it to a fallen angel. The
moralist Defoe, in his *Political History of the Devil*, was preaching,
tabulating and scrutinising, often choosing delicious raillery and
devastating wit, the evasions that man had, from the beginning of
time, deployed in order to acquit himself of sin by finding Lucifer
guilty. The psychic mechanism of projection which operates when
we reject or refuse to admit to ourselves feelings, qualities and
wishes which govern us and, disavowing them, expel and locate
them in another, has never been more insightfully explored in
English literature than in this work of Defoe.

It was 170 years later that Freud gave his first description of this
psychic mechanism,[3] and so gave the phenomenon a significant
place in psychoanalytical theory; but so many of the various psychoanalytical presentations of the exculpatory nature of the phenomenon are explicitly anticipated by Defoe that it is tempting to
challenge, in this particular respect, the priority psychoanalysts
award Freud and to affirm that perhaps Defoe can lay claim to
the accolade of being the first depth psychologist; the clinical
assessments made by psychoanalysts which lead them to identify

the precipitates triggering off projective thinkings in their patients are indeed to be found richly illustrated in *The Political History of the Devil*.

So many of Freud's contributions are devastatingly innovative that it is quite unnecessary to add false claims and to deny the contributions of his precursors. Perhaps Freud himself is to blame that this occasionally occurs; in a congratulatory birthday greeting to Einstein he enviously suggests that Einstein has the good fortune of being "a completer" whereas he was "a pioneer", that it was one matter to open a new field in science and technology but quite another to open up virgin territory in psychology:

> Without specialised preparation no one can permit himself a judgement in astronomy, physics or chemistry. . . . This does not hold for psychology. Every man is a connoisseur of the mind, every man knows just as well, or better, without having gone to any trouble. And since they have arrived at their opinions so cheaply, they cannot believe that someone else has gone to greater expense on the matter.[4]

Freud is acknowledging Einstein as the last and greatest of a long line while claiming that he himself had no such lineage; his self-image as a lonely figure, a foundling lacking ancestors, is a conceit; he had debts to predecessors and, although he was unaware of him, one of those forerunners was Daniel Defoe. Far more convincing is the acknowledgement made by Freud on his seventieth birthday: "The poets and philosophers before me discovered the unconscious. What I discovered was the scientific method by which the unconscious can be studied."

Like Defoe, Freud found it necessary to personify the evil and destructive forces which man, fearing their implosion, endeavours to project outwards; Defoe entitles them "the Devil", Freud named them "Thanatos", the Greek god of death and destruction. The poetic metaphors are of the same ilk; the pseudonyms should not confuse us; both of them are concealing descriptions of the same reality; both Defoe and Freud, in their various fashions, are mocking the superstitions that men, unable to tolerate the burdens of their lusts, have displaced on to mythic figures. Bluntly, Freud tells us: "I believe that a large part of the mythological view of the world, which extends a long way into most modern religions, is nothing but psychology projected into the external world."[5] Freud draws that conclusion from his delving into the mind of the paranoiac; there, the sick man's fears, desires and homicidal impulses are not fought and overcome; they are projected outwards and, there suspended, they ceaselessly persecute the victim. In what Freud describes as an analogous mode of thinking,

> Psychical factors and relations in the unconscious are mirrored in the construction of a supernatural reality, which is destined to be changed back once more by science into the psychology of the unconscious. One could venture to explain in this way the myths of paradise and the fall of man, of God, of good and evil, of immortality, and so on, and to transform metaphysics into metapsychology.[6]

Though Freud and Defoe are engaged in a similar exercise—that of freeing men from the chains of superstition—their ultimate goals differ. Freud was a man of his times, over-valuing in early twentieth-century fashion the potential of science to bring rationality to mankind, and ever hostile to theistic religious belief, considering that it told of man's continuing infantile dependence, of his immaturity; his derision of superstition was that of a godless Jew. Defoe's debunking was of a different order; he was the unswerving English Protestant of the eighteenth century determined to defend the wisdom of God at a time when he believed it was in danger of being buried in the clutter of "Papist" superstitions and trampled upon by sceptics and empiricists. The perspective of the theologian Nicholas Hudson well explicates Defoe's motivations:

> Defoe's discussions of the devil and providence illustrate the conflicts and perplexities which accumulated when English Protestants began to insist on a theology that seemed acceptable to reason and commonsense, a demand inseparable from the rise of empiricism and the increased liberty to question established doctrines which followed the political events of 1688 and 1714.[7]

Freud, in Nietzschean mode, had looked forward to a distant rational day when man would declare God was dead. Meanwhile, he counselled us to follow the advice of Heine, "one of his comrades in disbelief":

Let us leave the heavens
To the angels and the sparrows.[8]

Similar advice had in his day been proffered to Defoe. He well knew the strength of the argument; and indeed early in *The Political History of the Devil* in deliciously comic speech he stages a debate between "Two gentlemen of quality, and both men of wit too, one a non-believer, the other affirming his belief in the devil." Defoe provides the doubter with ammunition to defend his position, allowing him to quote from "the incomparable noble genius My Lord Rochester", who "upon the subject unfeignedly sings":

After death nothing is,
And nothing death.

Pressing his argument, the non-believer thrusts: "Is it not wiser to believe no Devil than to be always terrify'd at him?" But Defoe would not allow his believer to capitulate; and when the dialogue is completed, he sums up:

The Truth is, God and the Devil, however opposite in their nature and remote from one another in their place of abiding, seem to stand pretty much upon a level in our faith; For, as at to our believing the reality of their existence, he that denies one generally denies both; and he who believes one necessarily believes both.

Very few, if any of those who believe there is a GOD, and acknow-ledge the debt of homage which mankind owes to the Supreme Governor of the World doubts the existence of the Devil, except here and there one, to whom we call practical Atheists; and 'tis the character of an Atheist, if there is such a creature on Earth, . . . he believes neither god or devil.[9]

For Defoe the Devil defined God; he rejected any Heine-like injunc-tion to leave the heavens to the sparrow; to have followed such advice could only lead to faithless despair. No one would deter Defoe from his explorations of life in the heavens, where good angels and wicked dissidents clashed, where demographic prob-lems always prevailed as erring denizens were rejected and far fewer souls ascended to replenish the heavenly hosts, where in the

civil wars prevailing the Devil was ever present with his incite-
ments. And all this Defoe subtly, and some may say miraculously,
depicted without lapsing into anthropomorphism; on the contrary,
he de-anthropomorphised some of the most tenaciously held fictions
of mankind.

The sophistication of the treatise makes one keenly aware how
misplaced were the assessments by his literary peers of the man and
his works: Jonathan Swift anathematised Defoe as a "stupid, illiter-
ate fanatic" and Joseph Addison dismissed him as a "false, prevari-
cating rogue". So compelling are some passages in this *History* that
one can only conclude that spleen, not genuine literary criticism,
determined their judgements.

In one of the most arresting passages in the whole work, focusing
upon the cloven hoof so widely attributed to the Devil, we see Defoe
ridiculing the superstitions hindering awareness of the real forces
moving man to evil; he mocks at man's attempts to domesticate the
Devil and so evade recognition that he is at work in himself:

'tis the Cloven-Foot understood by us not as a bare Token to know
Satan by, but as if it were a Brand upon him, and like the Mark God
put upon Cain, it was given him for a Punishment, so that he cannot
leave to appear without it, nay cannot conceal it whatever other
Dress or Disguise he may put on; and as if it was to make him as
ridiculous as possible, they will have it be, that whatever Satan has
Occasioned to dress himself in any humane Shape, be it of What
Degree soever, from the King to the Beggar, be it of a fine Lady or
an Old woman (the Latter it seems the oftenest assumed) yet still he
not only must have this Cloven-Foot about him, but he is oblig'd to
shew it too; nay, they will not allow him any Dress, whether it be a
Prince's Robe, a Lord Chancellor's Gown, or a Lady's Hoops and
long Petticoats, but the Cloven-Hoof must be show'd from under
them; they will not so much as allow him an artificial shoe, or a
jackboot, as we often see contrived to conceal a Club-Foot or a
Wooden-Leg; but that the devil may be known wherever he goes, is
bound to shew his Foot; they might as well oblige him to set a Bill
upon his Cap, as Folks do upon a House to be let, and have it written
in capital Letters, I am the DEVIL.

It must be confess'd this is a very particular, and would be very
hard upon the devil, if it had not another Article in it which is some

Advantage to him, and that is, that the fact is not true; but the Belief of this is so universal, that all the World runs away with it; by which Mistake the good People miss the devil many times when they look for him and meet him often where they did not expect him, and when for want of this Cloven-Foot they do not know him.[10]

Commenting on this passage the Defoe scholar Laura Curtis, whose work so differs from the obsessive and arid discursive textual analyses of his writings afflicting so many English departments of universities (particularly in the United States), has emphasised its significance:

> The central action of this passage from *The Political History of the Devil* is a caricature of the central action of Defoe's writing. The "Folks" or "good People" are translating the non-quantifiable aspects of life, in this case evil, into a humble physical equivalent, the cloven hoof, and thereby ejecting from their world, or refusing to consider, the uncontrollability and the complexity of evil. The cloven hoof exists only in the simplified and ideal world of their limited imaginations. . . . The notion of the cloven hoof, frightening to the unsophisticated, amusing to the thoughtful, misrepresents Satan's real nature, which is internal to the individual, intangible, and complex, and thus leads people astray; they are powerless to recognise the presence of evil when Satan does appear in their midst.[11]

Satan, Defoe is warning us, as Curtis presents it, is "internal to the individual"—be he a Lord Chancellor or a beggar. By a circuitous route, Defoe has found the same source of man's compulsion to project and concretise the Devil as does Freud,[12] who saw him as the personification of the repressed unconscious instinctual life within every man. But there is one essential difference between the two men. Each has reached the same destination but they have travelled on different roads, having different experiences. Freud, en route, killed off God, but Defoe, on his highway, good Protestant as he was, challenged and warded off the Devil and rehabilitated the Almighty.

★   ★   ★   ★   ★   ★   ★   ★   ★   ★

The contributions of Defoe in his *Review*, justifying him being awarded the accolade of "Father of Journalism",[13] are collated in twenty-two books and in over five thousand double-columned pages written over nine busy years, from 1704 to 1713. For twelve years Laura Curtis trawled this corpus of Defoe's work before advancing the thesis which she founded on her reading of those works;[14] she saw a Defoe divided between an ideal world of order and rational control and a real world of disorder and impulse. In the *Review*, as "Mr Review", the meliorist ceaselessly presents his blueprints of the ideal society he advocated; simultaneously he vividly depicts in the real world all the deceptions, transgressions and irreverences to which he was attracted and condemns. In *The Political History of the Devil* the same utopian hopes and the same ambivalences towards vitality and destructiveness find expression. But in *The Political History of the Devil*, more than in any of his works, Defoe forges a viable compromise between his ideal and real worlds, between his idealised and real selves; the tumultuous world, the uncontrolled satanic world, with all its deviance and lustful temptations and terrifying energy, which Defoe always feared would overwhelm him, was allowed a measured release; he gave the Devil his due, and thus respected, the Devil was ready to share with Defoe his élan and put his creative guile at Defoe's service. With the Devil identified, Satan becomes less threatening and Defoe is sufficiently relaxed to jostle and laugh with him as together they mock the foibles of mankind. Here in this work, exceptionally, the Devil is less fearsome than when he tempts the heroes and heroines of his novels; those fictional characters are ever walking precariously on a tightrope with frightening mysterious elemental forces poised to tip them and send them to their doom; they and their creator are well depicted by the Defoe scholar George Starr when he writes

> Such mastery as the Defoedian hero achieved over himself and his world is quite precarious; it involves insulation and repression rather than openness and liberation, an imposing of order on everything alien and threatening rather than that benign acceptance of the facts of otherness and disorder (or order beyond man's contriving) which we find at the conclusion of a Sophoclean or Shakespearian tragedy.[15]

Sometimes too in Defoe's non-fiction, as we have seen in our scrutiny of *The Storm*,[16] the syndrome Starr identifies results in aesthetic failure; Defoe's over-determined need to maintain such a tight control of his passions, to keep rigidly in place the "insulation" upon which Starr remarks, means we are presented with a desiccated work, impressively researched but lacking élan. Such defects, however, are not to be found in *The Political History of the Devil*; the Devil, the repository of all repressed desires, is not excluded; on the contrary, here Defoe and the Devil become allies. Defoe identifies the targets, and then sets Satan to execute his devilish destructive assaults upon them.

Too often, however, as we know to our cost in our unhappy twenty-first century, the Devil, not through indolence but through a desire to continue enjoying the iconoclastic pleasures of a sadistic demolisher, never completed his tasks. When Defoe tells us of the work of his ally at the time of the Crusades, we are aware, as Bush and his puppet Blair wage their presidential crusade, how the Devil continues to insinuate himself. Defoe, when employing the Devil to incite religious fundamentalism and Western arrogance, gives us a piquantly ironic commentary as chasteningly apposite today as when it was written:

> It is plain Satan has very often had a share in the method, if not in the design of propagating christian faith; For example

> I think I do no injury at all to the Devil, to say that he had a great hand in the old holy war, as it was ignorantly and enthusiastically call'd, and in stirring up the christian princes and powers of Europe to run a madding after the Turks and Saracens, and make war with those innocent people above a thousand miles off, only because they enterd into God's heritage when he had forsaken it, graz'd upon his ground when he had fairly turned it into a common, and laid it open for the next comer; spending the nation's treasure, and embarking their kings and peoples, I say, in a war about a thousand miles off, filling their heads with their religious madness, call'd in those days holy zeal to recover the sancta, the sepulchres of Christ and the Saints, and as they called this falsly, the holy city, tho' two religions say it was the accurs'd city, and not worth spending one drop of blood for.

> This religious Bubble was certainly of Satan who, as he craftily drew them in, so like a true Devil, he left them in the lurch when they came there, fac'd about to the Saracens, animated the immortal Saladin against them, and manag'd so dextrously that he left the

bones of about thirteen or fourteen thousand Christians there as a
trophy of his infernal politicks; and after the christian world had run
a la santa terra, or in English, a saunt'ring about a hundred years, he
dropt it to play another game less foolish, but ten times the wickeder
than that which went before it, namely turning the Crusadoes of the
christians one against another and . . .

Made them fight like mad or drunk,
For dame religion as for punk

Here, as in so many of his depictions of the ingenious machinations
of his ally, Defoe is informing upon him, giving warning of his presence, providing copious illustrations of his technique and declaring,
like a Zarathustra, "thus has Satan abused the Reason of Man".

Defoe is no dabbling amateur; always the perpetual spy, no matter what disguise the Devil assumes, he is determined to unmask
him. He has grasped that when the Devil reveals himself in exotic
form, he is engaged in a distraction, leaving him free to pursue his
mischief elsewhere. Alerting us, therefore, to the Devil's protean
nature, Defoe, as is his fashion, turns to admonitory scriptural texts:

It is thus express'd in Scripture, where the person possess'd,
Matt.14,24 [sic], is first said to be possess'd of the Devil (singular) and
our Saviour asked him, as speaking to a single person, What is thy
name? and is answered in the plural and singular together, My name
is Legion, for we are many.

But Defoe has no qualms in betraying his ally in whatever form he
may appear. His main purpose in consorting with the Devil is to
collect the information that will subvert him:

for 'tis a great mistake in those who think that in an acquaintance
with the affairs of the Devil may not be made very useful to us all;
They that know no evil can know no good; and, as the learned tell us,
that a stone taken out of the head of a Toad is a good antidote against
poison, so a competent knowledge of the Devil and all his ways may
be the best help to make us defie the devil and all his works.

To achieve the task Defoe set himself, to be equipped to defy man's
destroyer, he endeavoured to collect everything then believed about

Beelzebub. Much source material was available to Defoe. From his childhood he had been enveloped in the imagery of the Bible; he would have known the disguises the Devil had assumed, as Gog, the archetype of evil in Ezekiel,[17] as the mighty horn of the great Beast who waged war against the saints and prevailed against them in the visions of Daniel,[18] and, above all, as Satan in the futurist apocalyptic eschatology of Revelation. Literate in the diabolic, Defoe proceeds to take us from the glory days when Satan was an

> angel of light, a glorious Seraph, perhaps the choicest of all the glorious Seraphs down to the time of his failed rebellion when, choked with rage that God had proclaimed His Son Generalissimo, and with himself supreme ruler in Heaven, giving the dominion of all his works of creation, as well already finish'd as not then begun, to him; which boasts of honour (say they) Satan expected to be conferr'd on himself as next in honour, majesty and power to God the Supreme;

And then Defoe recalls for us how, having fallen from his blessedness, the Devil:

> continued with his whole army in a state of darkness before the creation of man. 'Tis supposed it might be a considerable space, and that he was part of his punishment too, being all the while unactive, unemploy'd, having no business, nothing to do but gnawing his own Bowels, and rolling in the agony of his own self reproaches, being a Hell to himself in reflecting on the glorious state from whence he was fallen. How long he remained thus, 'tis true that we have no light into from history, and but little from tradition; . . . Rabbi Judah says, The Jews were of the opinion, that he remained twenty thousand years in that condition, and that the world shall continue twenty thousand more, in which he shall find work enough to satisfy his mischievous desires. . . . Indeed, let the devil have been idle as they think he was before, it must be acknowledg'd that now he is the most busy, vigilant and diligent, of all God's creatures and very full employment too, such as it is.

With the same vividness as Defoe tells us of the Destroyer's wickedness even before the creation of man, we find illustrated, as the work unfolds, the deceptions practised even up to Defoe's day by Lucifer upon mankind. By thus using the traditional myths to de-mythologise the very myths he was deconstructing, Defoe was compelling attention to be focused on the self-deceptions and rationalisations employed to evade personal responsibility and to shift it elsewhere; and, even more, he was unveiling the motivations hidden behind the pretensions of nobility, nationalism, religious enthusiasms and ideological fundamentalism, so that he could then assert that it was Man himself who was creating hell on earth. The over-riding purpose of Defoe's extraordinary collation of tales of the Devil was to provide insight into the unselfconscious conduct of purblind Man who, lacking that insight, encompassed his own destruction, a victim of the Devil within him.

Defoe was relentless in his betrayal of the secrets he had wrested out of his unsuspecting ally. Now the Devil cowered under the searchlight that Defoe directed upon him; the Devil had been fooled, and ere Defoe concluded recounting the Destroyer's escapades, it was Defoe not the Devil who was in control. And Defoe was possessed of the same elation as we have witnessed[19] when he triumphed over the Devil, then operating in consort with Thanatos, in his defiant work *Journal of the Plague Year*.

The resonances with the completed book were immediate. Notwithstanding a large first edition, a second edition appeared within a year, in 1727, another in 1728 and yet another in Dublin. By 1729 a translation was published in Amsterdam and was speedily reprinted; before long a German edition was issued in Frankfurt. It may be that some of its success was due to a prurient readership attracted to the diverting anecdotes of the Devil's antics which laced the work; but it is a weighty tome and its emancipatory impact must surely have registered with a serious audience welcoming and sharing the liberation it brought; for such a work, helping to free man from thraldom to unbridled passions and involuntary aggression, and assisting man, unbedevilled by hindrances, towards the achievement of rationality, would have brought relief to many readers, as indeed it did to Defoe; it is infinitely more comfortable, although less exciting, to travel when the ego, not the id in the form of the Devil, is in the driving seat.

       ★ ★ ★ ★ ★ ★ ★ ★ ★ ★

Stabilised, after the temporary subjugation of the Devil in *The Political History*, Defoe, for the little time left to him, successfully continued on to write a few optimistic, melioristic works; but the

Devil, biding his time, knowing the weaknesses of his betraying erstwhile ally, was plotting revenge. The Devil was set to lure him, to proffer him the masochistic delights which for Defoe were ever irresistible temptations. What Defoe found intolerable was success; it was the sweet smell of defeat that intoxicated him; punishment had to be sought for his earliest infantile fantasised sins so deeply buried in his unconscious that even the brilliant insights into motivations displayed in *The Political History of the Devil* had not turned them up. Nothing therefore gave him greater delight than when the adversities he courted fell upon him; he revelled in his stoicism. He had once written: "He that cannot live above the scorn of scoundrels, is not fit to live; dogs will bark, malice will rage, slander will revile—and they shall; without lessening one moment of my tranquillity."[20] Defoe's boast that he was invulnerable was soon to be sorely tested; for a handful of years the ageing Defoe held the Destroyer at bay but the avenging Devil was relentless and persistent, determined to exact his revenge. In the end, Defoe's carapace cracked. He was left exposed; the destructive forces of revenge invading his imagination turned in upon himself. Thus with no defences, he succumbed, and masochistically submitted to the tainted delights that none knew better than he were the dangerous accompaniments of indulgence in what he once described as the "luscious" passion of revenge:

> I might enlarge here, and very much to the Purpose, in describing spherically and mathematically that exquisite Quality called a devilish Spirit, in which he would naturally occur to give you a whole Chapter upon the glorious Articles of Marriage, and Envy, and especially upon that luscious, delightful, triumphant Passion call'd REVENGE; How natural to Man, nay even to both Sexes; How pleasant in the very Contemplation, tho' there be not just at that Time a Power of Execution; How palatable it is in its self, and how well it relishes when dish'd up with its proper Sauces, such as Plot, Contrivance, Steam and Confederacy, all leading to Execution; How it possesses humane Soul in all the most sensible Parts; how it empowers Mankind to sin in Imagination, as effectually to all future Intents and purposes (Damnation) as if he had sinned actually; How safer practice it is too, as to Punishment in this Life, namely that it empowers us to cut Throats clear of the Gallows, to slander Virtue, reproach Innocence, wound Honour and stab Reputation; and in a

Word to do all the wicked Things in the World, out of the Reach of
the Law.

It also requir'd some few Words to describe the secret Operations
of those nice Qualities when they reach the humane Soul; how
effectually they form a Hell within us, and how imperceptibly they
assimilate and transform us into Devils, mere humane Devils, as
wary Devils, as Satan himself, or any of his angels; and that therefore
'tis not so much out of the Way as some imagine, to say such a Man is
an incarnate Devil; for as crime makes Satan a Devil, who was before
a bright immortal Seraph, or Angel of Light, how much more easily
may the same Crime make the same DEVIL, tho' every Way meaner
and more contemptible, of a man or a woman either.

Such meditations on the qualities and operations of the Devil may
seem quaint to faithless modern man; for Defoe it was axiomatic that
a true belief in God was unsustainable without belief in the Devil.
He inhabited a different world from that of today's vapid believers
and half-hearted atheists; the Devil was no exhausted over-worn
metaphor, he was a reality, albeit found in oneself.

Perceptions of Satan have changed before in the history of Western man; indeed, the whole notion that men could become angels
filling the gaps left in heaven by the fall of Lucifer and his hosts
was a seventeenth-century innovation uncanvassed by mediaeval
theologians;[21] but it was an ideality that possessed the Puritan
imagination. The nascent Enlightenment had not yet done its worst
and created a space between the spiritual and secular life; for Defoe
there was no such space, no realm of neutrality or middle ground for
action that was not a commitment to one side or other in the great
battle between God and Satan.

With our tin ears, only exceptionally do we now hear the clamour
of that battle; it is too far away from us, but when a blessed wind
carries it to us, then we are aware of the nobility of the struggle. It is
Defoe's contemporary, the Protestant composer Johann Sebastian
Bach, following the 200-year-old instructions of Martin Luther, who
still attunes us to the battle cries. The Bach scholar James Gaines has
told us:

As with Luther, God and Satan were vividly alive for Bach, and his
own life was their battleground. It is difficult to listen to his music—by

turns gruesome and angelic, tormented and enraptured, mournful and exuberant—without hearing the warfare raging inside him, just as it had raged in Martin Luther; and in that respect his sacred and secular music were the same.[22]

Defoe's life too was the site of a battle between God and Lucifer or, as the Freudians would say, between Eros and Thanatos. But the result of the battle was far different; in Bach's scenario God triumphs, in Defoe's victory goes to the Devil. Often with Bach we have works which are at first of almost unbearable sadness, music from a cold and distant darkness but which as it comes closer begins to sing a quiet song which, although full of pain, speaks of hope. His wondrous oratorios too end in redemption and resurrection. But Defoe, fated to be a heroic loser, was to end in hopelessness. His triumph was to be posthumous, in the endurance over the centuries of his works, but in his lifetime, in the end, he suffered the sweet and sour bitterness of defeat.

Despite, with extraordinary precision, having self-mockingly traced the repulsive suppurative liniments of "devilish spirits", still he was not able to free himself from their fatal attractions; yet again, he exemplified the adage that not all are free who mock their chains. In his last days Satan took over and Defoe eagerly submitted to the consequent flagellation.

The Devil's lashings were unsparing; as Defoe approached his seventieth year the world's hostility, and his own hostility to himself, intensified. He had presaged years before in one of the last editions of *The Review* that friendlessness was to be his ultimate lot, the price he would pay for his independence:

> He that writes against the sense of two potent, contending, and violent parties, is likely to be censured by both, and certain to be crushed by one—As I thank God I have never written for any party yet, so I find myself almost writing against every party now; and doubt not I may be a sacrifice to both, or at least to the fury of that which shall prevail, let it be which it will.

Now the times had ominously moved on and his prophecy was fulfilled; there was no principled king, patron or faction to whom he could turn; he was alone in a world that had become, for the great moralist, cruelly out of joint. As the blows fell upon him, no solace to still his anguishes would be available from an indifferent selfish ruling group increasingly preoccupied with ensuring its own sordid survival. The reign of the first Hanoverian had been followed by George II, who presided over a court as depraved as that of his predecessor; the aristocrats and the gentry lived in elegance and luxury but the London in which Defoe dwelt was a stinking, filthy, mud-bespattered metropolis, pullulating with slums, where infants died like flies, tuberculosis was rampant and successive waves of smallpox ravaged the populace. Life was cheap, death a lottery; furious gambling obsessed both men and women, and an abundance of low-priced gin, not faith, was the dangerous anodyne for the miseries of the poor. With the serious concerns of politics reduced only to conflicts arising from the placing of sons and nephews in lucrative positions around the court, this was the society where the Devil and his works were unchallenged. It was later in the century, after Defoe's death, that the industrious middle classes really flexed their muscles and demanded reform to bring order and thrift, the necessary components of the society they sought; but meanwhile, Satan, unchecked, was footloose, spreading disorder, eulogising violence and encouraging self-destruction. He did not fail to include Defoe as one of his victims.

Now the sick and ageing Defoe, loaded with the misfortunes he was continuing to provoke, lacked sufficient strength to resist the Devil's assaults; the defiant defences, once bulwarks against the pounding neurotic guilts of the infantile fantasy crimes he had imagined, collapsed. He yielded to his enemy. His masochism, now untempered, inflamed his rheumatism, his arthritis; gout afflicted him; some form of bladder, kidney disease or gallstones brought excruciating pain: "exceedingly ill", he was too distracted to correct his manuscripts; "fits of Fever" were exhausting him. No greater torture could befall him than, as now, to be compelled to put down his pen. In despairing mood he told his daughter Sophia that he saw himself "Sinking under the Weight of Affliction too heavy for my Strength, and looking on myself as Abandon'd of every Comfort, every Friend, and every relative, except only such as are able to give me no Assistance."[23] His tragic loneliness was self-inflicted; he had successfully managed to be estranged from his children. His heavy-handed treatment of his wilful son, Benjamin, progenitor of seventeen children, had provoked the rebellious anti-social conduct that led to that son being gaoled. When his other son, Daniel Jr, attempted to curb Defoe's commercial extravagances, which threatened financial ruin for the whole family, a bitter and lasting quarrel ensued. Meanwhile, he brought his favourite daughter, Sophia, to a nervous breakdown through his endeavours to cheat her husband, Henry Baker, of part of an agreed dowry; the outraged Baker told his wife that her father was "dark and hideous". And, to add to the destructive turmoil he was producing, he became embroiled in disastrous litigation arising out of an old embezzlement of trustee funds of which he was guilty. No one could have pursued his own ruination with greater zeal than the ageing Defoe; the Devil had more than his pound of flesh.

Once Defoe had mourned: "We come weeping into the World and go groaning out of it." He was determined, despite all the temporary triumphs and successes, literary and political, that had punctuated his life, that in the end the tragic trajectory he forecast should be fulfilled. The failed litigation resulted in court orders to repay his ill-gotten gains or face imprisonment for debt. Defoe refused the options; he fled. For the last six months of his life he went into hiding, hunted like an animal by his debtors' agents.

His nemesis was nigh. The punishment for the Great Sin could not be mitigated; for the abomination of imagined incestuous homosexual fulfilment as a babe, a savage Jehovah decreed there could only be one sentence, death. For seventy years in frenetic activity and wondrous creativity Defoe had used every stratagem to delay that decreed execution but the death instinct, an instinct which, to the dismay of many of his followers, Freud was to insist uncompromisingly was an irreducible biological determinant in all our lives, now inexorably embraced the afflicted man. It was the imaginative early dissident psychoanalyst Wilhelm Stekel who, in identifying the death-wish, was the first to name that instinct Thanatos.[24] Stekel, knowing neurotic guilt to be Thanatos' accomplice, counselled us: "Cultivate a robust conscience"; but counselling of that order, even if it had been in his time available to Defoe, would have been fruitless; his guilt was too profound, his conscience too scarred. The burdened Defoe carried his guilt with him as, pursued by his creditors' sleuths, he shifted from one lodging-house to another; he was alone, unable even to communicate with his ailing wife lest his whereabouts should become known.

Finally he quit his hiding-place in Kent and, as if anticipating his return to the womb from which he had sprung, crept back to London to the area of his boyhood ramblings; and there, in a mean house in one of the labyrinthine lanes through which he could, if discovered, flee, he remained in severe depression. And now, lacking the will to escape, ere long he gave himself up to the last enemy.

The rumbustious, aggressive, gregarious man of seemingly inexhaustible manic energy faded out and, isolated, in his sleep, quietly departed this world; the doctor accurately attributed the cause of death to "languor". It was only one of the ironies attending Defoe's death and burial; the hyperactive man, however, even in the grave, could not for long rest in peace; posthumously he provoked his last public storm. More than a century later, in 1871, on the occasion at his graveside of a dedication service marking the erection of a monument to the author of *Robinson Crusoe*, his skeleton, as a preliminary to its reburial, was disinterred. A riot ensued; a gaping public fought the police as they tried to clear bones off the skeleton. A fierce denouncer of Roman Catholic cults was now being treated as a saintly relic.

Nothing could have been more repugnant to him. Sainthood for him was the coward's reward for choosing martyrdom; he scorned those who, unlike him, dodged a genuine confrontation with their own self-destructiveness by praying at and empathising with the shrines of martyred saints. That was for pusillanimous Papists; for the proud Protestant there was to be no intermediary, no priest, no saint, no Mary to intercede; his relationship with God, the Father, was exclusive; he would not tolerate any interlopers, jealous of the love he gave to his beloved, nor would he share with them either the love or the punishment bestowed upon him by the Almighty. The brave and passionate anti-Catholic doctrinal commitment of the great Dissenter, the dynamic behind so many of his works and political activities, was an elaborate epiphenomenon sustained by the intensity of his earliest fantasised transgressive incestuous relationship with his own biological father. And in the end, when he wrote the despairing letters to his daughter telling of his feelings of abandonment, we hear the voice of the crucified son crying out and asking why the father has forsaken him. But we know too that this guilty son has half-understood the sin which brought the punishment upon him: he had loved to excess the forbidden object of his homosexual desires.

Notes

1. *Serious Reflections during the Life and Surprising Adventures of Robinson Crusoe: with His Vision of the Angelik World*, 1720.
2. Bowerman, R. M., Head note, in *The Political History of the Devil*, Stoke Newington Daniel Defoe edition, 2003.
3. Freud, S., *Draft H—Paranoia*, SE, Volume 1, pp. 206–12.
4. Forrester, J., A tale of two icons: Jews all over the world boast of my name, comparing me with Einstein, *Psychoanalysis and History*, 7, 2 (2005).
5. Freud, S., Determinism and superstition, in *The Psychopathology of Everyday Life*, SE, Volume 6, pp. 258–9.
6. Freud, *Draft H—Paranoia*.
7. Hudson, N., Why God no kills the Devil?, *Review of English Studies*, 39 (1988), 494–541.
8. Freud, S., *Future of an Illusion*, SE, Volume 21.
9. Defoe, D., *The Political History of the Devil: as Well Ancient as Modern*, 1726.
10. Ibid.
11. Curtis, L., *The Elusive Daniel Defoe*, Vision, 1984.
12. Freud, S., *Character and Anal Eroticism*, SE, Volume 9, p. 174, quoted in Chapter 10, p. 147.
13. See Chapter 8.
14. Curtis, *The Elusive Daniel Defoe*.
15. Starr, G. A., Introduction to *Moll Flanders*, Oxford University Press, 1998.
16. See Chapter 7.
17. Ezekiel, 38: 2.
18. Daniel, 8: 7.
19. See Chapter 6, p. 74.
20. Defoe, D., *The Review*, 15, 341–2.
21. Rattray Taylor, G., *The Angel-makers*, Heinemann, 1958.
22. Gaines, J., *Evening in the Palace of Reason*, Fourth Estate, 2005.
23. Harris, G. (ed.), *The Letters of Daniel Defoe*, Letter No. 474, Clarendon Press, 1955.
24. Stekel, W., Beiträge zur Traumdeutung, *Jahrbuch der Psychoanalyse*, 1 (1999), 489.

CHAPTER NINETEEN

Epilogue

The eternal adversaries, Death and the Creator, have many aliases. In *The Political History of the Devil*, Defoe personified them as Lucifer and God. In an earlier epoch Empedocles, when enunciating the two fundamental principles he held to govern not only human beings but the whole universe, named them as νεῖκοξ (Strife) and φιλία (Love). Freud, having recourse to the classical education of his youth, chose to describe the conflicting protagonists as Thanatos and Eros. It was in the name of Wotan that Hitler slew millions. Carl Jung, in his abhorrent 1936 apologia for Nazism,[1] unashamedly, approvingly, but insightfully, told us that God in Germany had been displaced: "The god of the Germans is Wotan and not the Christian God." But, no matter under what name they fight, the catabolic and anabolic forces they symbolise are irreducible concomitants of the biology of man and of the politics of every society. They were the combatants who, amidst awesome hurricanes and terrifying earthquakes when, as John the Divine foretold,[2] heaven's stars fell to the ground, took up residence on our planet. Here they ceaselessly fight for mastery in every domain. Victory goes to the one who gains possession of man's psyche. In every generation, their tumultuous relationship precipitates storms and it was in the eye of such a storm that Daniel Defoe lived out his whole life.

Sociologists studying our society may regard Defoe's depiction of a continuous struggle between Satan and God as an irrelevant, archaic allegory; over-cautious historians, faced with Freudian claims that Eros and Thanatos are determinants never to be ignored in their theses, dismiss such attributions as baseless eschatology. The rebuttals of such academics are quaint; they seem to be based on a notion that, because Defoe finds the devil in the individual psychology of the protagonists peopling his novels, he leaps too hastily to conclude that the devil is similarly operating within larger groups, which is an extravagant extrapolation, they claim, both fanciful and evidentially unsound; in like manner, they charge Freud's conclusions with being founded on the psychology of individuals telling us on the couch in the privacy of a consulting-room of their neuroses and dreams well insulated from the social clamour without. Such criticisms tell us more of the irrational resistance to acceptance of Defoe's and Freud's uncomfortable findings, rather than providing us with demonstrations of allegedly flawed methodology. There can, in fact, be no more sociological work than Defoe's *Journal of the Plague Year*, in which he scrupulously catalogues group behaviour. And Freud, in 1905 in the earliest paper he published, taught us that every aspect of our individual lives is really a social one:

> It follows from the nature of the facts which form the material of psychoanalysis that we are obliged to pay as much attention in our case histories to the purely human and social circumstances of our patients as to the somatic data and the symptoms of the disorder.[3]

Defoe, the indefatigable fact-finder of the Storm,[4] and Freud, the persistent clinician, in their conceptualisations and personifications of the forces operating on man and mankind are presenting us with a distillation of their empirical findings, not indulging in chimerical fancies; the Devil and Thanatos are realities.

Eros and Thanatos are not to be regarded as mere simplistic symbols of goodness and badness; nor should they be depreciated as poetic polyvalent symbols embracing sex and death; rather, they are active, purposive forces possessed of a defined teleology; they are, like Defoe's Creator and the Devil, of transcendental significance.

On the analogy of animalism and catabolism, Freud regarded the operation of Eros as essentially a binding one, as the cells of a meta-zoon are bound together; union was its supreme aim, as that of the death instinct, Thanatos, was disintegration or separation.[5] Yet each force defined and needed each other; without Thanatos, Eros is barren. That was what I first learned at the knee of my Talmudic grandfather when he recounted to me the story told by the Rabbis of antiquity; there had been delight in the community when the evil urge was arrested and locked up until it was discovered that from that moment chickens stopped laying eggs.[6] The sages had commentated that without the evil urge, people would not marry, build houses or apply themselves to improve material conditions of their lives.

By boldly writing *The Political History of the Devil*, Defoe acknow-ledged, not denied, the vitality and the necessary existence of a devil, for Satan's existence was a prerequisite to his own creativity; but he knew too he would have to be ever wary of the destructive disposition of his galvaniser. Thus alerted, all his days, as the battle between the immortal adversaries raged within his interior life, Defoe uneasily but successfully was able to maintain his poise; he walked on a tightrope, knowing that if he hesitated, if he paused or if he contemplated returning the leering gaze of the constantly hovering Thanatos, he would be forced to slip and thus fall to his doom. The works of Defoe indeed stand as a tribute to his stamina and nerve, for not until he had passed his seventieth year, too frail to stay erect any longer, did he succumb and Thanatos had his triumph.

As we all must, in the end, Defoe capitulated to the Destroyer; death is inescapable. Even before man leaves the womb and, still more, even before relinquishing his infancy and reaching adult-hood, his fate, by his genes and early maturing, is humiliatingly programmed as he proceeds on an irrevocable journey to death: "There's a divinity that shapes our ends, Rough-hew them how we will."[7] Our rough-hewn efforts may tinker or modify the program-ming; but even the belligerent, ever resisting and resourceful Defoe had ultimately to yield; man is mortal; the grave awaits each of us. That is the fate of individual man, but what of the fate of mankind? Will universal death bring a closure to the evolution of the human race? That was the sombre question reluctantly posed by Defoe as he drew his political history to its conclusion; and, even more explicitly, it was Freud's final question when, in the latter years of his life, he completed his admonitory work *Civilisation and Its Discontents*.[8]

★   ★   ★   ★   ★   ★   ★   ★   ★   ★

Defoe, as a believer, always tried to distance himself from "atheistic" thoughts, and ends his *Political History of the Devil* with victory going to God, the Majesty of heaven overcoming the rebellious and devil-ish spirits, with the instigator, Satan, receiving the excruciating punishment Defoe reckoned he deserved. To justify that punishment he lists:

> Satan having been let loose to play his Game in this World, has improv'd his Times to the utmost; he has not fail'd on all Occasions to exert his Hatred, Rage, and Malice at his Conqueror and Enemy, namely, his maker; he has not fail'd from Principle of meer Envy and Pride to pursue Mankind with all possible Rancour in order to deprive him of the Honour and Felicity which he was created for, namely, to succeed the Devil and his Angels in the State of Glory from which they fell. . . . This Hatred of God and Envy at Man, hav-ing broken out in so many several Ways in the whole Series of Time from the Creation, must necessarily have encreased his Guilt; and as Heaven is righteous to judge him, must terminate in an Encrease of Punishment, adequate to his Crime, and sufficient to his Nature.[9]

Yet, despite his Christian faith, Defoe cannot bring himself to affirm that the victory is final. The "Devil's Empire" is vanquished, but there is a snag:

> The Devil himself and all his Host of Devils are immortal Seraphs, Spirits that are not embodied and cannot die, but are to remain in Being; the Question before us next will be, what is to become of him? what is his State to be? whither he is to wander, and in what Condition is he to remain to that Eternity to which he is still to Exist?

Defoe is here imaginatively but heretically departing from the text of the canon. John the Divine, or some other inspired Jewish poet in the turmoil of the Judaeo-Hellenistic age, gave us the frenzied numerology and visionary invective of the Apocryphya which is unequivocal and explicit; in his defeat, Satan was first to be bound and hurled into an abyss which would be "closed and sealed"; then, after one thousand years, he would be released for a while when, in the role of a warmonger, he would once again join battle with the Holy One, once again be defeated, but this time would be hurled into a lake of burning sulphur where he would forever, throughout the ages, be tormented day and night. Satan's defeat is recorded in the Apocrypha as being final, heralding the emergence of the New Jerusalem where the Elect, undisturbed by the Devil, would dwell with the Lord.[10]

But Defoe was too much of a realist to accept such a happy-ever-after scenario. We see Defoe's forebodings emerging. He feared the Devil in the future could wreak even greater hazards than he ever had in the past, an eighteenth-century fear that a modern reader, in the post-Hiroshima world, knows to have been only too well founded. But Defoe here is only prepared to diagnose our past and present ills; he shirks prognostication, lest it lead him to conclude that the Destroyer will end our world. He shifts responsibility for such terrible thoughts to others, and ends his work by limiting himself to warning us to take care lest those pessimists should, hideously, prove their case:

> Some have suggested, that there is yet a Time to come, when *the Devil* shall exert more Rage, and do more Mischief than ever yet he has been permitted to do; whether he shall break his Chain, or be unchain'd for a Time, they cannot tell, nor I neither; and 'tis happy for my Work, that even this Part too does not belong to his History; if ever it must be given an Account of by Mankind it must be after it has come to pass, for my part is not Prophesy or foretelling what the Devil shall do, but the History of what he has done.
>
> Thus, good People, I have brought the History of *the Devil* down *to your own Times;* I have, as it were, *rais'd him* for you, and set him in your View, that you may know him and have a Care of him.

In similar manner Freud, in his final words in *Civilisation and Its Discontents*, hesitated to affirm ultimate victory would go to Eros. He had always written in a vein of tempered optimism about the future of society and, initially, writing in 1930 at the height of the economic disasters that had overtaken the Western world, he ended the book with the hopeful words: "And now it may be expected that the other of the two 'heavenly forces', external Eros, will put forth his strength so as to maintain himself alongside of his equally immortal adversary."[11] Four years later, however, when the Germans had given us Hitler as their leader, he was far less sanguine. In revising the book he added the ominous sentence: "But who can predict his success and the final outcome?" Those last lines were written before the Holocaust, before the slaughter of the Second World War culminating in Hiroshima, before the proliferation of nuclear arms, before the folly and illegality of the Iraq War and its stimulation of suicide bombings in our streets; and before our awareness that we were contributing to a climate change threatening us with environmental disaster.

The absence in the works of Defoe and Freud of any note of triumphalism, confident Hosannas anticipating ultimate victory over the Destroyer, is indeed finding cruel justification in our twenty-first century. Defoe well knew Satan's talent to use and quote scripture for his own purpose and had the wit to read the Bible with suspicion and with care lest the devilish spirits had infiltrated the text; he was not prepared to share a diabolic, destructive, apocalyptic vision of a future world where all but a remnant of mankind must be wiped out to ensure the arrival and success of the Second Coming. He assumed such millenarian notions were, as we have seen,[12] ways in which the devil could insinuate himself into "holy wars" on earth even as he had done in heaven; and thus on guard, Defoe made his sceptical exegesis of Revelation, never conceding the possibility of final victory to either of the heavenly adversaries. He had the capacity to tolerate doubt.

It is only a literal reading of Revelation that ensures absolute certainty. Read thus, it is a frenzied, dangerous and divisive call to arms; we are invited to join the army of the elect at Armageddon, to look forward with enthusiasm to battle being joined, and after the ensuing slaughter, after the end of the days, we are promised we shall dwell in heaven for ever after; there, death will have no dominion. It is an apocalyptic incendiary incitement that has had dire consequences ever since, after fierce debate, it was included in the canon to become the last book of the Bible. Defoe's diffidence, his reluctance to endorse its conclusions, is not exceptional; there have been a thousand hermeneutical readings of the work designed to cloud the literal, bloodthirsty and intolerant story. Yet this first-century work, the inaugural document of hallucinatory triumphalism, with its vision of a righteous war, has today, in the United States and Britain, become the political manifesto of our fundamentalist, Bible-reading heads of government; not for them any exegetical interpretation. Their own poverty-stricken imaginations, as bereft as their rhetoric, have been perilously augmented by the wondrous recounting of the phantasmagorical scenes in the dreams of a maniacal Jew; their limited literacy protects them from self-awareness but endangers us as they read and act upon the text literally, never conscious of its mystical depths. It was after such a reading that Blair, in March 2003, invoked Armageddon by name and cast his decision to go to war against Iraq in visionary terms, declaring he had experienced a "revelation":

> September 11th was for me a revelation. The purpose was to cause such hatred between Muslims and the West, the religious *Jihad* became reality, and the world engulfed by it. The global threat to our security was clear. So was our duty; to act to eliminate it.[13]

The same apocalyptic perspective permeates the political consciousness of the White House. Marina Warner, in her elegant and profound Rodds Lecture, spoke of the dangers when Revelation is read in a highly literal way, as a blueprint for coming crises, and reminded us:

> Prophecies of retributive justice also strike again and again in the United States administration's proclamations, most notoriously in the Axis of Evil speech of January 29th 2002, in which Bush tellingly phrased his apocalypticism in semi-archaisms that move from ordinary American speech to a pretentious use of full auxiliary verbs; "We'll be deliberate, yet time is not on our side. I will not wait on events, while dangers gather. I will not stand by as terror draws closer and closer. . . . Our war on terror is well begun, but it is only begun. This campaign may not be finished on our watch—yet it must be and it will be waged on our watch.[14]

Bush's speechwriters, regular attenders of the Bible classes held in the White House, had provided with him with the Book of Revelation's constant exhortation "Be watchful". They had plagiarised Revelation's constant warning that the unwary will be taken by the enemy. It is indeed ironic, as we have seen, that the example given by Defoe of the satanic takeover of the Christian faith was the call of the popes to wage crusades against the "saracens".[15] The devil has indeed continued to find his dupes, not least in the ostentatious Christians Bush and Blair, as they abuse the language of the scripture to justify their catastrophic Iraq war. When Bush, in 2003, announced "God told me to end the tyranny in Iraq",[16] he was faithfully observing the orthodox apocalyptic doctrine so chillingly enunciated by Ronald Reagan in 1971 when responding to Gadaffi's coup in Libya:

> That's the sign that the day of Armageddon isn't far off . . . everything is falling into place. It can't be long now. Ezekiel said that fire and brimstone will be rained upon the enemies of God's people. That must mean that they will be destroyed by nuclear weapons.[17]

With the nuclear capacity to exterminate all mankind now in the hands of his blasphemous satraps, the Devil is poised for his ultimate victory; yet he is not unchallenged. Those arrayed against him may appear to be disparate but the binding force which Freud postulated could arise when Eros brought forth his strength so as to maintain himself against his eternal adversary may yet achieve for us the seemingly impossible; it is possible to hope Eros is bestirring himself. With Britain's major political parties in a state of incipient organisational collapse, the phenomenon of the decay of party has been accompanied by the growth of lobby; many are now marching who refuse to hold aloft the duplicitous banners of the clapped out political parties. In February 2003 a million people took to the streets in a life-affirming protest against being led to Armageddon by dangerously bemuddled zealots. By September 2005, echoing the increasing alarm among so many usually uninterested in, and indifferent to, the foreign policies of their government, even the Church of England, ever in the rear, tardily but lucidly and vigorously joined in the protest.

From the Church of England's House of Bishops came a weighty report showing an unblinking awareness of the devilish spirits that Defoe had so presciently identified; the Book of Revelation has become the mendacious manifesto of the Republican president who, like most US presidents since Jimmy Carter, claimed, before gaining office, to be "born again". The bishops condemned the appropriation and stigmatised the reading of Revelation by President Bush and his millions of fundamentalist evangelical supporters as "illegitimate". A true reading of the book, they said, "far from being a justification of American expansionism, is in fact a fierce critique of the imperial enterprise". More, the bishops, like Defoe centuries ago, warn us against futurology, against treating the Bible as a warranty, as a blueprint of a pre-ordained future where the victories and defeats in apocalyptic battles are already determined: "To read human history with a confidence that one knows precisely what God is doing through current events is an illegitimate extension of our limited, creaturely status and viewpoint. History outwits all our certitudes."[18] Such futurological certitudes, when expressed in political ideology or religious belief, are baits luring us to our destruction. Karl Marx, knowing the fatal attraction of millenarianism to his supporters, once surprisingly pronounced: "Whoever composes a programme for the future is a reactionary."

There is, however, no inevitability that Satan, although presently so advantaged and promising us that we are on the road to heaven, will succeed in leading us to hell. But if we dare to hope that Eros is bestirring himself, then that hope, to be authentic and creative, must essentially be rooted in the immediate; it is an affect needing present, personal commitment; it is actualised within all those burgeoning organised groups and lobbies whose concerns, and often ennobling goals, enhance both our society and their member participants. Men's and women's sexuality is a bountiful source of hope; from it can come the sublimated love found within a worthy common cause; the *terroirs* of such activities can promote growth; our stunted personal relationships and arrested societal values can, within such an environment, mature. These days single-issue bodies proliferate as never before. Some, it is true, are negative and self-interested, but most, whether they protest against a runway, a hospital closure, a bypass, the privatisation of the National Health Service, the state of our prisons, the poverty and disarray of our inner cities, the introduction of genetically manipulated foods, the desecration of the environment, the racialism and gender discriminations still prevailing, all these pressure groups are providing an opportunity for men and women to be libidinally bound together, to be, as Freud has put it, part of the civilising process: "In the service of Eros whose purpose is to combine single human individuals and after that families, then races, peoples and nations, into one great unity, the unity of mankind."[19]

The cynics or defeatists who would dismiss such aspirations as daydreams should not be left to enjoy their pessimism; the phenomenon first made visible in December 1999, when thousands of protesters from all over the world surrounded the meeting of the World Trade Organisation, has proved to be no spasm; the backlash against the devilish excesses of contemporary global capitalism with its indifference to the environment, to the starvation of millions in Africa and to the hazardous trade in nuclear armaments, is gaining greater force. Satan depends for his triumph on apathy, despair, avarice and narcissism; they are formidable supporters but they are not invulnerable; they can be fought and sometimes overcome. Those engaged in efforts to thwart them and their master can indeed gain much instruction from Daniel Defoe, for he was one of their most illustrious precursors, a man in whose life and works we find the experience of a battle-scarred, lifelong paid-up member of the anti-Satan party.

Those who falter, who fear in today's disordered, misgoverned, terrorist-ridden world that the battle is already lost to the Destroyer can wonder at this man and gain sustenance from his courage; almost to the last of his seventy years, Defoe refused to allow his impediments to defeat him; on the contrary, he used them as a stimulant. Every one of his social and personal handicaps—and they were many—he strove to turn to advantage. Born an outsider, distanced from the Establishment of his day as a son of a mere chandler who was a despised Dissenter, he treated his status as an act of serendipity, not as a disadvantage; never belonging to the political elite or the classically educated dominant literary clique, always apart from the unthinking compact majority, always an observer even when a participant, he retained his independent view and was ever ready, at great risk to himself, to challenge any attempt to drag the new and more democratic Britain, which he had helped to create, back to its former autocratic and theocratic governance; and more, since he waged war on many fronts, most unfashionably, in his later years he passionately assailed the vulgarities and promiscuities of the corrupt Hanoverian regime. Only a man fundamentally alienated by his handicaps from the mainstream could have possessed the dynamism to sustain such a lifelong critique of his society; he never mellowed, was never assimilated, never gave up the struggle.

He had one special disadvantage to spur him on: his physique. Alfred Adler, an early disciple of Freud who seceded and founded his own movement, gave us the term "inferiority complex", which has become the popular term for a sense of inadequacy, but which originally described the cluster of ideas and feelings which may arise in relation to a sense of what Adler called "organ inferiority"; and Defoe was certainly a tiny man, the same height as myself, not quite 5' 4", as was discovered when he was disinterred; short men are notorious for their over-compensated belligerence and Defoe was indeed a bantam boxer who successfully punched above his weight.

But the faint-hearted, fearing the destructive forces in today's turbulent world are too powerful to be defeated, may find even greater encouragement by observing the manner in which Defoe fought against, and often overcame, his worst handicap: the neurotic sense of guilt ever pressing down on him, the price he was forced to pay throughout his life for his infantile fantasy of enjoying exclusive congress with his own father. That sickness could have driven him to self-destruction; instead, like those other geniuses, Newton, Darwin, Proust and Freud, who in like manner dealt with their psychoneurotic afflictions, he turned his illness into a creative malady.[20]

Eros can be a cunning healer, so subtly regulating the poisonous potions which his adversary has prescribed that they miraculously become not lethal toxins but life-savers. Each time Defoe had been in danger of sinking under the weight of his afflictions, almost to the end, Eros had come to his rescue, so ministering Thanatos' potions that they became elixirs; with such boosters, though suffering relapses, Defoe had battled on. In his life he endured the humiliation of the stocks, he was confined in grim prisons and he suffered constant private travail as he wrestled with his demons; but he survived. He lives on as a giant in our literary canon, and as one of the significant architects of the unwritten British constitution protecting our liberties. But, more, in these dark days, when no rational man or woman can have confidence that the world that so narrowly escaped during the 1962 Cuban crisis will survive the twenty-first century, Defoe, with all his blemishes, stands out as an exemplar; his daring in his fearless identification of the destructive elements in the human condition, his readiness to confront the Devil and all his works, is a reproach to all today who, politically disenchanted, and covetous only for the baubles proffered in our meretricious society, retreat to their private, self-regarding worlds.

In a few months, the Great Reaper willing, I shall be ninety. My day is almost done; but will my grandchildren have the same opportunity to become nonagenarians? That now depends on younger generations than mine; some among them will surely have the stamina shown by Defoe in his battles against the despoilers of our world. Mindful of the setbacks they will endure, I send them the same encouraging valediction with which Freud was wont to end his communications to colleagues suffering painful disappointments: Corragio! Corragio!

Notes

1. Jung, C., Wotan, *Neue Schweitzer Rundeschau*, Zurich, BS111, March 1936; Jung, C. *Essays on Contemporary Events; Reflections on Nazi Germany*, Ark Paperbacks, 1988; and Abse, L., *Wotan My Enemy*, Robson Books, 1994.
2. Revelation, 6: 12–13.
3. Jones, E., *The Life and Work of Sigmund Freud, Volume 3*, Hogarth Press, 1957, p. 316; Freud, S., *Essays–A Case of Hysteria*, SE, Volume 7, p. 80.
4. See Chapter 7.
5. Jones, *The Life and Work of Sigmund Freud*, p. 296.
6. Brichto, S., *Apocalypse*, Sinclair-Stevenson, 2004.
7. Shakespeare, W., *Hamlet*.
8. Freud, S., *Essays*, SE, Volume 21.
9. Defoe, D., *The Political History of the Devil: As Well Ancient as Modern*, 1726.
10. Revelation, 20: 10–21.
11. Freud, S., *Civilisation and Its Discontents*, SE, Volume 21.
12. See Chapter 18, p. 271.
13. Blair, A., quoted by Warner, M., *Times Literary Supplement*, 19 August 2005.
14. Warner, M., Lecture given March 2004, University of Auckland, New Zealand, *Times Literary Supplement*, 19 August 2005.
15. See Chapter 18, p. 272.

16. Quoted in the *Guardian*, 7 October 2005.

17. Reagan, R., quoted in Northcott, M., *An Angel Directs the Storm: Apocalyptic Religion and American Empire*, I. B.Taurus, 2004, p. 59.

18. Church of England, *Countering Terrorism: Power, Violence and Democracy Post 9/11*, Church House, September 2005.

19. Freud, *Civilisation and Its Discontents*.

20. Pickering, G., Sir, *Creative Maladies*, Allen & Unwin, 1974.

INDEX